The Gödel Programming Language

The Gödel Programming Language

Patricia Hill
John Lloyd

The MIT Press
Cambridge, Massachusetts
London, England

This book was set in Computer Modern by the authors and was printed and bound in the United States of America.

Library of Congress Cataloging-in-Publication Data

Hill, Patricia, 1942–
    The Gödel programming language / Patricia Hill, John Lloyd.
        p.   cm. — (Logic programming)
    Includes bibliographical references and index.
    ISBN 0-262-08229-2
    1. Gödel (Computer program language) 2. Logic programming languages. I. Lloyd, John, 1947–   . II. Title. III. Series.
QA76.73.G17H55 1994
005.13'3—dc20   93-37158
                                                          CIP

To our families

Contents

Series Foreword

The logic programming approach to computing investigates the use of logic as a programming language and explores computational models based on controlled deduction.

The field of logic programming has seen a tremendous growth in the last several years, both in depth and in scope. This growth is reflected in the number of articles, journals, theses, books, workshops, and conferences devoted to the subject. The MIT Press series in logic programming was created to accommodate this development and to nurture it. It is dedicated to the publication of high-quality textbooks, monographs, collections, and proceedings in logic programming.

Ehud Shapiro
The Weizmann Institute of Science
Rehovot, Israel

Foreword

This splendid book presents Gödel, an equally splendid new relational logic programming language designed to diminish, if not to eliminate, the regrettable gap between 'pure' and 'applied' relational logic programming, a gap that has plagued the relational logic programming community since the birth of Prolog in the early 1970s. The functional logic programming community has tolerated a similar gap for even longer, since the introduction of Lisp around 1960, but is now quite close to closing it completely.

In both functional and relational logic programming, it has proved to be quite difficult to outgrow the inexorable influence of the Turing/von Neumann (TvN) computer architecture and of what one might call 'the TvN way of thinking' about computation. The TvN view of computation emphasizes the *activity* of computation ('how') whereas the declarative view emphasizes the *result* of computation ('what'). In a 'strong' declarative program the programmer need supply only the logical part of the program in the form of a set of definitions (of relations, or functions, or both), leaving all control information to be supplied automatically by the machine. Such contemporary 'pure' functional logic programming languages as Miranda and Haskell purport to fall into this category. By that very token, however, they tend to be regarded with scepticism by those programmers who must seek the last ounce of run-time efficiency that can be squeezed out of TvN engines. Such programmers are reluctant (with plenty of empirical justification, one has to admit) to hand over the entire burden of meeting stringent run-time efficiency criteria to the compiler writers and the machine architects.

Strong declarativeness is nevertheless a Good Thing that opens up the prospect of vast improvements in the *efficiency of the programming process* itself. Strongly declarative programs can be highly intelligible, simple, modular constructions. They can be rapidly composed out of 'large' conceptual units and are amenable to systematic logical analysis, verification, transformation, and debugging. However, we are not yet at the point where strongly declarative programming is a realistic, practical, and truly competitive alternative to the sort of TvN programming that people do in C and the like, when it comes to run-time efficiency. Reality forces designers of a practical logic programming language to compromise, to settle for some degree of 'weak' declarativity. In a weakly declarative logic programming language the programmer is offered facilities to supply control information in order to produce efficient run-time behavior, and in practice these facilities are copiously invoked.

The language described in this book is a beautifully engineered example of this compromise. Gödel programmers are provided with the notational means to supply, and are largely responsible for supplying, suitable control information (the machine can supply a limited amount). A pity, one cannot help feeling, but the truth is that in a TvN world there simply is no free lunch.

The situation is one in which there is both good news and bad news.

The bad news is that until the day when non-TvN, purely declarative, machines are both thoroughly understood and widely available as alternative run-time vehicles, logic programming language designers will apparently have to practise their art in the shadow of what seems to be a basic law of programming for TvN machines:

$$\text{(programming inefficiency)} \bullet \text{(runtime inefficiency)} \geq \text{constant.}$$

The good news is that the cost of TvN hardware is very rapidly decreasing whilst its performance and capacity are just as rapidly increasing. So the constant on the right-hand side of the inequality is getting smaller, and therefore the balance can be shifted acceptably toward seeking ways of reducing programming inefficiency at the expense, if necessary, of some increase in run-time inefficiency.

Apart from the virtues of pure declarativeness as such (simplicity, referential transparency, denotational semantics, and so on), today's declarative languages also offer (indeed, they enforce) strong typing, and they provide a notational facility for writing in modular style. If (as in the case of the Gödel language) the decision is made to retain a modicum of nondeclarativeness in order to allow the programmer to have at least some direct influence over run-time events, the requisite language facilities can at least be carefully designed so as to encourage a clear and intelligible style of control specification. In Gödel this is exactly what has been done.

The language's name – Gödel – aptly commemorates the twentieth century's greatest logician. I have long maintained that Kurt Gödel was both the world's first functional logic programming language designer and also its first serious functional logic programmer. In his great 1931 paper proving the essential incompleteness of formalized systems of arithmetic he set up (as a relatively small part of his overall argument) what was in effect an elegant functional programming language (the equational formalism of primitive recursive functions of natural numbers). In this language he then composed a suite of function and predicate definitions collectively comprising a computational presentation of the general syntax and proof machinery of formalized arithmetic. As a programming exercise it is a gem: concise, clear, powerful, and demonstrably correct.

In this book the reader will find the language Gödel laid out in full detail, together with the case for believing that the pioneer relational logic programming language Prolog must now be seen as nearing the end of its brilliant career. The authors' opinion is, clearly, that in a perfect world a logic programming system would directly embody what they call the central thesis of logic programming: *programs are first order theories, and computations are deductions from them.* They recognize, however, that in an imperfect world this marvellous idea must yield to the exigencies of the efficiency trade-off.

Robert Kowalski has famously said that *algorithm = logic + control.* Prolog programmers often worry rather more about the efficient control of the run-time search for solutions than about the clear expression of the logic of the problem. Gödel programmers will still be concerned with control, but they will be able to express their concern in a much more disciplined and structured way than is possible in Prolog. Gödel's control notations are simple and powerful. But then so is the entire Gödel language, and so is the exposition it receives in this book. The authors have met the test of Kurt Gödel's friend Albert Einstein: they have made everything 'as simple as possible, but no simpler'.

What more can one ask? Now read on . . . .

J. Alan Robinson
Tully, New York
September 1993

Preface

Would that I had unknown utterances and strange phrases,
In a new language that does not pass away,
Free from repetition,
Without a phrase of familiar speech which the ancestors spoke.

From *The Words of Khakheperreseneb*, around 1860 B.C.

Gödel is a declarative, general-purpose programming language in the family of logic programming languages. It is a strongly typed language, the type system being based on many-sorted logic with parametric polymorphism. It has a module system. Gödel supports infinite precision integers, infinite precision rationals, and also floating-point numbers. It can solve constraints over finite domains of integers and also linear rational constraints. It supports processing of finite sets. It also has a flexible computation rule and a pruning operator which generalizes the commit of the concurrent logic programming languages. Considerable emphasis is placed on Gödel's meta-logical facilities which provide significant support for meta-programs that do analysis, transformation, compilation, verification, debugging, and so on. The declarative nature of Gödel makes it particularly suitable for use as a teaching language, narrows the gap which currently exists between theory and practice in logic programming, makes possible advanced software engineering tools such as declarative debuggers and compiler generators, reduces the effort involved in providing a parallel implementation of the language, and offers substantial scope for parallelization in such implementations.

This book, which consists of two parts, describes the Gödel language. The first part gives an informal overview of the language and includes example programs. The second part contains a definition of the syntax and semantics of the language. We assume readers have some programming experience, have some acquaintance with logic programming concepts, and are familiar with the most basic material on the syntax and semantics of first order logic. We provide an appendix on polymorphic many-sorted logic for readers not familiar with this generalization of (unsorted) first order logic. At the end of the first chapter, we give, for those familiar with Prolog, a comparison between Gödel and Prolog. This provides much of the motivation for Gödel and explains why various design decisions were taken. We suggest readers follow the first nine chapters in order, looking ahead to the example programs in chapter 10 and referring to the formal definitions in the second part, as appropriate. Augmented by the reference manual of a particular implementation, the book contains everything a programmer needs to know to write large-scale Gödel programs.

Readers will notice that little is said about the procedural semantics of Gödel in this

book. This is a decision which probably requires some explanation, since one might
expect a book which gives a formal definition of a programming language to be rather
precise on this point. First, for the syntax and declarative semantics, we have tried to
be precise and comprehensive. The main criticism that could be made of our description
of the declarative semantics is that the specification of the system predicates is given
in English rather than some formal language. Our chosen method achieves conciseness,
but at the expense of some lack of precision. In contrast, for the procedural semantics,
we have adopted a different approach and merely specified that the implementation be
sound and satisfy some other conditions. (For example, the conditions under which a
control declaration will delay a call are specified, as is the effect on a search tree of the
pruning operator.)

The main advantage of specifying the procedural semantics in great detail is portability, so that one could port a program from one implementation to another and be
confident of identical behaviour of the program in the two systems. In spite of this,
we have decided not to follow this approach. The reason is that logic programming
language implementation is currently in a state of rapid development, so that whatever
detailed procedural semantics we might specify now is likely to look outdated and unnecessarily conservative in a couple of years. By leaving the details of the procedural
semantics so open, we hope to encourage, or at least not impede, this development. This
approach gives implementors of Gödel considerable freedom and, for example, admits
theorem proving methods which provide a more flexible handling of negation than the
usual SLDNF-resolution. However, the reference manual of an implementation will need
to discuss whatever further details on the procedural semantics are required to write
(reasonably) efficient programs.

The most likely difference between implementations of Gödel will be that programs
terminating on one implementation may flounder on another. The two places where this
will commonly happen are with constraint solving and the handling of negation. This is
because a considerable range of sophistication of constraint solvers for the integers and
rationals is possible. Also, an implementation employing safe negation may flounder on
calls which would run on an implementation employing a more flexible implementation
of negation. However, only completeness is affected: all implementations must be sound.

No programming language, certainly not Gödel, is ideal. Aware as we are that flaws and
gaps remain, we feel nevertheless that the language is sufficiently well-developed to appear
now in book form. We could have waited longer until the only existing implementation
was more complete, or we had worked out the details of a more declarative approach to
input/output, a parametrized module system, or a number of other potential facilities of
the language. But all of these things take time and the need for a successor to Prolog
grows more urgent. So we have decided that now is the time to try to make the language

available to a wider audience. Certainly, we believe that, while many people would have preferred us to have gone further, few would seriously object to the main thrust of the language. We hope that Gödel will be regarded as a good core language which encourages solid, long-lasting extensions – a step along the way to the unattainable, but always sought after, ideal general-purpose logic programming language.

It is hardly possible to design a new programming language without relying to a great extent on previous work. Gödel is no exception to this. First, we are greatly indebted to Alain Colmerauer who designed in 1972 the Prolog language, many features of which are clearly evident in Gödel. The intensional set terms of Gödel can be traced back to set processing facilities introduced around 1980 into Prolog by David H.D. Warren and IC-Prolog by Keith Clark and Francis McCabe. A particular case of the Gödel pruning operator first appeared in the Relational Language of Keith Clark and Steve Gregory in the early 1980's. We have also borrowed good ideas from more recent logic programming languages. In particular, we have adopted the if-then-else construct and the **when** control declarations of NU-Prolog. Both of these were introduced by Lee Naish around 1986. The type system is based firmly on many-sorted first order logic with the addition of polymorphism through parameters and constructors. The ideas of the polymorphic component of the type system go back (at least) to Robin Milner's work on ML in the 1970's and were first considered in the logic programming context by Alan Mycroft and Richard O'Keefe in 1983. The module system is based on standard ideas as elegantly embodied in Modula-2, for example, although many of the details seem to be new. The constraint-solving facilities were inspired by current research in this very active area which was pioneered by Alain Colmerauer, Joxan Jaffar, Jean-Louis Lassez, and Michael Maher in the mid-1980's. Finally, the key idea of the meta-programming facilities can be traced back to an influential paper of Kenneth Bowen and Robert Kowalski in 1982, which itself relied on much earlier work of logicians, particularly Kurt Gödel.

We owe a particular debt to Antony Bowers and Jiwei Wang, who have undertaken so successfully the substantial and demanding task of implementing the language. Corin Gurr helped with the implementation of the meta-programming modules. Also his work on self-applicable partial evaluators influenced the design of the language. Antony Bowers contributed to the design, especially of the meta-programming facilities, and introduced the concept of type lifting. Alistair Burt, who spent a year on the project, produced the first implementation of a subset of the language and also contributed to its design, especially the idea that the ground representation used by the meta-programming facilities should be handled like an abstract data type. Andrea Domenici contributed to an early implementation of the parser. Frank Defoort experimented at a formative stage with writing interpreters using the ground representation.

Various people commented on drafts of this book or the Gödel system itself. These include Dominic Binks, Antony Bowers, John Conery, Frank Defoort, André de Waal, Tony Dodd, Andrea Domenici, John Gallagher, Corin Gurr, Fergus Henderson, Henk Muller, Feliks Kluźniak, Micha Meier, Nicholas Moffat, Lee Naish, Alan Robinson, Vitor Santos Costa, Jeffrey Schultz, Zoltan Somogyi, Brian Stonebridge, Sten-Åke Tärnlund, Rodney Topor, Jiwei Wang, Geraint Wiggins, and several anonymous reviewers. Many improvements to the book resulted from these comments. The editorial advice and assistance of Terry Ehling of MIT Press was very helpful. Also Patrick O'Donnell provided much help with the MIT Press macros.

Cable and Wireless plc provided support for a WISE fellowship for the first author at the University of Bristol. This fellowship enabled her to return to an academic career, change her research field to logic programming, and participate in the preparatory research for the project. The first author is also particularly indebted to a number of people within the Division of Artificial Intelligence and the Centre for Theoretical Computer Science at the University of Leeds for encouraging her work on Gödel. The second author would like to thank many people, too numerous to mention, for many interesting discussions over the last decade, which have helped shape the form that Gödel has finally taken.

We are also indebted to Dr. Richard Parkinson of the Department of Egyptian Antiquities at the British Museum for the use of his translation of the above passage from the Words of Khakheperreseneb, which is preserved on a wooden writing tablet dating from the 18th Dynasty and is now in the British Museum (EA 5645). Khakheperreseneb is said to have been a priest of the city of Heliopolis. His name indicates that the text cannot predate the reign of Sesostris II (1895–1878 B.C.) in the Late Middle Kingdom.

The design and implementation of Gödel was partly supported by the ESPRIT Basic Research Action 3012 (Compulog) and Project 6810 (Compulog 2), SERC Grants GR/F/26256 and GR/H/79862, the University of Bristol, and the University of Leeds.

For details on obtaining an implementation of Gödel by ftp, send a message to `goedel@compsci.bristol.ac.uk`

I OVERVIEW OF GÖDEL

1 Introduction

In this chapter, we introduce briefly the main ideas of declarative programming, outline the main facilities of Gödel[1], and give a comparison of Gödel and Prolog.

1.1 Declarative Programming

Before getting down to the details of the Gödel language, we present a brief discussion of the general principles of declarative programming. The starting point for the programming process is the particular problem that the programmer is trying to solve. The problem is then formalized as an interpretation (called the *intended* interpretation) of a language which we assume here to be a (polymorphic many-sorted) first order language. The intended interpretation specifies the various domains and the meaning of the symbols of the language in these domains. In practice, the intended interpretation is rarely written down precisely, although in principle this should always be possible.

Now, of course, it is taken for granted here that it *is* possible to capture the intended application by a first order interpretation. Not all applications can be (directly) modelled this way and for such applications other languages and formalisms may have to be employed. However, a very large class of applications can be modelled naturally by means of a first order interpretation. In fact, this class is larger than is sometimes appreciated. For example, it might be thought that such an approach cannot (directly) model situations where a knowledge base is changing over time. Now it is true that the intended interpretation of the knowledge base is changing. However, the knowledge base should properly be regarded as data to various meta-programs, such as query processors or assimilators. Thus the knowledge base can be accessed and changed by these meta-programs. The meta-programs themselves have fixed intended interpretations which fits well with the setting for declarative programming given above.

Based on the intended interpretation, the *logic component* of a program is then written. This logic component is a particular kind of (polymorphic many-sorted) first order theory which is usually suitably restricted so as to admit an efficient theorem proving procedure. It is crucial that the intended interpretation be a model for the logic component of the program. This is because an implementation must guarantee that computed answers give instantiated goal bodies which are true in all models of the logic component of the program and hence are true in the intended interpretation. Ultimately, the programmer is interested in *computing truth in the intended interpretation*.

Typically, in logic programming languages, the logic component of a program is the

---

[1] The name Gödel is appropriate since the key concept of the language's approach to meta-programming is representation (i.e. naming), which was introduced by Kurt Gödel in his incompleteness result. Alternatively, Gödel can be regarded as an acronym formed from God's Own DEclarative Language.

theory obtained by completing the collection of program statements, that is, by adding to the program the only-if halves of the statements in the program. In other approaches to declarative programming different logics are used. For example, in functional programming, the logic component of a program can be understood to be a collection of formulas in the λ-calculus. However, while the logic used is different from that in logic programming, the underlying ideas of declarative programming from the functional programming perspective are the same.

Having written a correct logic component of a program, the programmer then turns to the *control component* of the program, which is concerned with the construction and pruning of search trees. Typically, the computation rule (which selects a subformula in a goal for an extension step) is partly specified by control declarations and the pruning of a search tree is specified by pruning operators. To some extent, it is possible to relieve the programmer of responsibility for the control component by the use of preprocessors which automatically generate appropriate control. Note that, in practice, control considerations may cause a programmer to go back and rewrite the logic component to improve the efficiency of a program. In any case, an important requirement of the control declarations and pruning operators of a program is that they can be stripped away and what remains is a correct logic component of the program.

Declarative programming can be understood in two main senses. In the weak sense, declarative programming means that programs are theories, but that a programmer may have to supply control information to produce an efficient program. Declarative programming, in the strong sense, means that programs are theories and all control information is supplied automatically by the system. In other words, for declarative programming in the strong sense, the programmer only has to provide the intended interpretation (or, perhaps, a theory which has the intended interpretation as a model). This is to some extent an ideal which is probably not attainable (nor, in some cases, totally desirable), but it does at least provide a challenging and appropriate target. Gödel itself is a contribution to declarative programming in the weak sense. Thus Gödel programs are (with some minor caveats) theories, but programmers are largely responsible for providing suitable control information.

In summary, declarative programming is much more concerned with writing down *what* should be computed and much less with *how* it should be computed. Ideally, in many circumstances, we would like to be able to dispense altogether with having to write down the "how" part (that is, the control part), but the current state of programming technology, including Gödel, does not permit this. Nevertheless, any significant progress towards declarative programming in the strong sense would make an important contribution to programming, fully justifying the considerable world-wide research effort which continues to be put into this area.

1.2 Gödel Facilities

Gödel is a declarative, general-purpose programming language in the family of logic
programming languages. Its main facilities are a type system, a module system, and
control, meta-programming, and input/output facilities. We now introduce each of these
in turn.

Types

The reasons for having types in logic programming languages are well known. The
major reason is for knowledge representation. Intended interpretations in most logic
programming applications are typed and hence using a typed language is the most direct
way of capturing the relevant knowledge in the application. Also, the information given
by the language declarations of a type system can be used by a compiler to produce
more efficient code. Furthermore, type declarations can help to catch programming
errors. For example, in an untyped language, simple typographical errors often lead to
bizarre program behaviour which can usually only be identified by laborious tracing of
the program. In contrast, in a typed language, such errors often lead to syntax errors
which can be caught by the compiler. It is nearly always easier to correct an error caught
by the compiler than it is to discover and correct an error that leads to wrong program
behaviour. Our experience with the Gödel type system supports the contention that it
greatly decreases the effort required for program development and greatly increases the
likelihood of correctness of programs compared with untyped languages.

There are two kinds of type system studied in logic. The first kind are type systems
suitable for higher order logics (for example, the type system of typed λ-calculus). These
provide the foundation for the type systems of functional languages and higher order
logic programming languages. The other kind of type system studied in logic arises from
many-sorted (first order) logic. It is many-sorted logic which provides the foundation for
type facilities in first order logic programming languages and it is an extension of this
logic that is used by Gödel. In the following, to conform to the usual terminology of
programming languages, we often refer to a sort as a type.

However, a many-sorted logic alone is not sufficiently flexible for a type system in a
logic programming language. The reason is that we want to write predicates which take
a variety of types of arguments. For example, the usual Append predicate will normally
be required to append lists each of whose elements has the same fixed but arbitrary type.
For this reason, Gödel allows a form of polymorphism, called parametric polymorphism,
familiar from functional programming languages. Parametric polymorphism necessitates
the introduction of type variables, which range over all types. By this means, a polymorphic version of Append, for example, can be written in a similar way to the functional

languages.

Gödel's type system is a strongly typed one, in the sense that each constant, function, proposition, and predicate in a program and its type must be specified by a language declaration. By contrast, variables have their types inferred from their context.

Modules

The usual software engineering advantages of a module system are well known and they apply equally well to Gödel. In its most basic form, a module system simply provides a way of writing large programs so that various pieces of the program don't interfere with one another because of name clashes and also provides a way of hiding implementation details. The Gödel module system is based on these standard ideas. A program is a collection of modules. A module generally consists of two parts, the export part and the local part. The export part of a module consists of language declarations for the symbols available for use in either part of the module and in other modules which import them, control declarations, and module declarations giving the symbols from other modules which are available for use in either part of the module and in other modules which import them. The local part of a module consists of language declarations for the symbols available for use only in this part, module declarations giving the symbols from other modules available for use in this part, control declarations, and definitions of those propositions and predicates specified by language declarations in the module.

There is a rich collection of system modules – 20 in all – provided by the Gödel language. These include modules that process numbers, lists, strings, and sets, modules that provide input/output, and modules that provide meta-programming facilities. Gödel also makes significant use of abstract data types, which are implemented by means of the module and type systems. An abstract data type consists of a type and a collection of operations on the type. The details of the way the type is represented and the way the operations are implemented are hidden from programmers. Abstract data types have many advantages for software engineering, including the provision of a higher level of abstraction for programmers and the ability to change the implementation of a type without affecting existing code. The Gödel system modules provide a number of important abstract data types, including `Unit` (the type of units which are term-like structures), `Flock` (the type of ordered collections of units), `Program` (the type of terms representing Gödel programs), and `Theory` (the type of terms representing polymorphic many-sorted first order theories). In each case, the corresponding module provides a collection of operations on the type and the module system is used to hide the implementation details of these operations. Furthermore, a number of other Gödel system modules provide types which are at least partly abstract. For example, the implementation of the operations on the types `Integer` and `Rational` are hidden from programmers. However, for pragmatic reasons, it is preferable to make explicit the symbols used to represent these types. For example, the constants representing the integers are made available to programmers. It would be possible to avoid this by having a predicate which returned the integer 0 and a predicate which returned the successor of an integer, but this is much more cumbersome for programmers than simply making the constants available. In any case, a good way to think about the Gödel language is that essentially it provides a rich collection of (mostly abstract) data types, useful for a variety of applications, and provides facilities for programmers to define their own abstract data types.

Control

Gödel has a flexible computation rule which may select, in a goal body consisting of a conjunction of literals, a literal other than the leftmost literal. The advantages of a flexible computation rule are that it can be used to ensure safeness (especially of negative calls), assist termination, assist efficiency, solve constraints, and control pruning. The computation rule is partly specified by means of **DELAY** control declarations, which cause certain calls to be delayed until they are sufficiently instantiated. Many Gödel system predicates have **DELAY** declarations. Furthermore, a programmer can encourage co-routining behaviour by means of these declarations.

Gödel has constraint-solving capabilities in the domains of integers and rationals. It can solve systems of (not necessarily linear) constraints which involve integers, variables which range over bounded intervals of integers, and the usual functions and predicates with integer arguments. It can also solve systems of linear rational constraints involving rationals, variables ranging over the rationals, and the usual functions and predicates with rational arguments.

We now discuss the Gödel pruning operator, called the commit, which can be used to prune away parts of a search tree and can thus affect the completeness of the search procedure. The commit is a powerful pruning operator and, in its full generality, is primarily meant for use by source-level tools, such as partial evaluators and program transformers. Thus Gödel provides two special cases of the commit with simplified notation for use by programmers. These are the one-solution commit and the bar commit. The one-solution commit prunes the search tree in such a way as to ensure (at most) one solution of the formula it contains will be found. The bar commit, which is similar to the commit of the concurrent logic programming languages, provides a means of pruning some of the branches emanating from a node in a search tree, where each branch corresponds to a statement in the program whose head unified with the selected atom in the goal labelling that node.

The commit is an effective tool for pruning away unwanted subtrees of search trees, but it can affect the declarative semantics of programs in the sense that correct answers can be pruned. Therefore, while commits are infrequently needed in Gödel programs because their effect can often be achieved with declarative constructs such as negation and if-then-else, their use does detract from the major aim of Gödel, which is to have programs with the best possible declarative semantics. However, as was argued in detail in [12], (sound) pruning operators *do* have an important place in logic programming languages, even though they may adversely affect the semantics of programs in which they appear. Furthermore, it is always possible to strip away all commits from a Gödel program to reveal its underlying logic component. In addition, the commit is sound and has been shown to have excellent procedural semantics. For example, a theorem in [12] shows that the commit is well-behaved under partial evaluation in the sense that, under reasonable conditions, the original program can be arranged to have the same set of computed answers as the partially evaluated program.

For an arbitrary computation rule, the pruning done by the commit, while correct according to its definition, may be very difficult for a programmer to understand and control. For example, if an insufficiently instantiated call is allowed to proceed, the system may commit to a branch of the search tree which is not intended and, as a consequence, the computation may later fail. Thus an important use of DELAY declarations is to control pruning. Appropriate DELAY declarations ensure calls only proceed if they are sufficiently instantiated, thus avoiding unexpected failure and, more generally, giving the programmer sufficient control over what is pruned.

The other facility provided by Gödel that gives a form of control is the IF-THEN-ELSE construct, which has several variations. This construct has a declarative meaning, but also provides the important control information that the condition in the IF part should be computed only once. This can result in an important saving if this condition is computationally expensive. One variation omits the ELSE part and another allows existentially quantified variables to appear in the IF and THEN parts. As the reader will see from the programs in this book, the IF-THEN-ELSE construct figures prominently in the Gödel programming style.

Meta-programming

The essential characteristic of meta-programming is that a meta-program is a program which uses another program (the object program) as data. Meta-programming techniques underlie many of the applications of logic programming. For example, knowledge base systems consist of a number of knowledge bases (the object programs), which are manipulated by interpreters and assimilators (the meta-programs). Other important kinds of software, such as debuggers, compilers, and program transformers, are meta-programs.

The Gödel approach to meta-programming is to exploit abstract data types. One of the main such types is Program which is the type of a term representing an object Gödel program. Terms of type `Program` are complicated terms which contain a representation of all the components of a Gödel program. So, for example, the module structure must be represented, as must all the language declarations and statements appearing in the program. The system module `Programs` provides a large number of operations on this abstract data type, including adding and deleting statements in a program, accessing language declarations, running goals to a program, and many others. There are two other major abstract data types for meta-programming. One is `Theory` which is the type of a term representing an object polymorphic many-sorted theory. The system module `Theories` provides operations on this abstract data type which can be used to implement theorem provers, for example. The other type is `Script` which is the type of a term representing an object Gödel script. A script is similar to a program except that it has no module structure. Scripts are particularly useful as the target for partial evaluators. The system module `Scripts` provides operations on the type `Script`. This approach to meta-programming is declarative – all the predicates providing the operations on the various abstract data types can be understood declaratively. This, combined with the fact that a large number of useful operations are provided by these modules, means that Gödel provides a congenial environment for meta-programming.

Input/Output

Unfortunately, at the interface between a program and the external world, the declarative semantics of a program can be severely compromised. To try to ameliorate such difficulties, we recommend that programmers exploit Gödel's module system. The idea is to have all the modules which use input/output predicates as high as possible in the module hierarchy. This means that modules not above or equal to these input/output modules will not make any calls to input/output predicates. Thus they will contain pure code together possibly with commits. In other words, it will actually be modules not above or equal to the input/output modules of a Gödel program which will have the significantly improved declarative semantics.

Summary

There are precisely two facilities, input/output and pruning, which adversely affect the declarative semantics of Gödel programs. Input/output introduces side-effects via read predicates. However, as was pointed out above, this problem can be ameliorated by appropriate use of the module system. Commit affects the declarative semantics because it can cause correct answers to be pruned. Fortunately, Gödel programs generally need few uses of pruning. Except where use is made of either of these two facilities, Gödel programs are declarative.

The declarative nature of Gödel programs provides a number of important advantages. First, Gödel is eminently suited as a teaching language partly because students can concentrate much more on writing down what it is they want to compute without being so concerned about how to compute it. Second, Gödel narrows the gap between theory and practice in logic programming. At the moment, most practical logic programming languages rely on a significant number of non-logical features for which there is no useful semantics. By greatly reducing the reliance on non-logical features, Gödel thus provides a solid bridge between theory and practice. Third, the fact that Gödel meta-programs are declarative makes some desirable applications possible. One of these is to build a compiler-generator by partial evaluating a (self-applicable) partial evaluator with respect to itself as input. Another such application is the use of a declarative debugger to debug Gödel programs. Declarative debugging is an attractive debugging technique which only requires that the programmer know the intended interpretation of a program to locate certain bugs. In particular, knowledge of the procedural behaviour of the Gödel system is not needed. Fourth, Gödel more easily allows a parallel implementation since there are only a couple of non-logical features to complicate matters. Finally, because the language has so few features (namely, input/output and pruning) which have side-effects or have global effects on a search tree, there is very little to unnecessarily impede the exploitation of parallelism in programs.

1.3 Comparison with Prolog

In this section, we make a detailed comparison between Prolog and Gödel. This comparison provides much of the motivation for various design decisions for Gödel. In particular, we examine those Prolog features which are non-logical, since these are the ones that need most attention. We begin by discussing some general requirements for any programming language.

Five desirable properties of any programming language are that it be high level, expressive, efficient, practical, and have a simple (mathematical) semantics. A high level language is one which provides concepts as close as possible to those which people like to use to express their thoughts and ideas. An expressive language is one which provides concepts that can be used to model real-world situations easily and concisely. An efficient language is one for which typical programs run at speeds and memory costs similar to competing languages. A practical language is one that can be used for large-scale, real-world applications. A language with a simple semantics is one for which programmers can relatively easily verify and debug their programs and be assured of the correctness of program transformations, optimizations, and so on.

Prolog has proved to be a great success in a wide variety of application areas. This success is undoubtedly due to the fact that Prolog is comparatively high level, efficient, and practical. Prolog's importance and widespread use is well justified by these properties. However, Prolog is not sufficiently expressive as the logic it uses is untyped. Furthermore, Prolog's semantics (and by Prolog, we mean the practical programming language as it is embodied in currently available Prolog systems, not the idealized pure subsets studied in [15], for example) is not at all satisfactory. The problems with the semantics are numerous and well known: the lack of occur check, the use of unsafe negation, the use of non-logical predicates, such as `var`, `nonvar`, `assert`, and `retract`, the undisciplined use of cut, and so on. These problematical aspects of Prolog cause many practical Prolog programs to have no declarative semantics at all and to have unnecessarily complicated procedural semantics. This means that the analysis, transformation, optimization, verification, and debugging of many Prolog programs is extremely difficult.

The solution to these semantic problems is to take more seriously the central thesis of logic programming, which is that

- a program is a (first order) theory, and
- computation is deduction from the theory.

It is crucially important that programs can be understood directly as theories. When this is the case, they have simple declarative semantics and can be much more easily verified, transformed, debugged, and so on. Each of the problematical aspects mentioned above causes difficulties precisely because it creates an impediment to the understanding of a program as a theory. A Prolog program which cannot be understood in some simple way as a theory has only a procedural semantics. This leaves us in no better position to understand the program than if it was written in a conventional procedural language.

Gödel directly addresses these semantic problems of Prolog. The main design aim of Gödel is to have functionality and expressiveness similar to Prolog, but to have greatly improved declarative semantics compared with Prolog. Gödel is intended to have the same relation to Prolog as Pascal does to Fortran. Fortran was one of the earliest high-level languages and suffered from a lack of understanding at that time of what were good programming language features. In particular, it had a meagre set of data types and relied on the `goto` for control. Pascal, which was introduced 10 years later, benefited greatly from a considerable amount of research into programming language design. In particular, Pascal had a rich set of data types and relied on structured control facilities instead of the `goto`. Similarly, Prolog was designed at the birth of logic programming before researchers had a clear understanding of how best to handle many facilities. Consequently, these facilities compromised its declarative semantics. In the period since Prolog first appeared, various research projects have shown how to design logic programming languages with

better software engineering facilities and greatly improved declarative semantics with all
the well-known advantages that these bring. Our aim has been to exploit this research
in the design of Gödel.

Now we turn to some problematical features of Prolog. To begin with, we discuss
Prolog's approach to meta-programming, which is one of its most unsatisfactory aspects.
Unfortunately, Prolog does not make a clear distinction between the object level and
meta-level, and does not provide explicit language facilities for representation of object
level expressions at the meta-level. Thus important representation (that is, naming)
and semantic issues are glossed over. As we show below, Prolog's meta-programming
problems can be traced to the fact that it doesn't handle the representation requirements
properly. A consequence of this is that it is not possible to (directly) understand most
Prolog meta-programs as theories and hence they do not have a declarative semantics.
The most obvious symptom of this is with **var**, which has no declarative semantics at
all in Prolog. However, within the framework of the appropriate representation, a meta-
program is a first order theory and the meta-logical predicates of Prolog, such as **var**,
nonvar, **assert**, and **retract**, have declarative counterparts.

We now point out precisely where Prolog's meta-programming problems lie. The first
problem is illustrated by one of the best known meta-programs, the standard **solve**
interpreter. This interpreter consists of the following definition for **solve**.

```
solve(empty).
solve(x and y) <- solve(x) & solve(y).
solve(x) <- clause(x,y) & solve(y).
```

together with a definition for **clause**, which is used to represent the object program. For
example, if the object program contains the clause

```
p(x,y) <- q(x,z) & r(z,y).
```

then there is a corresponding clause of the form

```
clause(p(x,y), q(x,z) and r(z,y)).
```

appearing in the definition of **clause**.

However, the declarative meaning of the **solve** interpreter is by no means clear. The
problem is that the variables in the definition of **clause** and the variables in the definition
of **solve** intuitively range over different domains [10]. Thus the intended interpretation
is simply not a model of the program. What is at stake here is whether it is possible to
give a simple and precise semantics to the **solve** interpreter and other meta-programs.
Without such a semantics, it is impossible, for example, to verify them or prove the
correctness of transformations performed on them.

If the different kinds of variable are intended to range over different domains, then there is a clear solution: we should introduce types into the language underlying the meta-program. The key aspect of the appropriate representation is that an object level variable is represented by a meta-level variable. This representation is called the *nonground* representation. Then, for example, using an appropriately typed version of the `solve` interpreter, it is possible to prove its soundness and completeness for both the declarative and procedural semantics [10].

However, Prolog has another problem related to the fact that an object level variable is (implicitly) represented by a meta-level *variable*. This leads to severe semantic problems with `var`, for example. With this representation, there seems to be no way of giving a declarative semantics to `var` (or, equivalently, `nonvar`). To see the difficulty, consider the goals

```
<- var(x) & solve(p(x)).
```

and

```
<- solve(p(x)) & var(x).
```

If the object program consists solely of the clause `p(a)` (a a constant), then (using the "leftmost literal" computation rule) the first goal succeeds, while the second goal fails.

These considerations lead to another representation, called the *ground* representation, in which object level expressions are represented by ground terms at the meta-level. In particular, in the ground representation, an object level variable is represented by a ground meta-level term. The ground representation is a standard tool in mathematical logic. Using this representation, it is possible to give appropriate definitions for declarative counterparts of the static meta-logical predicates of Prolog, such as `var` and `nonvar`.

We remark that it is possible to identify two different uses of `var` in Prolog. The first is the "meta-logical" use which can be understood as above. This use of `var` is exemplified by the unification algorithm given on page 152 of [20]. The other use is the "control" use, which is exemplified by the program for `grandparent` given on page 148 of [20]. In Gödel, the meta-logical use of `var` is covered by a declarative replacement for it. Some of the control uses of `var` are covered by the provision of control declarations.

Meta-programs are often required to manipulate the representations of object programs, creating new object program representations dynamically. For example, a partial evaluator and a program transformer both do this. To do this declaratively, we need one further idea, which is that object programs should be represented not as meta-programs, but instead as meta-level terms [3]. Using this idea together with the ground representation, it is straightforward to set up the abstract data types used in the Gödel approach to meta-programming and to give appropriate definitions for declarative counterparts of the dynamic meta-logical predicates of Prolog, such as `assert` and `retract` [11].

We remark that the ground representation is easily the more important of the two representations. In fact, the non-ground representation seems useful mostly for the `solve` interpreter and various extensions of it. As soon as, for example, we want to do any significant manipulation of meta-level terms representing object level expressions, we must use the ground representation. This means that most of the important uses of meta-programming, such as compiling, transforming, partially evaluating, and debugging, will require the ground representation. Gödel does not provide any special support (other than the type system) for the non-ground representation. This means that, while it is straightforward to write in Gödel a `solve` interpreter and extensions of it in a similar way to Prolog, the non-ground representation of the object program must be given explicitly by the programmer. On the other hand, Gödel provides considerable support for the ground representation for the reasons given above.

Representing object level variables by ground meta-level terms means that we can no longer make direct use of the underlying unification of the system. In principle, much low-level computation, which is normally done directly and efficiently by the system, must now be done less efficiently by explicit Gödel code. However, as is demonstrated in [8] and [9], there is scope for dramatic improvement of the efficiency of Gödel meta-programs by partial evaluation. Furthermore, there is a major implementation advantage in making programs more declarative, which is that more declarative programs are more easily parallelized. In fact, we conjecture that the cost of implementing the ground representation will be more than repaid by the greater degree of parallelism available on the coming generation of parallel machines. In other words, we conjecture that ultimately Gödel meta-programs will run faster than corresponding Prolog meta-programs!

Next we turn to pruning. Prolog uses the cut as its pruning operator. However, cut has a number of semantic problems, which were discussed in detail in [12]. The first of these problems is that cut, at least as it is employed in existing Prolog systems, allows considerable uncertainty about what the underlying logic component of the program is. This is because programmers can exploit the sequential nature of cut to leave "tests" out and when this is done the logic component of the program cannot be obtained by simply removing all the cuts from the program. Furthermore, there is no convention for systematically putting back the omitted tests so as to define the logic component precisely. The second problem with cut is that its use, in the presence of negation, can be unsound, in the sense that a computed answer may not be correct with respect to the completion of the logic component of the program. The third problem is that the class of programs containing cut is not closed under program transformations.

For these reasons and because the commit of the concurrent logic programming languages [19] has better semantics, Gödel's pruning operator, also called commit, is based on the commit of the concurrent languages. In fact, the simplest form of the commit (denoted | and called bar commit) is similar to the commit of the concurrent languages. Consider the following definition of the proposition M, in which we write | as a connective with the declarative meaning of conjunction.

```
M <- Q | R.
M <- S | T.
```

The informal procedural meaning of bar commit is that it finds only one solution for the formula to its left in the body and prunes all branches corresponding to other statements in the definition which contain a bar commit. The order in which the statements are tried is not specified, so that bar commit does not have the sequentiality property of cut. For the above definition, if M is called and S succeeds, then only one solution will be found for S and the branch corresponding to the first statement will be pruned.

We now investigate the extent to which | supports program transformations. Consider the following program.

```
P <- M & L.
P <- N.
M <- Q | R.
M <- S | T.
N <- U | V.
```

How can we unfold on M and N in the definition for P? A first attempt might be the following definition for P.

```
P <- Q | R & L.
P <- S | T & L.
P <- U | V.
```

However, this is not correct as the | notation is unable to distinguish the commits in the first two statements from the commit in the third statement. This difficulty leads us to introduce a more flexible notation than |. This notation has the form {...}_1, where 1 is a label (which is a positive integer). In this notation, the previous program would be written as follows.

```
P <- M & L.
P <- N.
M <- {Q}_1 & R.
M <- {S}_1 & T.
N <- {U}_1 & V.
```

The brackets {...} capture the scope of the commit inside a statement. By convention, for | this scope is the formula to its left. The label captures the scope of the commit over the statements in the definition. When a formula $\{W\}\_1$ succeeds, all branches in the search tree corresponding to other statements in the definition which contain a commit labelled 1 are pruned. The other pruning that takes place is that only one solution is found for W. Now when we unfold on M and N in the definition for P, we obtain the following definition

```
P <- {Q}_1 & R & L.
P <- {S}_1 & T & L.
P <- {U}_2 & V.
```

in which the label in the commit in the definition for N has been standardized apart to avoid an unwanted coincidence with the label of the commits in the definition for M. Note that we have now correctly distinguished the commits.

The notation for the commit is very flexible. For example, we could have the following definition for P.

```
P <- {Q & {R}_2}_1.
P <- {S & {W}_2}_1 & T.
P <- {U & V}.
P <- W & V.
```

This definition illustrates that a single statement can contain several commits and that commits can be nested. Note also that the commit {...} in the third statement has no label. This is syntactic sugar for a commit with a label different from all other commit labels in the definition. This commit gives just one solution for the formula it contains but does not prune any branches corresponding to other statements in the definition. Thus the commit contains a one-solution operator as a special case. We envisage programmers writing almost all their programs with just the two important special cases of the commit – the bar commit | and the one-solution commit {...}. However, source-level tools, such as partial evaluators and program transformers, will require the flexibility of the general commit, since definitions as complex as the previous one can easily be obtained from definitions using the | notation after just a few unfolding steps.

Other problematical aspects of Prolog can be repaired comparatively easily. For example, Gödel requires a sound implementation of negation instead of Prolog's unsound version. A sound implementation of negation is not expensive or difficult to implement. Related to this, Gödel adopts the declarative and flexible if-then-else construct of NU-Prolog [21]. Also Gödel (at least in principle) does the occur check during unification.

However, the occur check is generally very expensive and so it is important for an implementation to avoid occur checks whenever possible. Fortunately, in practice the occur check very rarely causes the unification algorithm to fail, so there is considerable scope for reducing the occur check overhead by determining through program analysis the few places where the occur check may be needed. In this way, an implementation can be both sound and efficient.

Many extensions and variations of Prolog have been introduced and studied by the logic programming community over the last 15 years. These include concurrent languages, constraint languages, and higher order languages. Unfortunately, these languages have been essentially built on top of Prolog and therefore inherit many of Prolog's semantic problems. For example, most of these languages use Prolog's approach to meta-programming. We hope that the designers of future logic programming languages will see from Gödel that it really *is* possible to design and implement a logic programming language which is both practical and declarative.

2 Types

In this chapter, we discuss the Gödel type system, giving details of the various kinds of language declaration which are used to define the polymorphic many-sorted languages in which programs are written.

2.1 Many-Sortedness

The main purpose of this chapter is to explain the Gödel type system. However, since a program consists of a collection of modules, to do that it is convenient to introduce here the simplest form of module. Modules are explained in detail in Chapter 5.

A module consists of module declarations, language declarations, control declarations, and statements. Module declarations name modules and declare which symbols of the language are imported and exported. Language declarations define a polymorphic many-sorted language. Control declarations constrain the computation rule. Statements are the formulas in the language which define the propositions and predicates. To begin with, we only require the module declaration which consists of the keyword MODULE followed by the name of the module. For example, the following module has name M1.

Now let us turn to the Gödel type system, which is based on many-sorted logic with parametric polymorphism. We first discuss the many-sorted aspect of the type system. Consider module M1 below which defines the predicates Append and Append3 for appending lists of days of the week. Note that variables are denoted by identifiers beginning with a lower case letter and constants by identifiers beginning with an upper case letter.

In general, language declarations begin with the keywords BASE, CONSTRUCTOR, CONSTANT, FUNCTION, PROPOSITION, or PREDICATE. These declarations declare the *symbols* of the language, which belong in one of the *categories*: base, constructor, constant, function, proposition, or predicate. In module M1, the language declaration beginning with the keyword BASE gives the types of the many-sorted language of the module. It declares Day and ListOfDay to be *bases*, which are the only types of the language. (More complicated types will be introduced shortly.) The next three declarations declare the constants, functions, and predicates of the language. The first part of the CONSTANT declaration declares Nil to be a constant of type ListOfDay. The second part declares Monday, Tuesday, etc., to be constants of type Day. The FUNCTION declaration declares Cons to be a binary function which maps a tuple of arguments, where the first argument is of type Day and the second argument is of type ListOfDay, to an element of type ListOfDay. The PREDICATE declaration declares Append to be a ternary predicate each of whose arguments has type ListOfDay. It also declares Append3 to be a quaternary predicate each of whose arguments has type ListOfDay. Statements and goals are written in the language defined by the language declarations. A proposition is declared with

---

```
MODULE        M1.

BASE          Day, ListOfDay.

CONSTANT      Nil : ListOfDay;
              Monday, Tuesday, Wednesday, Thursday, Friday, Saturday,
              Sunday : Day.
FUNCTION      Cons : Day * ListOfDay -> ListOfDay.
PREDICATE     Append : ListOfDay * ListOfDay * ListOfDay;
              Append3 : ListOfDay * ListOfDay * ListOfDay * ListOfDay.

Append(Nil,x,x).
Append(Cons(u,x),y,Cons(u,z)) <-
              Append(x,y,z).

Append3(x,y,z,u) <-
              Append(x,y,w) &
              Append(w,z,u).
```

---

a `PROPOSITION` declaration. So, for example, a module may contain the declaration

`PROPOSITION   P,Q.`

which declares P and Q to be propositions.

In general, the identifier immediately after the keyword of a language declaration is called the *name* of the symbol being declared. Until the last section of this chapter, distinct symbols declared in the same module have distinct names. Thus, until then, in the context of a single module, a symbol can be uniquely identified by its name and we are free, as we have already done in the previous paragraph, to refer to a symbol via its name. Later we will introduce a more flexible mechanism which allows overloading, that is, the use of the same name for distinct symbols.

Module M1 forms a complete program on its own. Typical goals for this program could be as follows.

`<- Append3(Cons(Monday,Nil), Cons(Tuesday,Nil), Cons(Wednesday,Nil), x).`

`<- Append3(x, y, z, Cons(Monday,Cons(Tuesday,Cons(Wednesday,Nil)))).`

Next we introduce *constructors* using module M2, which is a variation of module M1. The main difference between the two modules is that in module M2 a unary constructor List has been declared. From the base Day and the constructor List, the set of all types of the language is obtained by forming all "ground terms" from the "constant" Day and the "function" List. Thus the types of the language are Day, List(Day), List(List(Day)), and so on. Note that a constructor itself is not a type.

```
MODULE        M2.

BASE          Day.
CONSTRUCTOR   List/1.

CONSTANT      Nil : List(Day);
              Monday, Tuesday, Wednesday, Thursday, Friday, Saturday,
              Sunday : Day.
FUNCTION      Cons : Day * List(Day) -> List(Day).
PREDICATE     Append : List(Day) * List(Day) * List(Day);
              Append3 : List(Day) * List(Day) * List(Day) * List(Day).

Append(Nil,x,x).
Append(Cons(u,x),y,Cons(u,z)) <-
            Append(x,y,z).

Append3(x,y,z,u) <-
            Append(x,y,w) &
            Append(w,z,u).
```

All bases and constructors of the language must be declared. If there is no constructor, then the set of all types is just the set of all bases. If at least one constructor is declared, then the set of all types is obtained by applying the above construction using the bases as "constants" and the constructors as "functions". For example, if a base Person were declared in addition to those bases declared in module M2, then the set of all types would be Day, Person, List(Day), List(Person), List(List(Day)), List(List(Person)), and so on. In mathematical treatments of many-sorted logic, there is no need for the types (i.e. sorts) to have any structure. They are usually considered to be simply (unstructured) elements of the set of types. In contrast, for programming languages, it is very convenient for types to have structured names as Gödel does.

Note also that if there is at least one constructor and one base declared, the set of types is (countably) infinite. In some cases, this may mean that the language contains more types than the programmer really wants. For example, in module M2, the only types of interest are Day and List(Day). It would be possible to have a more flexible way of specifying types so that, in the case that a programmer wanted only some subset of the types given by the above construction, this could be achieved. For example, a more flexible notation for language declarations could allow a programmer to have only the types Day and List(Day) in the language. In most cases, it is not worth the extra complication in the language declarations needed to achieve this since no great harm is done in assuming that the intended interpretation is augmented with the extra types.

Every symbol of the language must be declared. The types of variables and their corresponding (possibly implicit) quantifiers in a statement are not declared, but are assigned by the system. This type assignment must satisfy the requirement that the statement be a many-sorted formula. Since every symbol has a language declaration, such an assignment, if it exists, is unique. Within a single statement, each variable will be assigned a single type although there is no requirement that a variable be assigned the same type in different statements.[1] For example, for module M1, the variable x in the first statement is assigned the type ListOfDay. In the second statement, the variable u is assigned the type Day, and the variables x, y, and z are assigned the type ListOfDay. In the third statement, the variables u, x, y, and z are assigned the type ListOfDay. So the collection of declarations and statements of module M1 together do constitute a module.

However, the declarations

```
BASE          Day, Person.
PREDICATE     P : Day * Person.
```

and the statement

```
P(x,x).
```

(together with a MODULE declaration) do not constitute a module, since there is no type which can be assigned to x to satisfy the declaration for P.

---

[1]This notational flexibility is very convenient in a programming language. By a suitable renaming of variables, if necessary, it is straightforward to map a program employing this licence with variables to a many-sorted theory with the stricter variable restrictions of many-sorted logic.

2.2 Polymorphism

Next we introduce the second aspect of the type system, which is parametric polymorphism. It is common for a programmer to want to write a definition of a predicate for which the arguments of the predicate can have a variety of types. For example, the Append predicate is normally written so that it can append lists of any type. For this purpose, we add parametric polymorphism to the type system, as illustrated by module M3 below.

```
MODULE        M3.

BASE          Day, Person.
CONSTRUCTOR   List/1.

CONSTANT      Nil : List(a);
              Monday, Tuesday, Wednesday, Thursday, Friday, Saturday,
              Sunday : Day;
              Fred, Bill, Mary : Person.
FUNCTION      Cons : a * List(a) -> List(a).
PREDICATE     Append : List(a) * List(a) * List(a);
              Append3 : List(a) * List(a) * List(a) * List(a).

Append(Nil,x,x).
Append(Cons(u,x),y,Cons(u,z)) <-
              Append(x,y,z).

Append3(x,y,z,u) <-
              Append(x,y,w) &
              Append(w,z,u).
```

The logic on which module M3 is based is called *polymorphic many-sorted logic.* In module M3, a is a *parameter*, which is a type variable. Like variables, parameters are not declared. For a polymorphic many-sorted language, we need to extend the concept of a type. For such a language, a type is a "term" constructed using the bases as "constants", the parameters as "variables", and the constructors as "functions". Thus, for module M3, the following are types: a, List(a), and List(List(Day)). A *ground* type (also called a *monotype*) is a type not containing parameters. Thus the ground types for module M3 are Day, Person, List(Day), List(Person), List(List(Day)), and so on.

A symbol is *polymorphic* if its declaration contains a parameter; otherwise, it is *monomorphic*. A polymorphic symbol can be understood as representing a collection of (monomorphic) symbols. For example, the CONSTANT declaration for the polymorphic constant Nil in module M3 declares a countably infinite set of (monomorphic) constants of type List(τ), where τ ranges over all ground types. It is helpful to imagine the distinct constants in this collection as being subscripted by the corresponding value for τ. Thus the (monomorphic) constants declared by the declaration for Nil are $\mathrm{Nil}_{\mathrm{Day}}$ of type List(Day), $\mathrm{Nil}_{\mathrm{Person}}$ of type List(Person), $\mathrm{Nil}_{\mathrm{List(Day)}}$ of type List(List(Day)), and so on. There is a similar understanding of polymorphic functions and predicates.

The definition of a formula in a polymorphic many-sorted language is given in Section A.2. It is decidable whether an expression is a formula or not. A polymorphic formula can be understood as representing a collection of (monomorphic) formulas. For example, consider module M3. During checks that the statements in M3 are actually formulas, the variable u in the second statement for Append has the type a assigned, and the variables x, y, and z have the type List(a) assigned. Thus the second statement for Append represents the following collection of formulas:

$\mathrm{Append}_{\mathrm{Day}}(\mathrm{Cons}_{\mathrm{Day}}(\mathtt{u},\mathtt{x}),\mathtt{y},\mathrm{Cons}_{\mathrm{Day}}(\mathtt{u},\mathtt{z}))$ <- $\mathrm{Append}_{\mathrm{Day}}(\mathtt{x},\mathtt{y},\mathtt{z})$,

$\mathrm{Append}_{\mathrm{Person}}(\mathrm{Cons}_{\mathrm{Person}}(\mathtt{u},\mathtt{x}),\mathtt{y},\mathrm{Cons}_{\mathrm{Person}}(\mathtt{u},\mathtt{z}))$ <- $\mathrm{Append}_{\mathrm{Person}}(\mathtt{x},\mathtt{y},\mathtt{z})$,

$\mathrm{Append}_{\mathrm{List(Day)}}(\mathrm{Cons}_{\mathrm{List(Day)}}(\mathtt{u},\mathtt{x}),\mathtt{y},\mathrm{Cons}_{\mathrm{List(Day)}}(\mathtt{u},\mathtt{z}))$ <-

$$\mathrm{Append}_{\mathrm{List(Day)}}(\mathtt{x},\mathtt{y},\mathtt{z}),$$

and so on.

As another example, consider the module ParametricTypes below. The variable x has type a in the atom Q(x) and has type M in the atom P(F(x)). Thus the variable x has type M in P(F(x)) <- Q(x) because the types of the two occurrences of x in the statement can be unified to give the type M. Thus the argument F(x) of P has type L(M) in this statement.

We also need to extend the usual definitions of interpretation, model, logical consequence, and so on, from many-sorted to polymorphic many-sorted logic. For a polymorphic many-sorted language, an interpretation has a domain corresponding to every ground type and these domains are pairwise disjoint. Then a constant such as Nil in module M3 with polymorphic type List(a) is assigned a (countably infinite) set of domain elements, one in the domain of each ground type which can be obtained by replacing the a in List(a) by a ground type. This corresponds to the assignment as for a (monomorphic) many-sorted language of a single domain element to each of the (monomorphic)

```
MODULE          ParametricTypes.

BASE            M.

CONSTRUCTOR     L/1.

FUNCTION        F : a -> L(a).

PREDICATE       P : L(M);
                Q : a.

P(F(x)) <- Q(x).
```

---

constants which `Nil` represents. In a similar way, one can define the assignments to functions and predicates. The definitions of model, logical consequence, and so on, also generalize from a (monomorphic) many-sorted language to a polymorphic many-sorted language in a similar way. The details can be found in Section A.2.

For a module such as `M3` which does not depend upon other modules, the *language of the module* is the polymorphic many-sorted language defined by the language declarations in the module. In Chapter 5, we will extend this concept to the case where a module is one of a number of modules constituting a program.

A *statement*[2] in a module is a formula in the language of the module having the form either `A` or `A <- W`, where `A` is an atom, called the *head* of the statement, and `W` is a formula, called the *body* of the statement. Any variables in `A` and any free variables in `W` are assumed to be universally quantified at the front of the statement. In addition, each statement must satisfy a condition on the types of the arguments in the head. This condition will be given shortly.

A *goal*[2] for a program consisting of a single module[3] has the form `<- W`, where `W` is a formula in the language of the module. `W` is called the *body* of the goal. Any free variables in `W` are assumed to be universally quantified at the front of the goal.

Module `M3` forms a complete program on its own. Typical goals for this program could be as follows:

---

[2]In Chapter 7 we shall extend this definition to include commits.

[3]The module must also be open. See Chapter 5 for the definition of an open module.

```
<- Append3(Cons(Monday,Nil), Cons(Tuesday,Nil), Cons(Wednesday,Nil), x).
```

```
<- Append3(x, y, z, Cons(Fred,Cons(Bill,Cons(Mary,Nil)))).
```

When a goal is given for a program consisting of a single module[3], the goal is first checked to make sure it is a formula in the language of the module. A desirable requirement of a type system is that goals can then be run with no run-time type checking. However, we need to impose two conditions to ensure this property holds.

The first of these conditions is the head condition [17].

- A statement satisfies the *head condition* if the tuple of types of the arguments of the head in the statement is a variant of the type declared for the predicate in the head.

Note that the head condition is satisfied by the statement in module ParametricTypes and also each statement in module M3.

The second condition is transparency. To state this, some new terminology is convenient. The type appearing on the right of the -> in a function declaration is called the *range type*.

- A declaration for a function is *transparent* if every parameter appearing in the declaration also appears in the range type.

Then, under the assumptions that each statement satisfies the head condition and that each function declaration is transparent, it can be shown that no run-time type checking is needed with standard proof procedures. For example, no type error will occur if a program and goal are run under the usual (untyped) SLDNF-resolution. (See [17] or [13, Theorem 5.7].) The head condition and transparency are general and natural conditions, so their imposition rarely causes any inconvenience.

Lists are a common data structure. Thus Gödel provides, via the module system, a constructor List, a constant Nil, and a function Cons, whose declarations are as follows.

```
CONSTRUCTOR    List/1.
CONSTANT       Nil : List(a).
FUNCTION       Cons : a * List(a) -> List(a).
```

Gödel also provides a special list syntax which is syntactic sugar on top of Nil and Cons. This is the usual [...] and | syntax used in Prolog. Thus the list

```
Cons(Fred,Cons(Bill,Cons(Mary,Nil)))
```

can be written more conveniently as

[Fred,Bill,Mary].

Similarly, the list

Cons(Fred,Cons(Bill,x))

can be written as

[Fred,Bill|x].

The constructor List, the list notation, and the various list processing predicates are made available for use by the module Lists, which is provided by the system. In Lists, the constructor List is declared, as are the constant Nil and the function Cons. Also a collection of useful list processing predicates, including Append, is defined there. Another module can make these symbols available for use by means of an IMPORT module declaration. For example, in module M4 below, the IMPORT declaration imports into M4 the constructor List, the constant Nil, the function Cons, and various predicates including Append. Thus these symbols are available for use in M4. We shall see the way Lists exports these in Chapters 5 and 6. In general, if a module imports from another module, it imports *all* the symbols exported by the other module.

Modules M4, Lists, and Integers (see Chapter 4), which is imported by Lists, together form a program. Typical goals for this program could then be as follows.

<- Append3([Monday], [Tuesday], [Wednesday], x).

<- Append3(x, y, z, [Fred,Bill,Mary]).

<- Append3(x, y, z, [1,2,3]).

```
MODULE      M4.

IMPORT      Lists.

BASE        Day, Person.

CONSTANT    Monday, Tuesday, Wednesday, Thursday, Friday, Saturday,
            Sunday : Day;
            Fred, Bill, Mary : Person.
PREDICATE   Append3 : List(a) * List(a) * List(a) * List(a).

Append3(x,y,z,u) <-
            Append(x,y,w) &
            Append(w,z,u).
```

---

3 Formulas

As we indicated in Chapter 2, arbitrary formulas can be used in the bodies of statements and goals. In this chapter, we examine the use of this facility in more detail.

3.1 Quantifiers and Connectives

In Gödel, conjunction is denoted by &, disjunction by \/, negation by ~, (left) implication by <-, (right) implication by ->, and equivalence by <->. The universal quantifier is denoted by ALL and the existential quantifier is denoted by SOME. Each quantifier has two arguments, the first being a list of the quantified variables and the second the scope of the quantifier. Note that the types of the quantified variables in the body of a statement or goal are not declared. The types of these variables are assigned by the type checker along with the types of the other variables in the statement or goal.

As an example, module Inclusion below contains the definition of the predicate IncludedIn, which is intended to be true if and only if its first argument is a list of elements of some type and its second argument is a list of elements of the same type which includes all the elements appearing in the first argument. Thus, for example, the goal[1]

```
<- IncludedIn([1,3,2],[4,3,2,1]).
```

succeeds and the goal

```
<- IncludedIn([1,5,2],[4,3,2,1]).
```

fails.

```
MODULE        Inclusion.

IMPORT        Lists.

PREDICATE     IncludedIn : List(a) * List(a).

IncludedIn(x,y) <-
              ALL [z] (Member(z,y) <- Member(z,x)).
```

---

[1]Note that the integers are available in the module Inclusion since they are imported via Lists. See Chapter 6.

```
MODULE          DB.

BASE            Person.

CONSTANT        Fred, Mary, George, James, Jane, Sue : Person.

PREDICATE       Ancestor, Parent, Mother, Father : Person * Person.

Ancestor(x,y) <-
                Parent(x,y).
Ancestor(x,y) <-
                Parent(x,z) &
                Ancestor(z,y).

Parent(x,y) <-
                Mother(x,y).
Parent(x,y) <-
                Father(x,y).

Father(Fred, Mary).
Father(George, James).

Mother(Sue, Mary).
Mother(Jane, Sue).
```

Allowing an arbitrary formula to appear in the body of a goal is very useful for querying databases, such as module DB above. A typical goal to the program formed by this module could be the following:

Does every person with a mother also have a father?

```
<- ALL [x] (SOME [y] Mother(y,x) -> SOME [z] Father(z,x)).
```

Taking advantage of the notational convention that a variable name beginning with an '_' in the body of a statement or goal stands for a unique variable existentially quantified at the front of the atom in which it appears, the previous goal can be written more compactly as follows.

```
<- ALL [x] (Mother(_,x) -> Father(_,x)).
```

Another goal could be the following:
Find a mother who has no father.

```
<- SOME [z] Mother(x,z) & ~ SOME [y] Father(y,x).
```

Using the underscore notation, this can be written as follows.

```
<- Mother(x,_) & ~ Father(_,x).
```

A variable beginning with an underscore in the head of a statement stands for a unique variable universally quantified at the front of the statement.

Sometimes a programmer may only be interested in the values of a subset of the free variables in the body of a goal. In this case, the unwanted variables can be masked out using the following colon notation. For example, suppose the goal was as follows:
Find all grandparents of Jane.

```
<- x : Parent(x,y) & Parent(y,Jane).
```

The "x :" reads "find an x such that". In general, there can be zero or more variables before the colon, separated by commas. Actually, the "x,y,... :" can be replaced by "SOME [u,v,...]", as in

```
<- SOME [y] (Parent(x,y) & Parent(y,Jane)).
```

However, the colon notation is usually more convenient, since it expresses directly the variables of interest and is often shorter. It is an error if a variable appears before the colon but is not a free variable in the body of the goal. Note that the colon notation is only available for use in goals and is not available for use in statements.

3.2 Conditionals

The connectives and quantifiers introduced so far provide an expressive language in which to write goals and statements. However, there are situations for which it is advantageous to provide constructs with specialized procedural semantics. The most common such situation is when a programmer wants to use a formula of the form

(Condition & Formula1)   \/   (~Condition & Formula2)

in a body. Although this formula is written with the connectives introduced so far, this approach has the disadvantage that *Condition* may be computed twice. Obviously, if *Condition* is computationally expensive, this is undesirable. For this reason, Gödel also has `IF-THEN` and `IF-THEN-ELSE` constructs, called *conditionals*, which should be implemented in such a way as to avoid this inefficiency.

Each of these constructs has two forms. The first form of the `IF-THEN` construct is

`IF` *Condition* `THEN` *Formula*

where *Condition* and *Formula* are formulas. (If *Condition* has an existential quantifier at the top level, then *Condition* must be bracketed for this form of the `IF-THEN`. The reason for this will become clear shortly.) This formula is defined to mean

(*Condition* & *Formula*)   \/   ˜*Condition*

or, equivalently,

Condition -> *Formula*.

So this construct is redundant. It is included mainly because it completes the collection of conditionals.

Sometimes this first form of the `IF-THEN` construct is not suitable because *Condition* and *Formula* share local variables. For this reason, a second form of the `IF-THEN` construct due to Naish [18] is available. This is

`IF SOME` $[x_1, \ldots, x_n]$ *Condition* `THEN` *Formula*

where *Condition* and *Formula* are formulas. This formula is defined to mean

(`SOME` $[x_1, \ldots, x_n]$ (*Condition* & *Formula*))   \/   ˜ `SOME` $[x_1, \ldots, x_n]$ *Condition*.

Note carefully that this is a non-standard use of the connective `IF-THEN` in that the quantification extends over both *Condition* and *Formula*. However, from a programming viewpoint, this non-standard use is very convenient. An implementation of this form of `IF-THEN` should avoid the inefficiency of computing *Condition* twice, in the sense that *Condition* should be run to determine whether `SOME` $[x_1, \ldots, x_n]$ *Condition* or its negation is a logical consequence of (the completion of) the program, after which the appropriate component of the disjunct can be deleted.

Now we turn to the `IF-THEN-ELSE` construct. The first form of this is

`IF` *Condition* `THEN` *Formula1* `ELSE` *Formula2*

where *Condition*, *Formula1* and *Formula2* are formulas. (If *Condition* has an existential quantifier at the top level, then *Condition* must be bracketed for this form of the `IF-THEN-ELSE`.) This formula is defined to mean

(*Condition* & *Formula1*)   \/   (˜*Condition* & *Formula2*).

As an example of the use of this form of `IF-THEN-ELSE`, here is a definition of the predicate `Max`, which computes the maximum of its first two integer arguments.

```
Max(x,y,z) <- IF x =< y THEN z = y ELSE z = x.
```

Gödel has a second, more flexible, form of the `IF-THEN-ELSE` construct due to Naish [18], which is

IF SOME $[x_1, \ldots, x_n]$ *Condition* THEN *Formula1* ELSE *Formula2*

where *Condition*, *Formula1* and *Formula2* are formulas. This formula is defined to mean

(SOME $[x_1, \ldots, x_n]$ (*Condition* & *Formula1*)) \/

$\qquad\qquad$ (~ SOME $[x_1, \ldots, x_n]$ *Condition* & *Formula2*).

Implementations of both forms of `IF-THEN-ELSE` should avoid the inefficiency of computing *Condition* twice, in the sense described earlier.

If a programmer wants to make use of the first form of `IF-THEN`, but the condition has an existential quantifier at the top level, then explicit scoping must be indicated by using parentheses. Thus

IF (SOME $[x_1, \ldots, x_n]$ *Condition*) THEN *Formula*

means

((SOME $[x_1, \ldots, x_n]$ *Condition*) & *Formula*) \/ ~ SOME $[x_1, \ldots, x_n]$ *Condition*

and not

(SOME $[x_1, \ldots, x_n]$ (*Condition* & *Formula*)) \/ ~ SOME $[x_1, \ldots, x_n]$ *Condition*.

Similar remarks apply to the first form of `IF-THEN-ELSE`.

Nesting of these constructs is allowed, so that a conditional can appear inside another conditional. For example, a case statement can be simulated by a formula of the form

IF *C1* THEN *S1*

$\qquad$ ELSE IF *C2* THEN *S2*

$\qquad\qquad$ ELSE ...

$\qquad\qquad\qquad$ ELSE IF *Cn* THEN *Sn*.

Note that the ambiguity in a formula such as

IF *C1* THEN IF *C2* THEN *S1* ELSE *S2*

is resolved as

IF *C1* THEN (IF *C2* THEN *S1*) ELSE *S2*

that is, the `ELSE` is associated with the outermost `IF`. Rather than relying on this convention, programmers are encouraged to use parentheses when employing embedded conditionals to make their intentions clear. A construct such as

IF SOME $[x_1, \ldots, x_n]$ (*P1* & ... & *Pk*) THEN *S1* ELSE *S2*

can be written without the parentheses as follows:

IF SOME $[x_1, \ldots, x_n]$ *P1* & ... & *Pk* THEN *S1* ELSE *S2*.

The precise grammar for conditionals is given in Chapter 11.

As an example of the use of the IF-THEN-ELSE construct, consider the module **AssocList** below, which defines the predicate **Lookup** for looking up an association list. The list consists of pairs having an integer key in the first argument and a string in the second. (See the module **Strings** in Chapter 6.) The definition of **Lookup** is due to Naish [18]. **Lookup** is intended to be true if and only if either the association list in the third argument contains a pair whose elements are equal to the first two arguments and the fourth argument is equal to the third argument, or the association list in the third argument does not contain a pair whose first element is equal to the first argument and the association list in the fourth argument is equal to a list whose first element is the pair with elements corresponding to the first two arguments and the remainder is the association list in the third argument. Note the quantification of the variable v over the condition and the THEN part, and how this gives the required behaviour of **Lookup**. Thus, for example, the goal

```
<- Lookup(5, value, [Pair(5,"abc"), Pair(5,"xyz"), Pair(1,"lmn")], list).
```

has the answers

```
list = [Pair(5,"abc"),Pair(5,"xyz"),Pair(1,"lmn")]
value = "abc"
```

and

```
list = [Pair(5,"abc"),Pair(5,"xyz"),Pair(1,"lmn")]
value = "xyz"
```

while the goal

```
<- Lookup(4, "rst", [Pair(5,"abc"), Pair(2,"xyz"), Pair(1,"lmn")], list).
```

has the answer

```
list = [Pair(4,"rst"),Pair(5,"abc"),Pair(2,"xyz"),Pair(1,"lmn")].
```

The Gödel programming style makes significant use of conditionals. This is illustrated in Chapter 10 where several programs use statements involving complicated nested conditionals.

MODULE   AssocList.

IMPORT   Strings.

BASE   PairType.

FUNCTION   Pair : Integer * String -> PairType.

PREDICATE   Lookup : Integer * String * List(PairType) * List(PairType).

Lookup(key, value, assoc_list, new_assoc_list) <-
              IF SOME [v] Member(Pair(key,v), assoc_list)
              THEN
                  value = v &
                  new_assoc_list = assoc_list
              ELSE
                  new_assoc_list = [Pair(key,value) | assoc_list].

3.3 Operators

It is often convenient to employ prefix, infix, or postfix notation instead of the standard
logical notation for terms and atoms. For example, we usually prefer to write 1 + 2
instead of +(1,2), u < v instead of <(u,v), and u * v + w instead of +(*(u,v),w).
For this reason, Gödel provides a mechanism for declaring operators, which are functions
or predicates employing such notation.

FUNCTION declarations allow the optional declaration of fixity, precedence, and associativity of unary or binary functions via *function indicators*. The general form of an
indicator for an infix binary function is either $xFx(N)$, $xFy(N)$, or $yFx(N)$. Each of
xFx, xFy, and yFx is a *specifier*. The N, which is a positive integer, is the *precedence*.
The position of the F indicates that the fixity of the function is infix. We shall see shortly
how the x and y indicate associativity. Prefix and postfix binary functions are not allowed. For example, the module Integers provided by the system contains the following
function declarations.

FUNCTION   ^ : yFx(540) : Integer * Integer -> Integer;
              * : yFx(520) : Integer * Integer -> Integer;

```
+ : yFx(510) : Integer * Integer -> Integer;
- : yFx(510) : Integer * Integer -> Integer.
```

These declarations allow the use of infix notation. For example, the specifier yFx in the declaration for + in Integers indicates that + is infix so that u + v should be written instead of +(u,v), and u + (v + w) instead of +(u,+(v,w)).

However, with the fixity information alone, although we can use the infix notation, we must always bracket subterms with structure. For a term containing functions with distinct precedences, the precedence information is used to disambiguate the meaning of the term in the absence of parentheses. The precedence rule is that *the higher its precedence, the more strongly a function binds its arguments.* For example, the precedence 510 for + and the precedence 520 for * in Integers indicate that the term u * v + w means (u * v) + w and not u * (v + w). If the latter meaning is intended, then the term must be written with explicit bracketing to indicate this. In general, precedence (and associativity) information in indicators can always be overridden by explicit bracketing.

The associativity information is needed when a term contains functions with the same precedence. An x indicates that the argument in that position must have precedence strictly higher than the precedence of the function having the indicator, while a y indicates that the argument in that position must have precedence higher than or equal to the precedence of the function having the indicator. For this purpose, the precedence of a term is the precedence of its top-level function, where the precedence of a function without an indicator is taken to be (plus) infinity. The precedence of variables, constants, and terms enclosed in parentheses is also assumed to be (plus) infinity. Thus the specifier xFy means the function is right associative, yFx means the function is left associative, and xFx means the function is non-associative. For example, the indicator yFx(510) in the declaration for + in Integers declares it to be infix, left associative, and to have precedence 510. So the term u + v + w means (u + v) + w and not u + (v + w). Also the indicator yFx(520) in the declaration for * in Integers declares it to be infix, left associative, and to have precedence 520. So the term u * (v + w) * s means (u * (v + w)) * s. Since ^ (exponentiation) has indicator yFx(540), the term

u + 45 * w ^ s ^ r * 2

means

u + ((45 * ((w ^ s) ^ r)) * 2).

Indicators do provide notational convenience. However, this last example shows that it is possible to overdo their use. Often a set of well-placed parentheses, even if they are strictly redundant, greatly reduces the difficulty of understanding the meaning of a complicated term.

The general form of a unary function indicator is either xF(N), Fx(N), yF(N), or Fy(N), where the specifier is either xF, Fx, yF, or Fy, and N, which is a positive integer, is the precedence. Fx and Fy indicate prefix, and xF and yF indicate postfix. The x and y have the same meanings as for binary functions. For example, the module Integers also contains the following function declaration.

FUNCTION   - : Fy(530) : Integer -> Integer.

The indicator Fy(530) declares (unary) - to be prefix, right associative, and to have precedence 530. Thus the term -u + v means (-u) + v and the term - -u means -(-u).

PREDICATE declarations have an optional fixity declaration using a *predicate indicator*. Predicate indicators consist solely of a *specifier* which indicates the fixity of the predicate. The specifier for a binary infix predicate is zPz. Prefix and postfix binary predicates are not allowed. A specifier for a unary predicate is either Pz, indicating that the predicate is prefix, or zP, indicating that the predicate is postfix.

For example, Integers contains the following predicate declarations.

PREDICATE   > : zPz : Integer * Integer;
              < : zPz : Integer * Integer;
             >= : zPz : Integer * Integer;
             =< : zPz : Integer * Integer.

The indicator zPz in the declaration for =< declares it to be infix. Thus, for example, one should write the atom =<(u,v) in the more convenient form u =< v.

An *operator* is defined to be a function or predicate whose language declaration contains an indicator. The precise syntax of operators can be found in Chapter 11. The use of operators can lead to ambiguities in the parsing of expressions, as is illustrated in Chapter 5.

4 Equality and Numbers

In this chapter, we discuss the equality predicate and also the modules which provide the integers, rationals, and floating-point numbers.

4.1 Equality

Equality is a distinguished predicate in logic because it is so fundamental. The same is true of the equality predicate = in Gödel. Equality is built into the system and is available in every module without being imported. It has the following declaration.

```
PREDICATE  = : zPz : a * a.
```

A companion to equality is the disequality predicate ~= whose declaration and definition are as follows.

```
PREDICATE  ~= : zPz : a * a.
```

```
x ~= y <-> ~(x = y).
```

Disequality[1] is also built into the system and is available in every module without being imported.

The equality theory (for user-defined types) is given in Section A.3. We illustrate this here by giving the equality theory for the program which consists just of the module M3. Note that, in each of the following axioms, any variables in an axiom are assumed to be universally quantified at the front of the axiom. First, we have the axioms corresponding to the axiom (schema) 1 of the equality theory.

```
Monday ~= Tuesday.
```

```
Monday ~= Wednesday.
```

$$\vdots$$

```
Sunday ~= Saturday.
```

```
Fred ~= Bill.
```

```
Fred ~= Mary.
```

```
Bill ~= Mary.
```

There is nothing corresponding to axiom 2 since there is only one function in the language of module M3. Corresponding to axiom 3, we have the following axiom.

---

[1]As the previous definition shows, disequality is redundant. However, it is convenient (for syntactic reasons) to have this symbol available and we will use it in the various equality theories as an alternative to negating expressions containing equality.

```
Cons(x,y) ~= Nil.
```

The following axiom (schema) corresponds to axiom 4.

`Cons(s,t) ~= x`, where `Cons(s,t)` contains `x`.

Then comes the axiom corresponding to axiom 5.

```
(x1 ~= y1 \/ x2 ~= y2) -> Cons(x1,x2) ~= Cons(y1,y2).
```

Finally, there are the reflexivity and substitutivity axioms corresponding to axioms 6, 7 and 8.

```
x = x.
```

```
(x1 = y1 & x2 = y2) -> Cons(x1,x2) = Cons(y1,y2).
```

```
(x1 = y1 & x2 = y2) -> (x1 = x2 -> y1 = y2).
```

```
(x1 = y1 & x2 = y2 & x3 = y3) -> (Append(x1,x2,x3) -> Append(y1,y2,y3)).
```

```
(x1 = y1 & x2 = y2 & x3 = y3 & x4 = y4) ->
                          (Append3(x1,x2,x3,x4) -> Append3(y1,y2,y3,y4)).
```

The equality theory consisting of all the above axioms corresponds to "syntactic identity", that is, two (ground) terms of the same type are equal if and only if they are syntactically identical. It is often the case that an intended interpretation of such a theory is an Herbrand interpretation [15] with equality interpreted as identity. However, for some system-defined base types, such as `Integer`, `Rational`, and `Float` corresponding to the integers, rationals, and floating-point numbers, respectively, equality is handled differently. For these types, we do not want to treat equality as syntactic identity. To see this, consider the terms (of type `Integer`)

```
23 + (3 * 5)
```

and

```
40 - 2.
```

With the axioms of the equality theory of Section A.3, these two terms would not be equal. However, the domain of the intended interpretation is the integers and the intended interpretation of the functions in these terms are the usual arithmetic operations on the integers. For this (non-Herbrand) interpretation, the terms are equal because they both evaluate to 38. Consequently, for the type `Integer`, the corresponding = is given the standard meaning of equality on the domain of integers. The types `Rational` and

Float are treated similarly. More complicated types that involve Integer, Rational, and Float, as well as other bases and constructors, are handled in the obvious way. Consider, as an example, the type List(Integer). For this, the components of a term corresponding to the List component of the type (that is, Cons and Nil) are handled using syntactic identity and the components corresponding to the base Integer are handled using the intended meaning of equality on the integers. Thus, for example, the goal

```
<- [2+3,6] = [5,7-1].
```

succeeds because [2+3,6] = [5,7-1] is true in the intended interpretation.

One subtle point when using underscores with ~= is worth noting. Recall that a variable beginning with an underscore in an atom in a body means a unique variable existentially quantified at the front of the atom. If an underscore appears in S ~= T, where S and T are terms, we treat this as ~$(S = T)$, in which case the underscore becomes a unique variable *universally* quantified at the front of S ~= T. So, for example, F(x) ~= F(_) means ALL [y] F(x) ~= F(y), where y is a unique variable, and the call F(x) ~= F(_) will fail. Similarly, x ~= [_|_] means ALL [u,v] x ~= [u|v], where u and v are unique variables. Thus the call S ~= [_|_] succeeds if S is the empty list and fails if it is a non-empty list. Note that x ~= [_|_] should be distinguished from x ~= [y|z], for which the y and z are treated as ordinary variables. Thus, if, for example, x ~= [y|z] occurs as a top-level conjunct in the body of a statement and y and z do not occur elsewhere in the statement, then it is equivalent to SOME [y,z] x ~= [y|z].

In addition to the built-in predicates = and ~=, the system also has two built-in propositions, True and False. The definition of True is

```
True.
```

The proposition False has the empty definition. True and False are built into the system and are available in every module without being imported. So the complete list of built-in propositions and predicates is True, False, =, and ~=.

4.2 Integers

Gödel provides a comprehensive set of functions and predicates with numerical arguments via the modules Integers, Rationals, and Floats. We discuss the module Integers in this section and the modules Rationals and Floats in subsequent sections.

The base type Integer is provided by the module Integers. The export part (except for the control declarations) of Integers is given below. The complete export part

---

EXPORT	Integers.

BASE	Integer.

% CONSTANT	0, 1, 2, ... : Integer.

FUNCTION   ^ : yFx(540) : Integer * Integer -> Integer;
               - : Fy(530) : Integer -> Integer;
               * : yFx(520) : Integer * Integer -> Integer;
               Div : yFx(520) : Integer * Integer -> Integer;
               Mod : yFx(520) : Integer * Integer -> Integer;
               Rem : yFx(520) : Integer * Integer -> Integer;
               + : yFx(510) : Integer * Integer -> Integer;
               - : yFx(510) : Integer * Integer -> Integer;
               Abs : Integer -> Integer;
               Sign : Integer -> Integer;
               Max : Integer * Integer -> Integer;
               Min : Integer * Integer -> Integer.

PREDICATE   > : zPz : Integer * Integer;
               < : zPz : Integer * Integer;
               >= : zPz : Integer * Integer;
               =< : zPz : Integer * Integer;
               Interval : Integer * Integer * Integer.

---

of Integers is given in Chapter 13. The export part of a module contains language declarations for symbols that it makes available to other modules which import from it. The keyword EXPORT indicates the export part of a module.

The export part of the Integers "declares" the constants 0, 1, 2, and so on. Since there are infinitely many non-negative integers and since the syntax does not support the declaration[2] of infinitely many symbols of any kind, this "declaration" is simply indicated by a comment in the export part of Integers. The system knows that Integers is to be treated specially in this regard. The export part of Integers also contains declarations

---

[2]Such a syntax could be provided, but we do not consider it important enough.

of the prefix unary function - (minus), and the infix binary functions ^ (exponentiation), * (multiplication), `Div` (integer quotient), `Mod` (modulus), `Rem` (remainder), + (addition), and - (subtraction), each of whose arguments has type `Integer` and which map to an element of type `Integer`. `Integers` declares the unary functions `Abs` (absolute value) and `Sign` (sign), and the binary functions `Max` (maximum) and `Min` (minimum). It also declares the infix binary predicates >, <, >=, =<, and the ternary predicate `Interval` all having arguments of type `Integer`. The intended meaning of `Interval` is that it be true if and only if its second argument is greater than or equal to its first argument and less than or equal to its third argument.

The module `Integers` conforms to the standard for the data type Integer in the Language Independent Arithmetic Standard (LIAS) [1]. This is a draft international standard which has the goals of enhancing the portability of numeric programs across a wide range of numeric architectures and of helping programming language standards express the semantics of their numeric types. An implementation of Gödel must therefore conform to this standard. Furthermore, an implementation of the module `Integers` must be sound, that is, the body of a goal concerning the integers with a computed answer applied should be true in the intended interpretation.

To illustrate how equality for the integers is used, suppose a module which imports `Integers` defines a predicate P as follows.

```
PREDICATE    P : Integer * Integer.

P(x,x).
```

Then a goal such as

```
<- P(3 + 4, (17 Div 6) + 5).
```

succeeds. The reason it succeeds is, of course, because 3 + 4 = (17 Div 6) + 5 is true in the intended interpretation. Similarly, the goal

```
<- P(2*x-3, 5)
```

gives the answer x = 4.

As an example of the use of `Integers` consider the module GCD below. The predicate Gcd is intended to be true if and only if its first and second arguments are integers and its third argument is the greatest common divisor of the first two arguments. Note that GCD contains essentially a *specification* of Gcd rather than an efficient algorithm, such as the Euclidean algorithm. Note also that the system provides the usual mathematical syntax for expressing ranges of integers. A range expression of the form $r =< s =< t$, where r,

---

```
MODULE        GCD.

IMPORT        Integers.

PREDICATE     Gcd : Integer * Integer * Integer.

Gcd(i,j,d) <-
          CommonDivisor(i,j,d) &
          ~ SOME [e] (CommonDivisor(i,j,e) & e > d).

PREDICATE     CommonDivisor : Integer * Integer * Integer.

CommonDivisor(i,j,d) <-
          IF (i = 0 \/ j = 0)
          THEN
            d = Max(Abs(i),Abs(j))
          ELSE
            1 =< d =< Min(Abs(i),Abs(j)) &
            i Mod d = 0 &
            j Mod d = 0.
```

---

s and t are terms of type Integer, is compiled into the call Interval(r,s,t). Range expressions involving < are also compiled into calls to Interval by adjusting appropriate arguments of the expression by 1 so that =< can be used instead of <.

Gödel can solve systems of (not necessarily linear) constraints which involve integers, variables which range over bounded intervals of integers, and the functions and predicates exported by Integers (including, of course, = and ~=). The precise integer constraint solving capabilities available in Gödel are not specified but are implementation dependent. However, we give some examples of what could be considered as "minimal" capabilities that should be provided. For example, for the program consisting of the module Integers, the goals

```
<- 32*4 >= (130 Mod 4).
```

```
<- x + 43 = 73 + (34 Mod 4).
```

```
<- 0 =< x =< 10  &  0 < y =< 10  &  35*x + 33*y =< 34.

<- 0 < x =< 10  &  x ~= 2  &  x^2 < 12.
```

should succeed with the answer x = 32 for the second goal, answer x = 0 and y = 1 for the third goal, and answers x = 1 and x = 3 for the fourth goal.

One can also find Pythagorean numbers using the goal

```
<- x^2 + y^2 = z^2  &  0 < x < 50  &  0 < y < 50  &  0 < z.
```

This goal should give the answers

```
x = 3
y = 4
z = 5

x = 4
y = 3
z = 5

x = 5
y = 12
z = 13
```

and so on.

Note also that infinite precision integer arithmetic is provided. The only limit to the complexity of an arithmetic computation is the limit on the memory available to the Gödel system. A computation involving very large integers may eventually exhaust the stack or heap space available, in which case the computation will halt with an error message. Also, an attempt to divide by zero will cause the computation to halt with an error message.

4.3 Rationals

Next we discuss the module Rationals which provides a similar collection of functions and predicates with rational arguments, as does Integers for integer arguments. The intended domain is the rationals Q. The various functions, such as +, −, etc., have their usual interpretation as mappings from $Q \times Q$ (or Q, as appropriate) into Q. Similarly, the various predicates, such as >, <, etc., have their usual interpretation on $Q \times Q$. The export part (except for the control declarations) of Rationals is given below.

EXPORT   Rationals.

IMPORT   Integers.

BASE   Rational.

FUNCTION   // : yFx(520) : Integer * Integer -> Rational;
                ^ : yFx(540) : Rational * Integer -> Rational;
                - : Fy(530) : Rational -> Rational;
                * : yFx(520) : Rational * Rational -> Rational;
                / : yFx(520) : Rational * Rational -> Rational;
                + : yFx(510) : Rational * Rational -> Rational;
                - : yFx(510) : Rational * Rational -> Rational;
                Abs : Rational -> Rational;
                Sign : Rational -> Rational;
                Max : Rational * Rational -> Rational;
                Min : Rational * Rational -> Rational.

PREDICATE   > : zPz : Rational * Rational;
                < : zPz : Rational * Rational;
                >= : zPz : Rational * Rational;
                =< : zPz : Rational * Rational;
                StandardRational : Rational * Integer * Integer.

The function // of type Integer * Integer -> Rational is the infix function which is used in the usual mathematical construction of the rationals from the integers. The notation N//M means the rational with numerator N and denominator M. As a useful notational convention, a rational of the form N//1 can be written more simply as N. The system will assume by default that a number N, which could be an integer or a rational, is a rational if no other information can resolve the ambiguity. Since rational division in Gödel is denoted by /, this convention means that, in many situations, the usual mathematical notation for rationals can be used instead of //. For example, it is possible to write 2/3 with the usual mathematical meaning. Here the numerator 2 is understood as the rational 2//1 and the denominator 3 as the rational 3//1. Thus 2/3 is indeed the rational 2//3. Using these conventions, for the program consisting of the modules `Rationals` and `Integers`, the goal

```
<- x = 5 + 9/7.
```

succeeds with answer x = 44/7 and the goal

```
<- x = 4/3 + 2/3.
```

succeeds with answer x = 2.

When giving answers, the system returns (non-zero) rationals in the form `N/M`, where `M>0` and `Gcd(N,M) = 1`. For example, the goal

```
<- x = 120/25.
```

succeeds with answer x = 24/5 and the goal

```
<- x = -4/(-5).
```

succeeds with answer x = 4/5.

Notice that a goal such as

```
<- x//y = 4/5.
```

has infinitely many answers and hence may flounder. (This depends on the implementation.) However, Gödel does provide a way to get the numerator and denominator of a rational in standard form. Let us say a rational is in *standard form* if the greatest common divisor of the numerator and the denominator is 1, and the denominator is positive. Then the predicate `StandardRational` is intended to be true if and only if its second and third arguments are the numerator and denominator of the standard form of the rational in the first argument. Thus the goal

```
<- StandardRational(34/(-8),x,y).
```

gives the answer x = -17 and y = 4.

Gödel solves systems of *linear* rational constraints involving rationals, variables of type `Rational`, and the functions and predicates exported by `Rationals`. For this class of constraints, there are polynomial time algorithms for deciding solvability. (See, for example, [14].) However, the precise rational constraint solving capabilities provided are implementation dependent. The following examples give an indication of what may be provided. For example, the goals

```
<- 3*x + 2*y = 3  &  (7/2)*x + y = 0.
```

```
<- 4*x + 5 >= 16  &  -x =< 2.
```

```
<- 3*x + 4*y = 1  &  x - 2*y = 2  &  x >= 0.
```

should succeed with answer x = -3/4 and y = 21/8 for the first goal, answer x >= 11/4 for the second goal, and answer x = 1 and y = -1/2 for the third goal. Note that infinite precision rational arithmetic is provided.

4.4 Floats

The module Floats provides floating-point numbers and a large set of functions and predicates with floating-point arguments. Part of the export part of Floats is given below. The complete export part of Floats is given in Chapter 13. The module Floats conforms to the standard for the data type Floating-Point in LIAS [1]. It also conforms to the ANSI/IEEE Standard for Binary Floating-Point Arithmetic 754–1985 [2]. An implementation of this module must therefore conform to both these standards.

The intended interpretation of the symbols in this module is as follows. The domain of the intended interpretation is the finite set F of floating-point numbers characterized by a fixed radix, a fixed precision, and fixed smallest and largest exponent. Thus F is the finite set of numbers that can be represented as either 0 or $\pm 0.f_1...f_p * r^e$, where r is the radix, p is the precision, e is the exponent, and each f_i satisfies $0 \leq f_i < r$. Note that the LIAS boolean *denorm* is true. Thus denormalized floating-point numbers are provided.

The language of Floats contains finitely many constants, exactly one corresponding to each floating-point number in F. However, for the convenience of the user, there is some syntactic sugar used instead of these constants. This is the usual decimal number notation, with or without an exponent. Typical decimal numbers without exponent are 3.1416 and 0, and typical decimal numbers with exponent are -2.345619E-12 and 674328.89E+2. Such decimal numbers are converted (according to the ANSI/IEEE standard 754–1985) by the system to floating-point numbers in the form above. Then the convention is that a decimal number is syntactic sugar for the constant whose interpretation is the floating-point number obtained from the decimal number. This means that there is more than one way of denoting each of these constants. For example, both 3.1416 and 314.16E-2 denote the same constant. Similarly, when answers are displayed by the system, floating-point numbers are converted back to a more convenient decimal form.

This module is intended for straightforward numerical computation and no (nontrivial) constraint solving capabilities are provided. For example, for the program consisting of the modules Floats and Integers, the goals

```
<- x = Sin(Sqrt(23.45812E+23) + 4.56E-13/0.432167E-2).
```

```
EXPORT       Floats.
% Part of the export part of Floats.

IMPORT       Integers.

BASE         Float.

% CONSTANT   Finitely many constants, one for each number in the finite
% set of floating-point numbers determined by the radix, precision, and
% smallest and largest exponent.

FUNCTION     ^ : yFx(540) : Float * Float -> Float;
             - : Fy(530) : Float -> Float;
             * : yFx(520) : Float * Float -> Float;
             / : yFx(520) : Float * Float -> Float;
             + : yFx(510) : Float * Float -> Float;
             - : yFx(510) : Float * Float -> Float;
             Abs : Float -> Float;
             Max : Float * Float -> Float;
             Sqrt : Float -> Float;
             Sign : Float -> Float;
             Successor : Float -> Float;
             Truncate : Float * Integer -> Float;
             Round : Float * Integer -> Float;
             IntegerPart : Float -> Float;
             Sin : Float -> Float;
             ArcSin : Float -> Float;
             Exp : Float -> Float.

PREDICATE    IntegerToFloat : Integer * Float;
             TruncateToInteger : Float * Integer;
             Exponent : Float * Integer;
             Radix : Integer;
             MaxExponent : Integer;
             MaxFloat : Float;
             > : zPz : Float * Float.
```

```
<- Exp(-2.0389E+1) < ArcSin(0.7349001).
```

both succeed, with answer x = -0.99172602406708 for the first goal. Similarly, suppose
a module which imports Floats defines a predicate P as follows.

```
PREDICATE     P : Float * Float.
```

```
P(x,x).
```

Then a goal such as

```
<- P(3.345 + 4.89E+2, x + 23.8889).
```

succeeds with answer x = 468.4561.

4.5 Numbers

The module Numbers is provided as a convenient way of loading all the number modules
together with the module Strings (described in Chapter 6). The export part of Numbers
is given below. It contains two predicates for converting between rationals and floating-
point numbers. The conversion functions for integers/rationals are in Rationals and
the conversion predicates for integers/floats are in Floats. It also contains predicates
for converting integers, rationals, and floating-point numbers to strings, and *vice versa*.

```
EXPORT        Numbers.

IMPORT        Rationals, Floats, Strings.

PREDICATE     RationalToFloat : Rational * Float;
              FloatToRational : Float * Rational;
              IntegerString : Integer * String;
              RationalString : Rational * String;
              FloatString : Float * String.
```

---

5 Modules

Gödel is intended to be used for the development of large and complex programs. For this, there needs to be a means of constructing a program from smaller components that have been developed independently, as far as possible. Also there needs to be a way of avoiding interference between the components because of name clashes and a way of hiding the implementation details of the components. In Gödel, these components are called modules. We now turn to an explanation of the Gödel module system, which satisfies these requirements.

5.1 Importing and Exporting

In general, modules consist of two parts, an export part and a local part. The *export part* of a module is indicated by an export declaration, which is either an EXPORT or CLOSED declaration. The *local part* of a module is indicated by a local declaration, which is either a LOCAL or MODULE declaration. In these declarations, the keywords EXPORT, CLOSED, LOCAL and MODULE are followed by the name of the module. In fact, a module may have a local and an export part, or just a local part, or just an export part. The other kind of module declaration is the import declaration, which is either an IMPORT or LIFT declaration. In these declarations, the keywords IMPORT and LIFT are followed by the name of a module.

The export part of a module begins with an export declaration and contains zero or more import declarations, language declarations, and control declarations. The local part of a module begins with a local declaration and contains zero or more import declarations, language declarations, control declarations, and statements. If a module consists *only* of a local part, then this is indicated by using a MODULE declaration instead of a LOCAL declaration. The use of a CLOSED declaration instead of an EXPORT declaration will be explained shortly.

We now introduce the concepts of importation, accessibility, and exportation in an informal way, ignoring the concept of type lifting which is discussed later. The precise definition of these concepts is given in Section 5.2.

We say a part of a module *declares* a symbol if the part contains a language declaration for that symbol. We say a module *declares* a symbol if either the local or export part of the module declares the symbol. We say a part of a module *imports* a symbol if the part contains an IMPORT declaration with the module name N, say, and either the module N declares this symbol in its export part or, inductively, N imports the symbol into its export part. We say a symbol is *accessible to* the local (resp., export) part of a module if it is either declared in, or imported into, a part of the module (resp., the export part of the module). We say a module *exports* a symbol if the symbol is accessible to the export part of the module.

Subject to the module conditions given in Section 5.2, a symbol accessible to a part
of a module is available for use in that part of the module. More precisely, a base
or constructor accessible to a part of a module can appear in a CONSTANT, FUNCTION,
or PREDICATE declaration in that part of the module. Similarly, a constant, function,
proposition, or predicate accessible to a part of a module can appear in a statement in
the module. Of course, a symbol can only be used according to its language declaration.

We illustrate these concepts with the modules M5 and M6 below. Module M5 has an
export part and a local part. The export part of M5 makes all the symbols it declares or
imports available for use by other modules, such as M6. In particular, the declarations
for the bases Day and Person, the declarations for the constants Monday, Fred, and
so on, and the declaration for the predicate Append3 make these symbols available for
use by other modules which import M5. The IMPORT declaration in the export part of
M5 makes the symbols exported by Lists available for use in M5. It also makes the
symbols exported by Integers available for use in M5, since the export part of Lists
imports Integers. Any module which imports M5 automatically imports all the symbols
exported by Lists and Integers and hence does not need to import Lists or Integers
explicitly to make these available for use. The local part of M5 contains the definition of
the predicate Append3, which uses the definition of Append from Lists.

```
EXPORT      M5.

IMPORT      Lists.

BASE        Day, Person.

CONSTANT    Monday, Tuesday, Wednesday, Thursday, Friday, Saturday,
            Sunday : Day;
            Fred, Bill, Mary : Person.
PREDICATE   Append3 : List(a) * List(a) * List(a) * List(a).
```

By contrast with module M5, module M6 has only a local part. Hence its first module
declaration uses the keyword MODULE instead of LOCAL. It imports all the symbols exported
by M5, which include Append3 together with all the symbols exported by Lists and
Integers. Module M6 contains the definition of the predicate Member2. Member2(x,y,z)
is intended to be true if and only if z is a list which contains x and y as members so that

```
LOCAL        M5.

Append3(x,y,z,u) <-
             Append(x,y,w) &
             Append(w,z,u).
```

```
MODULE       M6.

IMPORT       M5.

PREDICATE    Member2 : a * a * List(a).

Member2(x,y,z) <-
             Append3(_,[x|_],[y|_],z).
```

x precedes y in the list.

Informally, a *program* consists of a set of modules $\{M_i\}_{i=0}^n$ ($n \geq 0$), where M_0 is a distinguished module called the *main* module and $\{M_i\}_{i=1}^n$ is the set of modules which appear in import declarations in M_0 or appear in import declarations in these modules, and so on. (A formal definition is given in Section 5.4 and Chapter 11.) For the above example, {M6, M5, Lists, Integers} is a program with main module M6.

Certain modules are provided by the system and hence are called *system modules*. For example, Integers and Lists are system modules. The complete set of system modules is given in Chapter 13. Other modules are called *user modules*. Note that the export declaration in the export part of a system module may contain the keyword CLOSED instead of EXPORT. A module is *closed* if its export part contains a CLOSED declaration and *open* if its export part contains an EXPORT declaration. In closed modules the visibility of symbols accessible to the local part of the module is restricted. (The precise restrictions are given later in the definition of goal language and in the specification of certain predicates in the module Programs.) This effectively increases the range of implementations available. For example, the local part of a closed module does not have to be implemented in Gödel. An implementation of Gödel may make some or all of the system modules closed. Furthermore, an implementation may also allow user modules to be closed, although normally these modules would be open. A likely reason for wanting a user module to be closed would be to allow it to contain an interface to another language.

In general, symbols declared in, or imported into, the local part of a module are not available for use in the export part of the module. However, there are occasions when it is desirable that selected bases and constructors imported into the local part of a module should also be available for use in its export part (and hence other modules that import it). For this reason, Gödel has a facility called *type lifting*. We illustrate how type lifting works in Figure 5.1 below. The base B is declared in the export part of N and we want to lift B from the local to the export part of M. To do this, we import N into the local part of M, but by means of a LIFT declaration instead of an IMPORT declaration. The LIFT declaration imports N, as an IMPORT declaration does, but also provides the opportunity to lift bases and constructors exported by N so as to make them accessible to the export part of M. This is achieved by redeclaring in the export part of M the bases and constructors that are to be lifted. For the example, the base B is redeclared in the export part of M. In general, a base or constructor is *redeclared* by repeating its declaration in the export part of the module in which it is being lifted. The symbol is thereby made accessible to the export part of the module. Only bases and constructors can be lifted.

Type lifting has several desirable properties which we illustrate with the example. First, the fact that the base B is exported from M is made explicit by repeating its declaration in the export part of M. In fact, since a user who only has access to the export part of M cannot tell whether the declaration declares or redeclares B and since it makes no difference anyway, the user might just as well assume B is actually declared there. Second, we can change the details of N without affecting in any way the users of M. This includes changing the name of N or even removing N altogether, if this became possible. Third, other symbols exported by N which are needed just for the implementation of M are hidden from the users of M.

5.2   Module Declarations and Conditions

We now give a precise meaning to the various module declarations and also give the module conditions which every module must satisfy.[1]

A *symbol* is a base, constructor, constant, function, proposition, or predicate.

A *type symbol* is a base or constructor. Other symbols are *non-type symbols*.

A part of a module *refers to* a module N if it contains a declaration of the form

---

[1]For the purposes of the definitions which follow, it is convenient to assume that all modules have *both* a local and an export part, and that, rather than be absent, one of these parts may contain nothing other than a local or an export declaration.

```
┌─────────────────────────────┐
│ EXPORT M.                   │
│ BASE B.                     │        ←   B is redeclared here.
│                             │
│      ⋮                      │
│                             │
│                             │
└─────────────────────────────┘


┌─────────────────────────────┐
│ LOCAL M.                    │
│ LIFT N.                     │        ←   N is imported and B is lifted here.
│                             │
│      ⋮                      │
│                             │
│                             │
└─────────────────────────────┘


┌─────────────────────────────┐
│ EXPORT N.                   │
│ BASE B.                     │        ←   B is declared here.
│                             │
│      ⋮                      │
│                             │
│                             │
└─────────────────────────────┘


┌─────────────────────────────┐
│ LOCAL N.                    │
│                             │
│      ⋮                      │
│                             │
│                             │
│                             │
└─────────────────────────────┘
```

Figure 5.1   Type Lifting

IMPORT N.

or (in the case of a local part)

LIFT N.

A module M *refers to* a module N if either the local or export part of M refers to N.

The local part of a module M *1-imports* a symbol S *via* a module N if S has a declaration in the export part of N and the local part of M refers to N.

The export part of a module M *1-imports* a symbol S *via* a module N if S has a declaration in the export part of N and either (i) the export part of M refers to N, or (ii) the local part of M refers to N by means of a LIFT declaration, S is a type symbol, and there is a declaration for S in the export part of M. In the latter case, the export part of M also *1-redeclares* S.

The local part of a module M *n-imports*, $n > 1$, a symbol S *via* a module N if there is a module L such that the export part of L $(n - 1)$-imports S via N and the local part of M refers to L.

The export part of a module M *n-imports*, $n > 1$, a symbol S *via* a module N if there is a module L such that the export part of L $(n - 1)$-imports S via N and either (i) the export part of M refers to L, or (ii) the local part of M refers to L by means of a LIFT declaration, S is a type symbol, and there is a declaration for S in the export part of M. In the latter case, the export part of M also *n-redeclares* S.

A part of a module M *imports* a symbol S *via* a module N if the part of M n-imports S via N, for some $n \geq 1$.

A module M *imports* a symbol S *via* a module N if either the local or export part of M imports S via N.

The export part of a module *redeclares* a type symbol S if it n-redeclares S, for some $n \geq 1$.

The export part of a module *declares* a type symbol if it contains a declaration for, but does not redeclare, the symbol. It *declares* a non-type symbol if it contains a declaration for the symbol.

The local part of a module *declares* a symbol if it contains a declaration for the symbol.

A module *declares* a symbol if either the local or export part of the module declares the symbol.

A part of a module M *imports* a symbol S *from* a module N if the part of M imports S via N and the export part of N declares S.

A module M *imports* a symbol S *from* a module N if either the local or export part of M imports S from N.

A symbol is *accessible to* the local (resp., export) part of a module if it is either declared in, or imported into, the module (resp., export part of the module).

A module *exports* a symbol if the symbol is accessible to the export part of the module.

Now let us turn to the *module conditions*, M1 to M5, given below, which are enforced by the system. The first of these ensures that the module structure of a program is non-circular and hence greatly simplifies compilation. To state this condition, we introduce a new concept. We define the relation *depends upon* between modules to be the transitive closure of the relation refers to. So, for example, module M6 depends upon the modules M5, Lists, and Integers.

M1: No module may depend upon itself.

The next module condition ensures that, in any given module part, the only names that can appear are names of symbols that are accessible.

M2: For every name appearing in a part of a module, there must be a symbol having that name accessible to that part.

Overloading is a useful programming language facility. For example, it is convenient to use the name − for both unary and binary minus, and the name + for addition of integer, rational, and floating-point numbers. For this reason, Gödel has a flexible scheme for overloading. The only condition on naming symbols enforced by the system is the following module condition (in which the arity of a base, constant, or proposition is 0).

M3: Distinct symbols cannot be declared in the same module with the same category, name, and arity.

The next module condition ensures that, for example, every constant of type a base, B say, and every function of range type B is declared in the module where B is declared.

M4: In a module, the type in a constant declaration or the range type in a function declaration must be either a base type declared in the module or a type with a top-level constructor declared in the module.

For example, module condition M4 means that a user module, which imports Lists, is not allowed to declare a constant of type List(τ), for any type τ.

The final module condition ensures that no definition of a proposition or predicate can be split across several modules.

M5: A module must declare every proposition or predicate defined in that module.

5.3   Ambiguity

The enforcement of module condition M3 avoids gratuitous ambiguity, but at the same time allows considerable flexibility in overloading. The system uses all type and indicator information available to try to disambiguate the use of a name which could refer to different symbols and, in most cases, will be able to resolve the ambiguity. In those circumstances where it cannot resolve the ambiguity, an overloading error message is issued. Note carefully that a precondition for an overloading error is the *use* of a name for which there is more than one accessible symbol having this name. By the *use* of a name in a module we mean any appearance of the name except as the identifier after the keyword of a language declaration. So, for example, it is always legal for a module to import two distinct symbols with the same name or to import a symbol with the same name as a symbol declared in the module if the name of these symbols is not used anywhere in the module. This requirement reduces the reporting of overloading errors to those that cause genuine difficulty.

As an example of a situation where module condition M3 is satisfied but where an ambiguity cannot be resolved, consider the module M7 and the export parts of the modules M8 and M9 below. The system has no way of determining which symbol with name Q is the one intended in the body of the statement for P. The only way to fix the problem in modules M7, M8, and M9 is to change the name of one of the predicates with name Q in modules M8 and M9.

Another cause of ambiguity is the use of operators, which can lead to ambiguities in the parsing of expressions. Suppose a local part of a module has two symbols accessible to it with the following declarations.

```
PREDICATE    P : zPz : Integer * Integer.
FUNCTION     P : xFy(500) : Integer * Integer -> Integer.
```

Then the expression u P v P w, used for example in a place where an atom should appear, is ambiguous.

Also, if the function with name F1 and indicator yFx(500), and the function with name F2 and indicator xFy(500) are accessible to the same module, then the expression u F2 v F1 w is ambiguous. Similarly, if the function with name F3 and indicator yF(400), and the function with name F4 and indicator Fy(400) are accessible to the same module, then the expression F4 u F3 is ambiguous. However, such ambiguities can always be avoided by adding appropriate parentheses to the expression.

```
MODULE        M7.

IMPORT        M8, M9.

PROPOSITION   P.

P <- Q(x).
```

```
EXPORT        M8.

BASE          B1.

PREDICATE     Q : B1.
```

```
EXPORT        M9.

BASE          B2.

PREDICATE     Q : B2.
```

5.4   Programs and Goals

A *program* consists of a set of modules $\{M_i\}_{i=0}^n$ $(n \geq 0)$, where $\{M_i\}_{i=1}^n$ is the set of modules upon which M_0 depends and where each module satisfies the module conditions given in Section 5.2. The module M_0 is called the *main* module of the program.

To define a statement, we introduce the language of a module in a program.

- The *language* of a module M in a program is the polymorphic many-sorted language given by the language declarations of all symbols accessible to the local part of M.[2]

---

[2]Some care must be taken with this definition and the two that follow. The reason is that, because of ambiguity, a symbol may not be uniquely identified by its name. For example, there is a predicate with

We will also need the export language of a module.

- The *export language* of a module M in a program is the polymorphic many-sorted language given by the language declarations of all symbols accessible to the export part of M.

To define a goal, we introduce the goal language of a program.

- The *goal language* of a program P is the language of the main module M_0 of P, if M_0 is open, or the export language of M_0, if M_0 is closed.

A *statement*[3] in a module M in a program is a formula in the language of M having the form either A or A <- W, where A is an atom, called the *head* of the statement, and where W is a formula, called the *body* of the statement. Any variables in A and any free variables in W are assumed to be universally quantified at the front of the statement. Each statement in a module must satisfy the head condition given in Chapter 2.

A *goal*[3] for a program has the form <- W, where W is a formula in the goal language of the program. W is called the *body* of the goal. Any free variables in W are assumed to be universally quantified at the front of the goal.

As an example, typical goals for the program {M6, M5, Lists, Integers} could be

```
<- Member2(x,y,[Fred,Bill,Mary]).
```

```
<- Member2(1,4,[56,7,3,4,5]).
```

```
<- Append3([1,-1],[2,-2],[3,-3],x).
```

If, as a result of solving a goal, a variable in the goal becomes bound to a term which contains a subterm not in the goal language of the program, then only the type of the subterm is given in an answer. For example, consider the program consisting of the modules Hidden1 and Hidden2 below. The goal

```
<- Father(x).
```

produces the answers

---

name Q declared in the module M8 and another predicate with the same name declared in module M9 and both these symbols appear in the language of M7. It is understood that a formula is only admitted by the language of a module if the use of each name in the formula can be disambiguated. Later, for the ground representation (see Chapter 9), we will introduce flat names to avoid such problems. The flat name of a symbol is a quadruple consisting of the name of the module in which the symbol is declared, the name of the symbol, its category, and its arity. Module condition M3 ensures that the flat name of a symbol in a program uniquely identifies it.

[3]This definition will be generalized in Chapter 7 to the case when commits are present in the body.

```
x = Individual(Bill)
x = Individual(<Name>)
```

where the phrase `<Name>` indicates that the argument of `Individual` is a term with a top-level constant or function which is not accessible and that this term has type `Name`.

```
MODULE       Hidden1.

IMPORT       Hidden2.
```

```
EXPORT       Hidden2.

BASE         Name, Person.

CONSTANT     Bill : Name.

FUNCTION     Individual : Name -> Person.

PREDICATE    Father : Person.
```

```
LOCAL        Hidden2.

CONSTANT     Fred : Name.

Father(Individual(Bill)).
Father(Individual(Fred)).
```

---

6 Various Data Types

In this chapter, we discuss six fundamental data types: lists, strings, sets, tables, units, and flocks; and also the system modules which provide them. Many of the system predicates discussed in this chapter are described in an informal procedural way. Their more formal, declarative descriptions are all given in Chapter 13.

6.1 Lists

The symbols exported by the system module Lists are shown below in its export part (which is complete except for the control declarations). The constructor List is used to give a type to domains whose elements are lists. Thus, for example, the domains of the intended interpretation for the program {Lists, Integers} are the integers (having type Integer), all lists of integers (having type List(Integer)), all lists of lists of integers (having type List(List(Integer))), and so on. Note that the elements of a list must all be of the same type, so, for example, it is not possible for a list to have some of its elements integers and some of its elements lists of integers. If a programmer would like to form a list having some elements of type A and some of type B, say, then this can in essence be achieved, as follows. Declare a new type, say,

```
BASE          Element.
```

and two new functions, say,

```
FUNCTION      F : A -> Element;
              G : B -> Element.
```

Then a list of elements of type Element can be formed, each member of which "packages up" an element of type A or B. In fact, the existence of F and G facilitates the processing of the elements of such lists and is good programming practice.

The module Lists provides a collection of useful list processing predicates. As an illustration of the use of lists, consider the module Qsort below. The predicate Quicksort in Qsort is intended to be true if and only if its first argument is a list of integers and its second argument is the list of integers occurring in the list in the first argument sorted into non-decreasing order. The predicate Partition is intended to be true if and only if its first argument is a list L of integers, its second argument is an integer n, its third argument is the list of integers in L which are less than or equal to n, and its fourth argument is the list of integers in L which are greater than n.

6.2 Strings

Next we turn to strings. A base type String is defined in the system module Strings which provides a collection of useful predicates for processing strings. The export part

---

EXPORT   Lists.

IMPORT   Integers.

CONSTRUCTOR   List/1.

CONSTANT   Nil : List(a).

FUNCTION   Cons : a * List(a) -> List(a).

PREDICATE   Member : a * List(a);
                MemberCheck : a * List(a);
                Append : List(a) * List(a) * List(a);
                Permutation : List(a) * List(a);
                Delete : a * List(a) * List(a);
                DeleteFirst : a * List(a) * List(a);
                Reverse : List(a) * List(a);
                Prefix : List(a) * Integer * List(a);
                Suffix : List(a) * Integer * List(a);
                Length : List(a) * Integer;
                Sorted : List(Integer);
                Sort : List(Integer) * List(Integer);
                Merge : List(Integer) * List(Integer) * List(Integer).

---

of **Strings** (except for the control declarations) is given below. Note that there is no type for characters.

The module **Strings** exports infinitely many constants which are in one-to-one correspondence with all possible strings. Gödel provides the standard double quotes notation for these constants. Thus **"ABC"** is the constant whose interpretation is the string whose first character is **A**, second character is **B**, and third character is **C**. Similarly, **""** is the constant whose interpretation is the empty string. By abuse of language, we usually refer to such constants as strings. A double quote can appear in a string by escaping it with a \, as in **"This is a string with a \" in it."**. To include a \ in a string, use \\; to include a backspace, use \b; to include a tab, use \t; and to include a newline, use \n. Tabs and newlines may also appear directly in a string. A single \ (not escaping a

---

```
MODULE        Qsort.

IMPORT        Lists.

PREDICATE     Quicksort : List(Integer) * List(Integer);
              Partition : List(Integer) * Integer * List(Integer) *
                          List(Integer).

Quicksort([],[]).
Quicksort([x|xs],ys) <-
              Partition(xs,x,l,b) &
              Quicksort(l,ls) &
              Quicksort(b,bs) &
              Append(ls,[x|bs],ys).

Partition([],_,[],[]).
Partition([x|xs],y,[x|ls],bs) <-
              x =< y &
              Partition(xs,y,ls,bs).
Partition([x|xs],y,ls,[x|bs]) <-
              x > y &
              Partition(xs,y,ls,bs).
```

\, b, t, n, or ") in a string is ignored. The function ++ is used to concatenate strings, so that the call x = "MOD" ++ "ULE" would bind x to the string "MODULE". The type String has an equality theory appropriate for strings that is different from the theory corresponding to "syntactic identity", as the answer to the last call illustrates.

The predicate Width gives the number of characters in a string, so that the call Width("Fred" ++ ".prm", x) would bind x to 8. The predicate StringInts allows conversion between a string and the list of ASCII codes of characters in the string. Thus the call StringInts(x, [77,111,110,100,97,121]) would bind x to the string "Monday". The predicate < is lexical less than, > is lexical greater than, and so on.

```
EXPORT      Strings.

IMPORT      Lists.

BASE        String.

% CONSTANT  Infinitely many constants which are in one-to-one
% correspondence with all possible strings.

FUNCTION    ++ : yFx(500) : String * String -> String.

PREDICATE   StringInts : String * List(Integer);
            FirstSubstring : String * Integer * String;
            LastSubstring : String * Integer * String;
            Width : String * Integer;
            > : zPz : String * String;
            < : zPz : String * String;
            >= : zPz : String * String;
            =< : zPz : String * String.
```

6.3 Sets

By a "set", we understand the usual mathematical concept. However, Gödel handles only *finite* sets and so "set" means "finite set" throughout. The export part (excluding the control declarations) of the system module **Sets** is given below. **Sets** exports the constructor **Set**, which plays a role for sets that is analogous to the role played by the constructor **List** for lists. Thus, for example, the domains of the intended interpretation for the program {**Sets**, **Integers**} are the integers (having type **Integer**), all sets of integers (having type **Set(Integer)**), all sets of sets of integers (having type **Set(Set(Integer))**), and so on.

Two kinds of set terms are allowed: extensional set terms and intensional set terms. We first consider extensional set terms. The module **Sets** exports the constant **Null** and the function **Inc**, which are used to form extensional set terms. (This is similar to the treatment of finite sets in [6].) The intended meaning of **Null** is the empty set (of the appropriate type). The intended meaning of **Inc** for some type τ is the mapping *Include*

EXPORT   Sets.

IMPORT   Integers.

CONSTRUCTOR   Set/1.

CONSTANT   Null : Set(a).

FUNCTION   Inc : a * Set(a) -> Set(a);
                * : yFx(120) : Set(a) * Set(a) -> Set(a);
                + : yFx(110) : Set(a) * Set(a) -> Set(a);
                \ : yFx(100) : Set(a) * Set(a) -> Set(a).

PREDICATE   In : zPz : a * Set(a);
                Subset : zPz : Set(a) * Set(a);
                StrictSubset : zPz : Set(a) * Set(a);
                Size : Set(a) * Integer.

---

such that $Include(d, S) = \{d\} \cup S$, where d is an element from the domain of type τ and S is a set of elements of type τ. Thus, the intended meaning of the term

Inc(6,Inc(5,Inc(6,Null)))

is the set $\{5, 6\}$.

In a similar way to lists, some notational sugar for sets is provided. An expression of the form

{}

stands for the constant

Null.

An expression of the form

$\{t_1, \ldots, t_n\}$

stands for the extensional set term

Inc(t_1, Inc(t_2, ... , Inc(t_n, Null) ...)).

An expression of the form

$\{t_1, \ldots, t_n \mid s\}$

stands for the extensional set term

Inc(t_1, Inc(t_2, ... , Inc(t_n, s) ...)).

It is important to appreciate that an extensional set term is *not* a set.[1] However, *its intended meaning is a set* and this is the reason for the use of the brackets { and } in the above notation.

A special equality is required for sets because the order of elements in a set is irrelevant and because sets do not have duplicate elements. Thus, for example, the following equalities are true in the intended interpretation:

{5,6} = {6,5}

and

{5,6} = {5,6,6}.

The module Sets also provides some standard set processing functions and predicates. Set-theoretic intersection is given by the function *, union by the function +, and difference by the function \. Set membership is given by the predicate In, inclusion by the predicate Subset, and strict inclusion by the predicate StrictSubset. The cardinality of a set is given by the predicate Size.

For the program {Sets, Integers}, the goal

<- x = Inc(1,Inc(2,Inc(1+1,Null))).

gives the answer x = {1,2} and the goal

<- x = {1,2,3,4,5} + {4,5,6,7,8} \ {3,4,5,6}.

gives the answer x = {1,2,7,8}.

As a further example of set processing, consider the module SetProcessing below, which defines two predicates Sum and Max. The predicate Sum is intended to be true if and only if its second argument is the sum of the integers in the (non-empty) set in its first argument. Thus the goal

---

[1] Actually, we could make a similar point about lists. An expression such as [1,2] is not a list, but notational sugar for the term Cons(1,Cons(2,Nil)). However, the intended meaning of this term is a list. It is pedantic to insist on this distinction for lists, but the more complicated equality for sets makes the distinction important in the latter case. It explains why it makes sense to write such things as {1,2,1}, where elements are repeated.

```
MODULE      SetProcessing.

IMPORT      Sets.

PREDICATE   Sum : Set(Integer) * Integer.

Sum(s,y) <-
       x In s &
       Sum1(s\{x},x,y).

PREDICATE   Sum1 : Set(Integer) * Integer * Integer.

Sum1({},x,x).
Sum1(s,x,x+w) <-
       z In s &
       Sum1(s\{z},z,w).

PREDICATE   Max : Set(Integer) * Integer.

Max(s,y) <-
       x In s &
       Max1(s\{x},x,y).

PREDICATE   Max1 : Set(Integer) * Integer * Integer.

Max1({},x,x).
Max1(s,x,y) <-
       z In s &
       IF z>x THEN Max1(s\{z},z,y) ELSE Max1(s\{z},x,y).
```

```
<- Sum({1,2,3,3},s).
```

gives the answer s = 6. The predicate Max is intended to be true if and only if its second argument is the maximum of the integers in the (non-empty) set in its first argument. Thus the goal

```
<- Max({1,2,3},m).
```

gives the answer `m = 3`. A further example of this kind of set processing appears in Chapter 10, where a solution of the wolf-goat-cabbage problem is given.

Next we discuss intensional set terms. These have the form

$\{T : W\}$

where T is a term with free variables $y_1, \ldots, y_n$, say, and W is a formula (not involving commits) which has $y_1, \ldots, y_n$ amongst its free variables. The variables $y_1, \ldots, y_n$ must be local to $\{T : W\}$. The free variables of $\{T : W\}$ are the free variables of W other than $y_1, \ldots, y_n$. (Note that T may itself be an intensional set term and that it is possible for n to be 0.) Informally, $\{T : W\}$ means "the set of all instances of T corresponding to the instances of W which are true".

The precise meaning of a term $\{T : W\}$ (not containing other intensional set terms) appearing in a statement or goal whose body is a conjunction of literals is given by the following transformation: $\{T : W\}$ is replaced by a new variable, s say, and the formula

```
ALL [x] (x In s   <->   SOME [y₁,...,yₙ] ((x = T) & W))
```

is added as an additional conjunct to the body of the statement or goal. This semantics for intensional set terms was first given in [5]. The general case for arbitrary bodies is given in Chapter 12. An implementation of intensional set terms must guarantee that it is sound, although it does not have to explicitly use the above transformation, of course.

Now we give some examples of processing with intensional set terms. Consider the program {Sets, Integers}. Then the goal

```
<- x = {s : s Subset {z : n Mod z = 0 & 1 =< z < 10}} & n = 10.
```

gives the answer `x = {{},{1},{2},{5},{1,2},...,{1,2,5}}` and the goal

```
<- x = {{n^2 : 1 =< n =< m} : 1 =< m =< 5}.
```

gives the answer `x = {{1},{1,4},{1,4,9},{1,4,9,16},{1,4,9,16,25}}`.

As another example of the use of intensional sets, consider the module **SetProcessing** again. The goal

```
<- Sum({x : 100 Mod x = 0 & 1 < x < 100}, s).
```

gives the answer `s = 116` and the goal

```
<- Max({x^2 + y^2 : -100 =< x =< 20  &  -10 =< y =< 30}, m).
```

gives the answer `m = 10900`.

Consider finally the module **Sports** below. Then the goal

```
MODULE      Sports.

IMPORT      Sets.

BASE        Person, Sport, PersonSports.

CONSTANT    Mary, Bill, Joe, Fred : Person;
            Cricket, Football, Tennis : Sport.

FUNCTION    Pair : Person * Set(Sport) -> PersonSports.

PREDICATE   Likes : Person * Sport.

Likes(Mary, Cricket).
Likes(Mary, Tennis).
Likes(Bill, Cricket).
Likes(Bill, Tennis).
Likes(Joe, Tennis).
Likes(Joe, Football).
```

```
<- x = {p : Likes(p,Tennis)}.
```

gives the answer x = {Mary, Bill, Joe}, the goal

```
<- x = {s : Likes(Fred,s)}.
```

gives the answer x = {}, the goal

```
<- x = {p : Likes(p,s)} & s In {Cricket,Football}.
```

gives the answers

```
s = Cricket, x = {Mary,Bill}
s = Football, x = {Joe}
```

and the goal

```
<- x = {Pair(p,y) : y = {s : Likes(p,s)} & p In {Mary,Bill,Joe,Fred}}.
```

gives the answer

```
x = {Pair(Mary,{Cricket,Tennis}), Pair(Bill,{Cricket,Tennis}),
                    Pair(Joe,{Tennis,Football}), Pair(Fred,{})}.
```

6.4 Tables

A table is a data structure containing an ordered collection of nodes, each of which has
two components, a key and a value. The key must be a string, but the value can have
any type. However, all nodes in a table must have values of the same type. The key in a
node uniquely identifies the node in the table. Furthermore, the lexical ordering of the
keys in a table provide a natural ordering of the nodes.

   A table is treated as an abstract data type and the system module Tables (see below)
provides various operations on this type. The module Tables provides a constructor
Table of arity 1 for constructing the type of a table. Thus, if the type of the values of
the nodes is τ, then the type of the table is Table(τ). EmptyTable is intended to be true
if and only if its argument is an empty table. NodeInTable is used to search for a node in
a table, InsertNode to insert a node into a table, and DeleteNode to delete a node from
a table. UpdateTable is intended to be true if and only if its first argument is a table,
its second is the key of a node in the table, its third is a new value to be associated with
this key, its fourth is the table with the node updated, and the fifth is the old value that
was associated with the key. AmendTable is a variation of UpdateTable which can be
used when the key in the second argument is not necessarily present in the table. If it is,
AmendTable behaves similarly to UpdateTable. If it is not, a new node with this key is
inserted into the table. JoinTables joins two tables by adding to the first table all nodes
in the second table whose keys are not already present in the first table. To display a
table as a pair of a list of keys (lexically ordered by the keys) and a list of corresponding
values, the predicate ListTable is used. FirstNode gives the first node in a table and
LastNode the last node (according to the lexical ordering of keys). NextNode finds the
node next in this ordering after a specified node and PreviousNode finds the previous
one.

   As an example of the use of the module Tables, the module DoubleTable below
contains the definition of a predicate Double, which is intended to be true if and only
if its first argument is a table of nodes with integer values and its second argument
is a table which differs from the first only in that all nodes whose key has width > 5
have a value double that of the value in the corresponding node in the table in the first
argument. Since it is necessary to check the width of every key in the table, the module
DoubleTable uses ListTable to produce a list of the keys and a list of the corresponding

---

EXPORT   Tables.

IMPORT   Strings.

CONSTRUCTOR   Table/1.

PREDICATE   EmptyTable : Table(a);
               NodeInTable : Table(a) * String * a;
               InsertNode : Table(a) * String * a * Table(a);
               DeleteNode : Table(a) * String * a * Table(a);
               UpdateTable : Table(a) * String * a * Table(a) * a;
               AmendTable : Table(a) * String * a * a * Table(a) * a;
               JoinTables : Table(a) * Table(a) * Table(a);
               ListTable : Table(a) * List(String) * List(a);
               FirstNode : Table(a) * String * a;
               LastNode : Table(a) * String * a;
               NextNode : Table(a) * String * String * a;
               PreviousNode : Table(a) * String * String * a.

---

values, makes a pass through the lists to find the keys which have width > 5 (and their corresponding values), and uses UpdateTable to update those nodes which have a key satisfying this condition.

6.5   Units

Units are term-like structures having the following grammar:

Unit $\longrightarrow$ Identifier
                | Identifier $<\text{`('}> <\text{`)'}>$
                | Identifier $<\text{`('}>$ UnitSeq $<\text{`)'}>$

UnitSeq $\longrightarrow$ Unit $\{<\text{Comma}>$ Unit$\}$

where the notation $\{\ldots\}$ indicates 0 or more occurrences of the included item and $|$ indicates alternative forms. Identifiers can be quite complicated and, for example, include quoted and double quoted identifiers, such as 'ABC' and "string_ident". The grammar

```
EXPORT     DoubleTable.

IMPORT     Tables.

PREDICATE  Double : Table(Integer) * Table(Integer).
```

```
LOCAL      DoubleTable.

% PREDICATE  Double : Table(Integer) * Table(Integer).

Double(table, new_table) <-
        ListTable(table, keys, values) &
        Double1(table, keys, values, new_table).

PREDICATE  Double1 : Table(Integer) * List(String) * List(Integer) *
                     Table(Integer).

Double1(table, [], [], table).
Double1(table, [k|ks], [v|vs], new_table) <-
        DoubleNode(table, k, v, next_table) &
        Double1(next_table, ks, vs, new_table).

PREDICATE  DoubleNode : Table(Integer) * String * Integer *
                        Table(Integer).

DoubleNode(table, key, value, next_table) <-
        IF (SOME [w] (Width(key,w) & w > 5))
        THEN
          UpdateTable(table, key, 2*value, next_table, value)
        ELSE
          next_table = table.
```

for identifier is given in Section 11.2. For example, each of the following is a unit:

```
F(A,x)
ABC
f(g(a,b),1,h(x,y)).
```

The module `Units` (see below) provides the type `Unit` as an abstract data type. Thus there is a representation of units, which is hidden from the programmer, and some operations on this type which are available to the programmer. `StringToUnit` is intended to be true if and only if its first argument is the string representation of a unit and its second argument is this unit. `UnitToString` is intended to be true if and only if its first argument is a unit and its second argument is the string representation in a standard form of this unit. `UnitParts` is intended to be true if and only if its first argument is a unit, the second argument is the string representation of the top-level identifier of this unit, and the third argument is the list of top-level subunits of this unit. For example, for the program with main module `Units`, the goal

```
<- new_string :
      StringToUnit("F(A,x)", unit) &
      UnitParts(unit, _, arguments) &
      UnitParts(new_unit, "G", arguments) &
      UnitToString(new_unit, new_string).
```

gives the answer

```
new_string = "G(A,x)".
```

If the first argument of `UnitParts` is just an identifier, then the third is the empty list. Thus the goal

```
<- identifier, arguments :
      StringToUnit("ABC", unit) &
      UnitParts(unit, identifier, arguments).
```

gives the answer

```
identifier = "ABC"
arguments = [].
```

Units are useful for a variety of applications. For example, it is easy to write a first order formula as a unit. Similarly, clauses in a Prolog program can be regarded as units. In fact, the reason for the introduction of quoted and double quoted identifiers is to have identifiers general enough for the latter application. Once an expression such as a formula or Prolog clause is written as a unit, it can be conveniently manipulated by the predicates in `Units`.

EXPORT   Units.

IMPORT   Strings.

BASE   Unit.

PREDICATE   StringToUnit : String * Unit;
              UnitToString : Unit * String;
              UnitParts : Unit * String * List(Unit);
              UnitArgument : Unit * Integer * Unit.

6.6 Flocks

Units often congregate in flocks, which are ordered collections of units. There is a system
module `Flocks` (see below) which provides some operations on the abstract data type
`Flock`. `EmptyFlock` checks whether a given flock is empty or creates an empty flock.
`Extent` gives the number of units in a flock. `UnitInFlock` and `UnitWithIdentifier`
allow a program to access units in a flock. `InsertUnit` inserts a unit into a flock and
`DeleteUnit` deletes a unit from a flock. Furthermore, there is a utility `flock-compile`
which takes a file containing a flock and produces a file containing the representation of
this flock employed by the abstract data type `Flock`. Another utility, `flock-decompile`,
reverses this process. The system module `FlocksIO` provides predicates to access this
representation. (This is discussed in more detail in Chapter 8.)

The module `Flocks` is useful for many applications. For example, suppose that a
programmer wanted to use Gödel as a meta-programming language for transforming
Prolog programs. First, the programmer would use a utility (which may be supplied by
the system) to convert a Prolog program into a flock. (The main thing that has to be done
is to write all operators in standard form.) The utility `flock-compile` would then be used
to produce the representation of this flock and predicates in the module `FlocksIO` would
be used to access this representation. The module `Flocks` then provides much low-level
support for doing whatever transformation was required on the Prolog program. Finally,
`flock-decompile` would be used to produce a flock containing the transformed Prolog
program in standard form and another utility could be applied to change this back to the
usual form. A similar procedure could be applied to other programming languages, which
would also require utilities for converting between programs in the language and flocks.

```
EXPORT      Flocks.

IMPORT      Units.

BASE        Flock.

PREDICATE   EmptyFlock : Flock;
            Extent : Flock * Integer;
            UnitInFlock : Flock * Unit * Integer;
            UnitWithIdentifier : Flock * String * Unit * Integer;
            InsertUnit : Flock * Unit * Integer * Flock;
            DeleteUnit : Flock * Unit * Integer * Flock.
```

Theories in most logics can also be mapped rather easily into flocks. Thus the module Flocks provides a convenient tool for implementing theorem provers and proof editors of such logics. As an application of this kind, we give in Chapter 10 a tableau propositional theorem prover which exploits the utility flock-compile and the predicates in Units, Flocks, and FlocksIO.

7 Control

There are two main aspects to control in Gödel. The first of these is the computation rule. The second is Gödel's pruning operator which determines those subtrees that may be pruned from the search tree. We examine each of these in turn.

7.1 Computation Rule

In the context of a search tree, a computation rule selects some subformula in the body of the current goal for use by an extension step, which may involve expanding a selected atom with the definition of the predicate in the atom or some other kind of extension step. (See Chapter 12.) There are five reasons for employing a flexible computation rule. These are to ensure soundness, assist efficiency, assist termination, solve constraints, and control pruning. We discuss the first four of these in this section. The use of a flexible computation rule to control pruning will be discussed in the next section.

We begin by discussing the role of a flexible computation rule in ensuring soundness. The major requirement of any implementation of Gödel is that it be sound. This means that considerable care must be taken when implementing certain facilities, such as negation, conditionals, and intensional set terms, which are well-known to have difficulties in this regard. For example, a standard way of implementing negation (called *safe* negation) is to delay a negative literal until it is ground. Under this restriction, the soundness of the implementation can be proved. In any case, whatever sound implementation of negation is employed, programmers may need to know some details of the implementation since normally there are restrictions on what negative literals can be run. Similar remarks apply to the implementation of conditionals and intensional set terms.

Next we turn to a detailed discussion of the `DELAY` control facility of Gödel. The computation rule is partly under the control of the programmer through explicit `DELAY` declarations. We first motivate the use of `DELAY` declarations to assist efficiency and termination by various examples. After this motivation, the precise syntax and semantics of `DELAY` declarations will be presented.

Computation rules which allow coroutining between subformulas can be much more efficient than, for example, the "leftmost literal" computation rule. As an example of this, consider the module `Coroutine` below. `Coroutine` imports, in particular, the predicate `Permutation` from `Lists`. `Permutation` has the following declarations and could be implemented by the following definition.

```
PREDICATE    Permutation : List(a) * List(a).
DELAY        Permutation(x,y) UNTIL NONVAR(x) \/ NONVAR(y).
```

```
MODULE          Coroutine.

IMPORT          Lists.

PREDICATE       Slowsort : List(Integer) * List(Integer).

Slowsort(x,y) <-
                Sorted(y) &
                Permutation(x,y).
```

```
Permutation([],[]).
Permutation([x|y],[u|v]) <-
                Delete(u,[x|y],z) &
                Permutation(z,v).
```

The DELAY declaration is a *control* declaration. In fact, DELAY declarations are syntactic variants of when declarations, which are due to Naish [21]. The meaning of the DELAY declaration for Permutation is that calls to Permutation will delay until either the first argument is not a variable or the second argument is not a variable.

Coroutine also imports the predicate Sorted from Lists. The declarations and possible definition for Sorted are as follows.

```
PREDICATE       Sorted : List(Integer).
DELAY           Sorted([]) UNTIL TRUE;
                Sorted([_|x]) UNTIL NONVAR(x).
```

```
Sorted([]).
Sorted([_]).
Sorted([x,y|z]) <-
                x =< y &
                Sorted([y|z]).
```

The meaning of the DELAY declaration for Sorted is as follows. If the argument of a call to Sorted is not an instance of either [] or [_|x], then the call delays. Thus the call Sorted(x) delays. If the argument of a call to Sorted has the form $[S \mid T]$, where T is a variable, then the call delays. Thus the call Sorted([1|x]) delays. If the argument of a call to `Sorted` is either `[]` or has the form `[S | T]`, where T is not a variable, then the call can proceed. Thus the calls `Sorted([])`, `Sorted([x])`, and `Sorted([3,2|x])` can proceed.

Now, assuming the "leftmost literal" computation rule was employed, the statement for `Slowsort` would have to be written as follows

```
Slowsort(x,y) <-
            Permutation(x,y) &
            Sorted(y).
```

so that the call to `Permutation` would be run before the call to `Sorted`. Thus a goal such as

```
<- Slowsort([6,1,5,2,4,3],x).
```

would take time having order $n!$, where n is the length of the input list. However, if the above `DELAY` declaration on `Sorted` is employed, then the time taken for such goals for the module `Coroutine` can be considerably reduced. Note that, using the `DELAY` declaration for `Sorted`, the call to `Sorted` may have to be put before the call to `Permutation` in the statement for `Slowsort` to ensure that the desired coroutining behaviour is achieved. (This depends on the implementation.) First, `Sorted` delays, then `Permutation` computes the first couple of elements of the permuted list (assuming it has length greater than one), then `Sorted` checks if this much of the permuted list is sorted, and so on.

Next we discuss the use of `DELAY` declarations to assist termination. Consider the module M5 again. M5 imports the predicate `Append` from `Lists`, where `Append` has the following `DELAY` declaration

```
DELAY        Append(x,_,z) UNTIL NONVAR(x) \/ NONVAR(z).
```

Without this `DELAY` declaration for `Append`, the computation (using the "leftmost literal" computation rule) of a goal such as

```
<- Append3(x,y,z,[1,2,3]).
```

gives all possible ways of splitting `[1,2,3]`, but then goes into an infinite loop. However, with the above `DELAY` declaration on `Append` instead, the computation of the goal gives all possible ways of splitting the list and then terminates.

As another example, consider the predicate `Delete`, which the definition of `Permutation` uses and which has the following declarations and possible definition.

```
PREDICATE     Delete : a * List(a) * List(a).
DELAY         Delete(_,y,z) UNTIL NONVAR(y) \/ NONVAR(z).
```

```
Delete(x,[x|y],y).
Delete(x,[y|z],[y|w]) <-
            Delete(x,z,w).
```

Now, using the "leftmost literal" computation rule, the computation of a goal such as

```
<- Permutation(x,[1,2,3]).
```

will first return the answer x = [1,2,3] and then, upon backtracking, will go into an infinite loop. However, using the above DELAY declarations for Permutation and Delete instead, the system will return all 6 permutations of [1,2,3] and then fail.

As well as the condition NONVAR, a DELAY declaration can use the condition GROUND. For example. the predicate < in the module Floats has the following DELAY declaration.

```
DELAY         x < y UNTIL GROUND(x) & GROUND(y).
```

This declaration delays calls to < until both its arguments are ground.

The fourth reason for employing a flexible computation rule is to solve constraints. In general, a goal consists of a constraint and a non-constraint part, and coroutining between the two parts is usually necessary for efficiency. Furthermore, just the solving of a system of constraints alone may require coroutining. The control necessary for the efficient solving of constraints in the modules Integers and Rationals is exercised by the system itself and cannot be changed by the programmer.

We now turn to the definition of the syntax and semantics of DELAY declarations. A DELAY declaration has the form

```
DELAY         Atom    UNTIL    Cond.
```

where *Atom* is an atom, which is not a proposition, and *Cond* is given by the following grammar.

Cond	$\longrightarrow$	*Cond1*
		| *Cond1* <'&'> *AndSeq*
		| *Cond1* <'\/'> *OrSeq*

Cond1	$\longrightarrow$	<'NONVAR'><'('> *Variable* <')'>
		| <'GROUND'><'('> *Variable* <')'>
		| <'TRUE'>
		| <'('> *Cond* <')'>

$$AndSeq \quad\longrightarrow\quad Cond1$$
$$| \; Cond1 <\text{`\&'}> AndSeq$$

$$OrSeq \quad\longrightarrow\quad Cond1$$
$$| \; Cond1 <\text{`\backslash/'}> OrSeq$$

where *Variable* is a variable in *Atom*.

A DELAY declaration for a predicate can only appear in the module where the predicate is declared. Also, as is illustrated by the DELAY declaration for Sorted, a set of DELAY declarations can be compacted into a single one of the form

DELAY $Atom_1$ UNTIL $Cond_1$;
                          $\vdots$
              $Atom_n$ UNTIL $Cond_n$.

The following condition is placed on *Atom*.

D1: No pair of *Atom*s in the set of DELAY declarations for a predicate can have a common instance.

This condition simplifies the semantics of DELAY declarations. Without it, a situation could arise where one declaration allowed a call to proceed, while another delayed it. As a further simplification, another condition is imposed. We say an atom is *constraint-free* if every term in the atom of type Integer, Rational, Float, String, or Set(τ), for some type τ, is a variable. Then the condition is as follows.

D2: An atom in the head of a DELAY declaration must be constraint-free and must not contain repeated variables.

This condition allows an implementation to avoid being concerned about the special equality theories that some types have and to use unification (without the occur check) when checking DELAY declarations.

In the grammar for *Cond*, the reserved word & stands for conjunction, \/ stands for disjunction, TRUE stands for the truth value true, NONVAR is true if and only if its argument is a non-variable term, and GROUND is true if and only if its argument is a ground term. Now suppose an atom A is an instance by a substitution θ of an *Atom* (that is, $A = Atom\,\theta$) in a DELAY declaration. Then we say A *satisfies* the corresponding condition *Cond* in this DELAY declaration if, when θ is applied to the variables in *Cond*, the resulting condition has truth value true using the above meanings given to the various reserved words. Otherwise, we say A does *not satisfy* the corresponding condition. For example, the atom `Permutation(x,[1|y])` is an instance of the atom in the `DELAY` declaration for `Permutation` and satisfies the corresponding condition. Also `Sorted([1|y])` and `Sorted([1,3])` are both instances of the atom in the second (part of the) `DELAY` declaration for `Sorted` but only `Sorted([1,3])` satisfies the corresponding condition.

Then `DELAY` declarations cause calls to be delayed according to the following rules:

- An atom in a goal is delayed if it has a common instance with some *Atom* in a `DELAY` declaration but is not an instance of this *Atom*.
- An atom in a goal is delayed if it is an instance of an *Atom* in a `DELAY` declaration[1] but does not satisfy the corresponding condition *Cond*.

Thus `DELAY` declarations give programmers some influence over the computation rule and can be used to ensure that certain calls will not be run until they are sufficiently instantiated.

During a computation, the current goal may have the property that no subformula of the goal can be selected for an extension step because of the delaying effect of `DELAY` declarations (and, possibly, other restrictions on the computation rule depending on the implementation). In such a case, the goal is said to *flounder* and, depending on the implementation, the computation may be halted with an error message to indicate that a flounder has occurred.

As another example to illustrate the control facilities, we consider the predicate `Merge` in the module `Lists`. `Merge` has the following declarations and possible definition.

```
PREDICATE  Merge : List(Integer) * List(Integer) * List(Integer).
DELAY      Merge(x,y,z) UNTIL (NONVAR(x) & NONVAR(y)) \/ NONVAR(z).
```

```
Merge([],x,x).
Merge(x,[],x).
Merge([u|x],[v|y],[u|z]) <-
          u < v &
          Merge(x,[v|y],z).
Merge([u|x],[v|y],[v|z]) <-
          u >= v &
          Merge([u|x],y,z).
```

The `DELAY` declaration for `Merge` shows that it can be used to either merge two given lists or else split a given list. Thus the goal

```
<- Merge([1,4,8],[3,6,9],x).
```

---

[1]By the condition D1, there can be at most one such declaration.

has the answer x = [1,3,4,6,8,9], the goal

```
<- Merge(x,y,[1,4]).
```

has the answers

```
x = [], y = [1,4]
x = [1,4], y = []
x = [1], y = [4]
x = [4], y = [1]
```

and the goal

```
<- Merge(x,[1,4],z).
```

flounders.

Now let us return to the DELAY declaration for Sorted again. It is clear from the above definitions that the first part of this declaration can be omitted and the effect will be exactly the same. Thus the original DELAY declaration for Sorted could be replaced by

```
DELAY        Sorted([_|x]) UNTIL NONVAR(x).
```

The reason is that all calls to Sorted have the form either Sorted(x), or Sorted([]), or Sorted([$S\,|\,T$]). Thus there is no call to Sorted which would be delayed by the first part of the declaration and which would not be delayed by the second part. However, we prefer to keep the original form of the declaration for clarity and documentation purposes.

Note that it is not always true that DELAY declarations with the condition TRUE have no effect and hence can be omitted. For example, if a predicate has a single DELAY declaration with the condition TRUE, then all calls which have a common instance with the atom of the declaration, but are not an instance of the atom, are delayed.

It is also worth remarking that other DELAY declarations for Sorted ensure similar behaviour. The weakest declaration (that is, the one that delays the least) is

```
DELAY        Sorted(x) UNTIL NONVAR(x).
```

and a stronger one is

```
DELAY        Sorted([]) UNTIL TRUE;
             Sorted([_]) UNTIL TRUE;
             Sorted([x,y|_]) UNTIL NONVAR(x) & NONVAR(y).
```

The first declaration will allow some calls to Sorted to proceed and then delay at the subsequent call to =<, whereas the second declaration will delay less often at the subsequent call to =<. In fact, there is little to choose between the three declarations.

Finally, in the module EightQueens below, we give a Gödel version of the standard 8-queens program.

```
MODULE      EightQueens.

IMPORT      Lists.


PREDICATE   Queen : List(Integer).

Queen(x) <-
            Safe(x) &
            Permutation([1,2,3,4,5,6,7,8], x).

PREDICATE   Safe : List(Integer).
DELAY       Safe(x) UNTIL NONVAR(x).

Safe([]).
Safe([x|y]) <-
            NoDiagonal(x,1,y) &
            Safe(y).

PREDICATE   NoDiagonal : Integer * Integer * List(Integer).
DELAY       NoDiagonal(_,_,z) UNTIL NONVAR(z).

NoDiagonal(_,_,[]).
NoDiagonal(x,y,[z|w]) <-
            y ~= Abs(z - x) &
            NoDiagonal(x,y+1,w).
```

7.2 Pruning

The most general form of the Gödel pruning operator, called *commit*, has the form {...}_*n*, of which two special cases have the form | and {...}. We begin by explaining with examples the more familiar | commit, then we discuss the {...} commit, and finally give the most general form of the commit.

However, before going on to discuss the details of the pruning operator, we make the following important remark: *well-written Gödel programs generally have little need for pruning*. For example, apart from the programs in this chapter which are deliberately designed to illustrate various aspects of pruning, there are few occurrences of the commit in programs in this book. Programmers are strongly encouraged to avoid the use of (explicit) pruning wherever possible, as such avoidance generally results in programs which have clearer semantics and are more amenable to analysis and transformation. In particular, the "non-failing" programming style of the propositional theorem prover in Section 10.3 is worth studying as, when applicable, it often results in a program with clearer declarative semantics and no need for (explicit) pruning at all.

Now consider the module P1 below, which is a variation of the module Qsort in Chapter 6 and for which the predicate Quicksort is intended to be called with its first argument instantiated. Module P1 uses the | version of the commit, which we call the *bar* commit. Declaratively, | is just conjunction. However, for convenience, if either argument of | is True it can be omitted, as in the first statement for Quicksort3. Each statement can contain at most one |. The *scope* of | is the formula to its left in the body of the statement. The order in which the statements are tried is not specified, so that commit does not have the sequentiality property of cut. The procedural meaning of | is that only one solution is found for the formula in its scope and all other branches in a search tree arising from the other statements in the predicate definition which contain a | are pruned. Thus the meaning of | is close to the commit of the concurrent logic programming languages. Note that, while a | commit would normally appear in *every* statement of a definition for which at least one | appears, this is not obligatory.

The DELAY declarations in P1 enforce the intended use of Quicksort. Thus there are DELAY declarations for Quicksort and Quicksort3 which delay calls to these predicates until their first argument is not a variable. The DELAY declaration for Partition ensures that either the first argument of a call to Partition will have its first argument the empty list, or the first element of the list in the first argument and the second argument will be known so that an arithmetic comparison between these can be carried out. In fact, the following weaker DELAY declaration for Partition is also suitable.

```
DELAY        Partition(x,_,_,_) UNTIL NONVAR(x).
```

```
MODULE       P1.

IMPORT       Lists.


PREDICATE    Quicksort : List(Integer) * List(Integer).
DELAY        Quicksort(x,_) UNTIL NONVAR(x).

Quicksort(x,y) <-
             Quicksort3(x,y,[]).


PREDICATE    Quicksort3 : List(Integer) * List(Integer) * List(Integer).
DELAY        Quicksort3(x,_,_) UNTIL NONVAR(x).

Quicksort3([],xs,xs) <-
             |.
Quicksort3([x|xs],ys,zs) <-
             |
             Partition(xs,x,l,b) &
             Quicksort3(l,ys,[x|ys1]) &
             Quicksort3(b,ys1,zs).


PREDICATE    Partition : List(Integer) * Integer * List(Integer) *
                         List(Integer).
DELAY        Partition([],_,_,_) UNTIL TRUE;
             Partition([x|_],y,_,_) UNTIL NONVAR(x) & NONVAR(y).

Partition([],_,[],[]) <-
             |.
Partition([x|xs],y,[x|ls],bs) <-
             x =< y |
             Partition(xs,y,ls,bs).
Partition([x|xs],y,ls,[x|bs]) <-
             x > y |
             Partition(xs,y,ls,bs).
```

If the first argument of a call to `Partition` is not a variable, the system can correctly commit to either the first statement in case this argument is the empty list or otherwise to one of the second and third statements. The commitment to either the second or third statement will be delayed until enough information is known to run the arithmetic tests.

For the intended use of `Quicksort`, the statements in the definition for `Quicksort3` are mutually exclusive, in the sense that the system can commit to at most one of these. The same is true for `Partition`. Thus no answer will be pruned – only useless computation will be pruned. So, in this case, the commits enhance efficiency without affecting completeness. More generally, the commits can prune answers.

Next we illustrate the Gödel one-solution commit, written {...}. Consider the module `P2` below. The intended meaning of `Perm` in `P2` is that it should be true if and only if its first argument is a list of integers and its second argument is a permutation of the list in the first argument. A goal such as

```
<- Perm([1,2,3],x).
```

will produce the answers

```
x = [1,2,3]
x = [1,3,2]
...
x = [3,2,1]
```

If instead the goal was

```
<- {Perm([1,2,3],x)}.
```

then only one of these answers would be produced. The scope of the one-solution commit {...} is the formula between the { and the }. When the scope is solved, all possible alternative solutions to the scope are pruned away. Of course, the one-solution commit can also be used in the bodies of statements in a program.

The bar commit and the one-solution commit provide programmers with powerful pruning facilities, which should suffice for the vast majority of programming tasks. However, source-level tools, such as program transformers and partial evaluators, have need of a more powerful pruning operator. The reason is that the class of programs containing | is not closed under even simple program transformations, such as unfolding. For this reason, Gödel has a more powerful pruning operator, $\{...\}\_n$, which includes the | and {...} as special cases, and which gives a class of programs closed under the usual program transformations. This pruning operator was introduced in [12].

To motivate the pruning operator, consider module `P3` below, which is a variant of module `P2`. Module `P3` can be used to *check* that one list is a permutation of another list. For example, the goal

---

```
MODULE      P2.

IMPORT      Lists.


PREDICATE   Perm : List(Integer) * List(Integer).
DELAY       Perm(x,y) UNTIL NONVAR(x) \/ NONVAR(y).

Perm([],[]).
Perm([x|y],[u|v]) <-
            Del(u,[x|y],z) &
            Perm(z,v).


PREDICATE   Del : Integer * List(Integer) * List(Integer).
DELAY       Del(_,y,z) UNTIL NONVAR(y) \/ NONVAR(z).

Del(x,[x|y],y).
Del(x,[y|z],[y|w]) <-
            Del(x,z,w).
```

```
<- Perm([1,2,3,4],[4,1,2,3]).
```

will produce the answer **Yes**.

The DELAY declaration for Perm in P3 will delay an atom with predicate Perm until its first argument is not a variable. This is sufficient to ensure commitment to the desired statement. In fact, the weaker DELAY declaration for Perm in P2 also ensures the desired commitment. Similarly, the DELAY declaration for Del in P3 will delay an atom with predicate Del until the desired commitment is ensured. (We assume here that all integer expressions appearing in a call to Del are either variables or ground terms. If this is not case, we would need to replace NONVAR by GROUND.)

As the previous paragraph indicates, an important heuristic for finding good DELAY declarations to control pruning is that they should be strong enough to avoid unexpected failure because of premature commitment to an inappropriate statement. For example, suppose the DELAY declaration for Del was omitted. Now consider the goal

---

```
MODULE      P3.

IMPORT      Lists.


PREDICATE   Perm : List(Integer) * List(Integer).
DELAY       Perm(x,_) UNTIL NONVAR(x).

Perm([],[]) <-
            | .
Perm([x|y],[u|v]) <-
            |
            Del(u,[x|y],z) &
            Perm(z,v).


PREDICATE   Del : Integer * List(Integer) * List(Integer).
DELAY       Del(x,[y|_],_) UNTIL NONVAR(x) & NONVAR(y).

Del(x,[x|y],y) <-
            | .
Del(x,[y|z],[y|w]) <-
            x ~= y |
            Del(x,z,w).
```

```
<- Del(x,[1,2,3],y) & x = 2.
```

The first atom in this goal unifies with the head of the first statement and so the system could commit to this statement. However, subsequently the call 1 = 2 will cause the goal to fail unexpectedly. If instead the call to Del had been delayed according to the DELAY declaration for it in P3, then the goal would have succeeded, as expected.

Now consider the program transformation task of unfolding (once) the call to Del in the second statement for Perm in module P3. For this purpose, we first rewrite the module using the more general commit. This is module P4 below. The scope of | is the formula in the body to its left. So each | is rewritten using { and } to indicate its scope inside a statement explicitly and a label, which is a positive integer, to indicate the scope across

---

MODULE   P4.

IMPORT   Lists.

PREDICATE   Perm : List(Integer) * List(Integer).
DELAY   Perm(x,_) UNTIL NONVAR(x).

Perm([],[]) <-
                {True}_1.
Perm([x|y],[u|v]) <-
                {True}_1 &
                Del(u,[x|y],z) &
                Perm(z,v).

PREDICATE   Del : Integer * List(Integer) * List(Integer).
DELAY   Del(x,[y|_],_) UNTIL NONVAR(x) & NONVAR(y).

Del(x,[x|y],y) <-
                {True}_2.
Del(x,[y|z],[y|w]) <-
                {x ~= y}_2 &
                Del(x,z,w).

---

the statements in each definition. The actual values of the labels in the two definitions are unimportant. It is only important that the two commits in the definition of **Perm** should have the same label and that the two commits in the definition of **Del** should have the same label. In module P4, the labels have been standardized apart in preparation for the unfolding step.

Now the unfolding step at the call to **Del** in the second statement for **Perm** can be performed. The result of this is given in module P5 below. The brackets {...} of a commit {$Formula$}_n indicate the scope of the commit inside a statement. The label n indicates the scope of the commit over the statements in a definition. When the formula *Formula* succeeds, all other statements in the definition which contain a commit labelled

```
MODULE        P5.

IMPORT        Lists.


PREDICATE     Perm : List(Integer) * List(Integer).
DELAY         Perm([],_) UNTIL TRUE;
              Perm([x|_],[y|_]) UNTIL NONVAR(x) & NONVAR(y).

Perm([],[]) <-
              {True}_1.
Perm([x|y],[x|v]) <-
              {True}_1 &
              {True}_2 &
              Perm(y,v).
Perm([x|y],[u|v]) <-
              {True}_1 &
              {x ~= u}_2 &
              Del(u,y,w) &
              Perm([x|w],v).


PREDICATE     Del : Integer * List(Integer) * List(Integer).
DELAY         Del(x,[y|_],_) UNTIL NONVAR(x) & NONVAR(y).

Del(x,[x|y],y) <-
              {True}_2.
Del(x,[y|z],[y|w]) <-
              {x ~= y}_2 &
              Del(x,z,w).
```

n are pruned. The other pruning which takes place is that only one solution is found for *Formula*. The commits which have been introduced into module P5 by the unfolding step are such that an answer computed for a goal to module P5 can also be computed for the same goal to module P4. Thus the transformation is sound for the procedural semantics. This follows from a theorem about partial evaluation in [12]. (See Theorem 3.1.)

Note that the DELAY declaration for Perm in module P5 has been strengthened compared with the one in module P4. This ensures correct commitment. For example, if the DELAY declaration for Perm in P5 is replaced by the weaker one for Perm in P4, then the goal

```
<- Perm([1,2,3],x) & x = [2,1,3].
```

could fail unexpectedly by committing to the second statement.

The unfolding in module P4 was carried out at an atom which was not inside the scope of the commit in the statement. For the case when the unfolding is carried out at an atom in the scope of all the commits in a statement (that is, the regularity condition in [12] is satisfied), a stronger soundness result applies. This is that, for any *set* of answers computed by the program resulting from the unfolding, the same set can also be computed by the original program. (See Theorem 3.2 in [12].) For a more detailed discussion about the interplay between pruning, the regularity condition, and partial evaluation, see [8].

The one-solution commit {...} is regarded as a special case of the commit {...}_n in that {...} is assumed to have a label that does not occur elsewhere in the definition in which it appears. Another aspect of the commit worth noting is that an implementation employing negation as failure (and variations of it) should disable all pruning during the subsidiary computation of a negated call (or at least ensure that no non-failed branch in the subsidiary tree is pruned). This ensures the soundness of the implementation.

We now describe the (top-level) syntax for statements and goals containing commits. For this, we need to give the (top-level) syntax for a body, which may be either the body of a goal or a statement. The grammar for a (non-empty) body is as follows.

Body	$\longrightarrow$	[CFormula(f)] <'|'> [CFormula(f1)]
		| CFormula(f)
CFormula(0)	$\longrightarrow$	<'('> CFormula(f) <')'>
		| <'{'> CFormula(f) <'}' ['_' Label]>
CFormula(2)	$\longrightarrow$	CFormula(f) <'&'> CFormula(f1) (f ≤ 1, f1 ≤ 2)
CFormula(f)	$\longrightarrow$	Formula(f)

where the notation [...] indicates 0 or 1 occurrences of the included item, Label is a positive integer, and Formula is a formula not involving commits.

Next, we describe how the bar commits and the one-solution commits are preprocessed away. The preprocessed versions of bodies will be useful for the ground representation and for describing the procedural semantics. According to the above grammar, only one bar commit is allowed in a body and it must not appear inside the scope of any other commit. So a body of the form $V \mid W$ (resp., $V \mid$, $\mid W$, $\mid$) is replaced by $\{V\}\_n \ \& \ W$ (resp., $\{V\}\_n$, $\{True\}\_n \ \& \ W$, $\{True\}\_n$), for a suitable positive integer n. If the bar commit is in the body of a goal, then n must be different from any other label in the goal. For bar commits appearing in a definition, n must be the same for all bar commits in the definition and different from the label of any other commits in the definition. Finally, any one-solution commits are given a label unique to the goal or definition in which they appear. After this preprocessing, all bodies contain only commits of the form $\{...\}\_n$.

Finally, we give a somewhat more formal description of the procedural semantics of commit. (More details can be found in Chapter 12 and, for the case of SLDNF-resolution, in [12].) First we need to introduce the concept of a search tree corresponding to some proof procedure. If P is a program and G a goal, a *search tree* for $P \cup \{G\}$ is a finite tree whose nodes are labelled by goals, the root being labelled by G. The children of a node in a search tree correspond to the children created by an extension step. There are various kinds of extension step, but the one of most interest here is an expansion step in which the selected subformula in the body of the current goal is an atom which is expanded using the definition of the proposition or predicate in the atom (by a straightforward generalization of a derivation step for SLD-resolution). We define an l-child as follows.

Definition Let T be a search tree, G_0 a non-leaf node in T, and G_1 a child of G_0. Then G_1 is an *l-child* of G_0 if **either**

1. G_0 contains a commit labelled l and the selected subformula in G_0 is in the scope of this commit, **or**

2. G_1 is derived from G_0 in an expansion step using a statement which contains a commit labelled l (after standardization apart of the commit labels).

G_1 is an l-child *of the first kind* (resp., *of the second kind*) if G_0 satisfies condition 1 (resp., 2) above.

Note the following properties of l-children.

1. A node can be an l-child of the first or second kind, but not both.

2. The l-children of a node are either all of the first kind or all of the second kind.

3. If one child of a node is an *l*-child of the first kind, then all children of the node are *l*-children.

4. A node can be an *l*-child and an *m*-child, where $l \neq m$.

The ideas of the previous definition are illustrated by module **P6**, for which the following is a search tree.

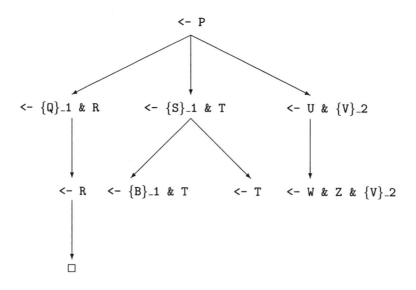

Then `<- {Q}_1 & R` and `<- {S}_1 & T` are 1-children and `<- U & {V}_2` is a 2-child of `<- P` of the second kind. The nodes `<- {B}_1 & T` and `<- T` are 1-children of `<- {S}_1 & T` of the first kind. The node `<- W & Z & {V}_2` is not a 2-child of `<- U & {V}_2`, as the selected atom is not in the scope of the commit.

Now we can define the concept of a pruning step, which gives the procedural meaning of the commit.

Definition Let S be a search tree. We say the search tree S' is obtained from S by a *pruning step* in S at G_0 if the following conditions are satisfied.

1. S has a node G_0 with distinct *l*-children G_1 and G_2, and there is a node G_2' in S which is either equal to or below G_2 and does not contain the commit labelled l.

2. S' is obtained from S by removing the subtree of S rooted at G_1.

```
MODULE        P6.

PROPOSITION   P,Q,R,S,U,B,W,Z,T,V.

P <- {Q}_1 & R.
P <- {S}_1 & T.
P <- U & {V}_2.
Q.
S <- B.
S.
U <- W & Z.
T.
R.
```

G_1 is the *cut node* and the pair (G_2, G_2') is an *explanation* for the pruning step.

Consider the preceding search tree. We can apply a pruning step to this tree to obtain the subtree S_1

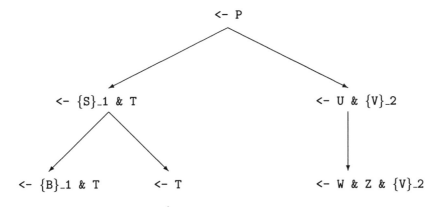

where the explanation for pruning the leftmost branch is the pair (<- {S}_1 & T, <- T). We can apply another pruning step to S_1 to obtain the subtree S_2

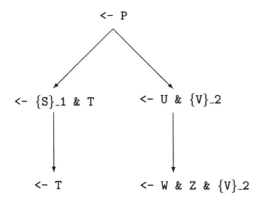

where the explanation for pruning the leftmost child of `<- {S}_1 & T` is the pair (`<- T`, `<- T`). No further pruning is possible.

We have defined a pruning step to be the smallest amount of pruning that could take place at any time. However, an implementation of Gödel may apply several pruning steps together. For example, if a pruning step at a node G_0 with cut node G_1 is possible because there is an explanation (G_2, G'_2), where G_1 and G_2 are l-children of G_0 and G'_2 does not contain a commit with label l, then it would also be possible to prune all other subtrees rooted at l-children of G_0 using the same explanation (G_2, G'_2). In the case when all children of G_0 are l-children, this amounts to removing the choice point at G_0. It is also possible to remove the choice points at each node on the branch to G'_2 at which the selected literal is in the scope of an l-commit. In fact, an implementation may do pruning *eagerly*, in the sense that when the scope of a commit is solved the system would perform as much pruning as is possible as a result of solving that scope.

8 Input/Output

The Gödel input/output facilities are provided by the system modules IO, NumbersIO, FlocksIO, ProgramsIO, ScriptsIO, and TheoriesIO. The first three modules are discussed in this chapter. The last three are relevant for meta-programming applications and so the discussion of these is postponed to Chapter 9.

8.1 IO

The basic input/output module is IO, the export part (except for the DELAY declarations) of which is given below. The types InputStream and OutputStream are provided, which are the types of input streams and output streams, respectively. To open a file for input, the predicate FindInput is used. Its first argument is the name of a file (given as a string) and the second argument contains either a term of the form In(*stream*), where *stream* is the new input stream, or the constant NotFound depending on whether the attempt to open the file was successful or not. Similarly, FindOutput is used to open a file for output. The two read predicates are Get and ReadChar. Get returns the ASCII code of the next character read from the open input stream or -1 if the end of the file has been reached. ReadChar returns a string of length 1 containing the next character read from the open input stream or the empty string if the end of the file has been reached. The write predicates are Put, which writes the character whose ASCII code is the second argument to the open output stream, and WriteString, which writes the string of characters in the second argument to the open output stream. The predicate EndInput closes an open input stream and EndOutput closes an open output stream. The constant StdIn of type InputStream represents the stream corresponding to standard input, with analogous meanings for the companion constants StdOut and StdErr. Thus, for the program {IO, Strings, Lists, Integers}, the goal

```
<- WriteString(StdOut, "Hello World\n").
```

produces the output

```
Hello World
```

As an example of the use of the module IO, the program with main module DisplayFile below reads a file as input and displays it on standard output.

Gödel's input/output facilities do not have a declarative semantics, so it is very important that input/output predicates are confined to as small a part of a program as possible. Let us say a module is an *input/output module* if it depends upon the module IO. The modules referred to by input/output modules, but not themselves input/output modules, form the main modules for programs which can be understood declaratively

---

EXPORT   IO.

IMPORT   Strings.

BASE   InputStream, OutputStream, ResultOfFind.

CONSTANT   StdIn : InputStream;
                  StdOut, StdErr : OutputStream;
                  NotFound : ResultOfFind.

FUNCTION   In : InputStream -> ResultOfFind;
                  Out : OutputStream -> ResultOfFind.

PREDICATE   FindInput : String * ResultOfFind;
                  FindOutput : String * ResultOfFind;
                  FindUpdate : String * ResultOfFind;
                  EndInput : InputStream;
                  EndOutput : OutputStream;
                  Get : InputStream * Integer;
                  ReadChar : InputStream * String;
                  Put : OutputStream * Integer;
                  WriteString : OutputStream * String;
                  NewLine : OutputStream;
                  Flush : OutputStream.

(apart from the commits). The basic idea is to maximize the size of these programs
and to keep the size and number of the input/output modules to a minimum. In fact,
a common module structure is to have just the main module of a program importing
system input/output modules together with one other non-input/output module. In
such a program, all the user modules other than the main module, together with any
system modules that they depend upon, form a program which has a declarative semantics. There is a strong incentive for programmers to adopt this kind of module structure,
since the purest forms of program transformation, declarative debugging, and so on, only
apply to modules that are not input/output ones. Since the order of input/output calls
is important, an implementation should indicate in what order such calls will be made.

```
EXPORT      DisplayFile.

IMPORT      Strings.

PREDICATE   Display : String.

DELAY       Display(x) UNTIL GROUND(x).

% Display displays on standard output the file whose name appears in its
% argument.
```

8.2 NumbersIO

The system module NumbersIO provides input/output facilities for integers, rationals, and floating-point numbers. The export part (except for the DELAY declarations) of NumbersIO is given below.

The predicate ReadInteger skips over layout characters to find the next token (or pair of tokens if the integer is negative) which should be an integer. If the next token (or pair of tokens) is not an integer, ReadInteger fails. If end of file has already been reached (or if there are only layout characters before the end of file), ReadInteger succeeds with 0 in the second argument and the constant EOF in the third. If end of file has not been reached and ReadInteger succeeds, then NotEOF is returned in the third argument. The predicates ReadRational and ReadFloat behave similarly. The predicates WriteInteger, WriteRational, and WriteFloat write numbers of the appropriate type to an output stream.

8.3 FlocksIO

So that a program can access a term representing a flock, Gödel provides a system module, called FlocksIO. The export part of FlocksIO is given below. FlocksIO imports IO so that the predicates there can be used to open and close files. The predicate GetFlock is intended to be called with its first argument ground and instantiates the second argument to the term representing the flock in the file with extension .flk corresponding to the input stream in the first argument. The predicate PutFlock is intended to be called with both arguments ground. It puts the term in the second argument into the file

```
LOCAL       DisplayFile.

IMPORT      IO.

% PREDICATE    Display : String.

Display(file) <-
            FindInput(file, result) &
            ProcessStream(result).


PREDICATE    ProcessStream : ResultOfFind.

ProcessStream(In(stream)) <-
            Get(stream, c) &
            DisplayStream(stream, c) &
            EndInput(stream).

ProcessStream(NotFound) <-
            WriteString(StdOut, "File not found\n").


PREDICATE    DisplayStream : InputStream * Integer.

DisplayStream(stream, c) <-
            IF c ~= -1
            THEN
              Put(StdOut, c) &
              Get(stream, c1) &
              DisplayStream(stream, c1).
```

EXPORT	NumbersIO.
IMPORT	IO, Numbers.
BASE	FileInfo.
CONSTANT	EOF, NotEOF : FileInfo.
PREDICATE	ReadInteger : InputStream * Integer * FileInfo; ReadRational : InputStream * Rational * FileInfo; ReadFloat : InputStream * Float * FileInfo; WriteInteger : OutputStream * Integer; WriteRational : OutputStream * Rational; WriteFloat : OutputStream * Float.

---

with extension .flk corresponding to the output stream in the first argument. The predicate FlockCompile is intended to be called with its first argument the name of a file containing a flock and produces the representation of this flock in its second argument. The predicate FlockDecompile is intended to be called with the representation of a flock in its first argument and the name of a file in its second argument. It writes the flock to this file.

Note that FlocksIO is an input/output module so it should be handled like the module IO. In particular, it is preferable to arrange the module structure of the program so that only its main module depends upon FlocksIO. A program illustrating the use of FlocksIO is given in Section 10.3.

EXPORT   FlocksIO.

IMPORT   IO, Flocks.

PREDICATE   GetFlock : InputStream * Flock;
              PutFlock : OutputStream * Flock;
              FlockCompile : String * Flock;
              FlockDecompile : Flock * String.

9 Meta-Programming

In the design of Gödel, particular attention has been paid to its meta-logical facilities. As we have already indicated, using the ground representation, a programmer can write in a declarative way many important kinds of meta-programs, such as program transformers, compilers, debuggers, abstract interpreters, program synthesizers, and theorem provers. We now turn attention to the various modules which provide meta-programming facilities via the ground representation.

9.1 Syntax

The ground representation is a scheme for representing object programs, modules, goals, theories, declarations, terms, and so on, as terms in a meta-language. The details of the ground representation are not made explicit. (For background on the ground representation, see [3], [10], or [11], and for a detailed discussion of a particular implementation of the ground representation for Gödel itself, see [4].) Instead, following an abstract data type approach, Gödel provides, via the system modules Syntax, Programs, Scripts, and Theories, a set of predicates which allow a meta-program to access and manipulate terms representing object expressions. The constants and functions actually used in the representation are hidden in the local parts of these modules. However, we emphasize strongly that, even though the details of the ground representation are hidden, all the predicates exported by these modules have definitions with fully declarative readings.

Gödel supports the ground representation of (object) programs, scripts, and theories. The first of these is given by the module Programs, the second by the module Scripts, and the third by the module Theories. We discuss these three modules in subsequent sections. In this section, we discuss the module Syntax which provides some facilities for the manipulation of the representations of (object) expressions common to all three of these ground representations.

First, Syntax imports all the symbols exported by the modules Integers, Lists, and Strings. It also declares (amongst others) the following bases, which are required by the ground representation of expressions of various kinds.

BASE   Name, Type, Term, Formula, TypeSubst, TermSubst, VarTyping.

Name is the type of a term representing the name of a symbol, Type is the type of a term representing a type, Term is the type of a term representing a term, Formula is the type of a term representing a formula, TypeSubst is the type of a term representing a type substitution, TermSubst is the type of a term representing a term substitution, and VarTyping is the type of a term representing a variable typing.

Note that two kinds of substitutions need to be represented. The first is the usual *term substitution* consisting of a set of term bindings, which are pairs of variables and

terms. The other kind is a *type substitution* consisting of a set of type bindings, which
are pairs of parameters and types. All the usual operations on term substitutions are
also provided for type substitutions. A *variable typing* is a set of bindings where each
binding consists of a variable together with the type assigned to that variable.

Before discussing the predicates provided by `Syntax`, we make some general points.
First, all bar commits and one-solution commits are preprocessed away, as explained in
Section 7.2, so that only commits with labels are present in object expressions. Second,
any subformula of an (object) formula may be bracketed by commits, so that commits are
not constrained to appear just around top-level conjuncts of a body. Third, the various
predicates in `Syntax` which manipulate types, terms, and formulas have no language
information and therefore cannot check whether the various expressions are types, terms,
or formulas in some language. Of course, the representation of a language could be
included as an argument to these predicates, but checking whether an expression is
properly formed in some language is expensive and is rarely needed, so this argument is
omitted. However, `Syntax` does provide predicates for explicitly checking that a formula
is a definite body, normal goal, and so on. Also there are predicates in the modules
`Programs`, `Scripts`, and `Theories` for explicitly checking that terms and formulas are
well-typed in certain languages.

We now discuss in some detail a representative selection of predicates provided by
`Syntax`. The complete export part of `Syntax` is given in Chapter 13. Throughout this
chapter, when giving the meanings of the various predicates, the phrase "true when"
always means "true in the intended interpretation if and only if".

The first collection of predicates is mainly concerned with the representation of the
connectives and quantifiers.

```
PREDICATE  And : Formula * Formula * Formula;
           All : List(Term) * Formula * Formula;
           Commit : Integer * Formula * Formula.
```

`And` is true when its first and second arguments are the representations of formulas, and
its third argument is the representation of the formula which is the conjunction of the
formulas in the first and second arguments. `All` is true when its first argument is a
list of the representations of variables, its second argument is the representation of a
formula, and its third argument is the representation of the formula which is obtained
by taking the universal quantification over the set of variables in the first argument of
the formula in the second argument. `Commit` is true when its first argument is a commit
label, its second argument is the representation of a formula, and its third argument
is the representation of the formula obtained by bracketing the formula in the second
argument with a commit having this label.

The next four predicates are concerned with the representation of variables and parameters.

```
PREDICATE   Variable : Term;
            VariableName : Term * String * Integer;
            Parameter : Type;
            ParameterName : Type * String * Integer.
```

Variable is true when its argument is the representation of a variable. Variable can only be used to *check* whether or not its argument is the representation of a variable. Variable names have the form name_n, where name is the *root* of the name of the variable and the non-negative integer n is called the *index* of the variable.[1] VariableName is true when its first argument is the representation of a variable, its second argument is the root of the name of the variable, and its third argument is the index of the variable. VariableName is used to create the representations of new variables and also to split a variable name into its root and index. Parameter names are analogous to variable names and have a root and index. Parameter is true when its argument is the representation of a parameter. ParameterName is true when its first argument is the representation of a parameter, its second argument is the root of the name of the parameter, and its third argument is the index of the parameter.

The next collection of predicates is mainly concerned with checking whether types, terms, and formulas have certain properties.

```
PREDICATE   NonVariable : Term;
            Atom : Formula;
            Statement : Formula;
            EmptyFormula : Formula.
```

NonVariable is true when its argument is the representation of a non-variable term. Atom is true when its argument is the representation of an atom. Statement is true when its argument is the representation of a standard statement. (See Section 11.7 for the definition of a standard statement and related concepts.) EmptyFormula is true when its argument is the representation of the empty formula.

The next two predicates are used to construct and pull apart the representations of terms and atoms. For these, we need some definitions. A term is *opaque* if it is a constant declared in the local part of a closed module or it has a top-level function declared in

---

[1]As an implementation point, we note that variable names of the form name_n allow a convenient and efficient way of creating new variables, renaming variables, and so on, both for the user and the system. Furthermore, an implementation must give an index to *all* object variables, even those not created by VariableName. This greatly increases the usefulness of the predicates FormulaMaxVarIndex and TermMaxVarIndex (see Chapter 13), which are often needed for renaming.

the local part of a closed module; otherwise, it is *non-opaque*. Opaque types and atoms
are defined analogously.

```
PREDICATE  FunctionTerm : Term * Name * List(Term);
           PredicateAtom : Formula * Name * List(Term).
```

FunctionTerm is true when its first argument is the representation of a non-opaque term
with a function at the top-level, its second argument is the representation of the name
of this function, and its third argument is the list of representations of the top-level
subterms of this term. A predicate OpaqueTerm is provided which can be used to find
out whether a term is opaque or not. PredicateAtom is true when its first argument
is the representation of a non-opaque atom with a predicate at the top-level, its second
argument is the representation of the name of this predicate, and its third argument is
the list of representations of the top-level terms of this atom.

   The final collection of predicates is useful for a variety of standard meta-programming
tasks. For the last of these, we will need a definition. A *resultant* is a formula of the
form *W1* <- *W2*, where *W1* and *W2* are formulas. *W1* is the *head* and *W2* is the *body* of
the resultant.

```
PREDICATE  RestrictSubstToTerm : Term * TermSubst * TermSubst;
           BindingToTermSubst : Term * Term * TermSubst;
           BindingInTypeSubst : TypeSubst * Type * Type;
           UnifyTerms : Term * Term * TermSubst * TermSubst;
           RenameFormulas : List(Formula) * List(Formula) *
                            List(Formula);
           VariantFormulas : List(Formula) * List(Formula);
           Derive : Formula * Formula * Formula * Formula * Formula *
                    TermSubst * Formula.
```

RestrictSubstToTerm is true when its first argument is the representation of a term,
its second argument is the representation of a term substitution, and its third argument
is the representation of this term substitution restricted to the variables in this term.
BindingToTermSubst is true when its first argument is the representation of a variable,
its second argument is the representation of a term, and its third argument is the representation of the term substitution containing just the binding in which this variable is
bound to this term. BindingInTypeSubst is true when its first argument is the representation of a type substitution, its second argument is the representation of a parameter in
the first component of a binding in this substitution, and its third argument is the representation of the type to which this parameter is bound in this substitution. UnifyTerms
is true when its first and second arguments are the representations of terms, its third

argument is the representation of a term substitution, and its fourth argument is the representation of the term substitution obtained by composing the term substitution in the third argument with a specific, unique most general unifier (mgu) for the terms which are obtained by applying the term substitution in the third argument to the terms in the first two arguments. RenameFormulas is true when its first and second arguments are lists of representations of formulas and its third argument is the list of representations of the formulas obtained by a specific, unique renaming of the free variables of the formulas in the second argument such that they become distinct from the free variables in the formulas in the first argument. VariantFormulas is true when its first argument is a list of representations of formulas and its second argument is a list of representations of formulas which are variants of the formulas in the first argument. Derive is true when its first argument is the representation of the head of a resultant, its second argument is the representation of the body to the left of the selected atom in the resultant, its third argument is the representation of the selected atom in the resultant, its fourth argument is the representation of the body to the right of the selected atom in the resultant, its fifth argument is the representation of a statement whose head unifies with the selected atom in the resultant, its sixth argument is the representation of a specific, unique mgu of the head of the selected atom and the head of this statement, and its seventh argument is the representation of the derived resultant.

As an illustration of the use of the above meta-level predicates, we give below a definition of the predicate MyUnifyTerms, which is essentially a special case of the system predicate UnifyTerms, using other predicates provided by Syntax.

```
EXPORT      Unify.

IMPORT      Syntax.

PREDICATE   MyUnifyTerms :

  Term          % Representation of a term.
* Term          % Representation of a term.
* TermSubst.    % Representation of an mgu for these terms.
```

```
LOCAL       Unify.

% PREDICATE  MyUnifyTerms : Term * Term * TermSubst.

MyUnifyTerms(t,t1,s) <-
          EmptyTermSubst(e) &
          UnifyingSubst(t,t1,e,s).


PREDICATE  UnifyingSubst : Term * Term * TermSubst * TermSubst.

UnifyingSubst(t,t1,s,s1) <-
          ApplySubstToTerm(t,s,ts) &
          ApplySubstToTerm(t1,s,t1s) &
          UnifyingSubst1(ts,t1s,s,s1).


PREDICATE  UnifyingSubst1 : Term * Term * TermSubst * TermSubst.

UnifyingSubst1(t,t,s,s).
UnifyingSubst1(t1,v,s,s1) <-
          Variable(v) &
          NotOccur(v,t1) &
          BindingToTermSubst(v,t1,r) &
          ComposeTermSubsts(r,s,s1).
UnifyingSubst1(v,t1,s,s1) <-
          Variable(v) &
          NotOccur(v,t1) &
          BindingToTermSubst(v,t1,r) &
          ComposeTermSubsts(r,s,s1).
UnifyingSubst1(t,t1,s,s1) <-
          t ~= t1 &
          FunctionTerm(t,x,tas) &
          FunctionTerm(t1,x,tas1) &
          UnifyingSubst2(tas,tas1,s,s1).
```

```
PREDICATE  UnifyingSubst2 : List(Term) * List(Term) * TermSubst *
                            TermSubst.

UnifyingSubst2([],[],s,s).
UnifyingSubst2([t|ts],[t1|ts1],s,s1) <-
         UnifyingSubst(t,t1,s,s2) &
         UnifyingSubst2(ts,ts1,s2,s1).


PREDICATE  NotOccur : Term * Term.

NotOccur(s,t) <-
         s ~= t &
         ALL [t1] (NotOccur(s,t1) <- Subterm(t,t1)).


PREDICATE  Subterm : Term * Term.

Subterm(t,t1) <-
         FunctionTerm(t,_,ts) &
         Member(t1,ts).
```

9.2 Programs

We will turn shortly to a discussion of the predicates provided by **Programs**. But before this, we need to introduce the concepts of the flat name of a symbol and the flat form of a program.

For clarity in this discussion, what we called before the *name* of a symbol, we will now call the *declared name* of the symbol. Since module condition M3 is enforced, a symbol can be uniquely identified by the quadruple consisting of the name of the module in which the symbol is declared, the declared name of the symbol, its category, and its arity. (For bases, constants, and propositions, the arity is extraneous, of course. We include it in these cases for uniformity.) Such a quadruple (M, S, C, A), where M is the name of a module, S is the declared name of a symbol which is declared in the module M, C is the category of S, and A is the arity of S, is called the *flat name* of the symbol.

The *flat form* of a program P is the "program" obtained from P by replacing each occurrence of the declared name of a symbol in P by the flat name of the symbol. The *flat language of a program* P is the polymorphic many-sorted language given by the set of language declarations in the flat form of P. The *flat language* of a module M in a program P is the subset of the flat language of P given by the set of language declarations of all symbols which have a language declaration in the language of M in P.[2] The *flat export language* of a module M in a program P is the subset of the flat language of P given by the set of language declarations of all symbols which have a language declaration in the export language of M in P.

Note carefully that, for the ground representation, it is the *flat form* of a program which is represented rather than the program itself. The reason is that the flat form of a program is much more convenient because it does not have any name clashes. Hence, such things as explicit derivation steps in an interpreter can be achieved by taking the current resultant, choosing an appropriate input statement, and doing a derivation step, without having to be concerned with name clashes.

Recall that bar commits and one-solution commits are preprocessed away, so that only the representations of commits with labels are present in the ground representation of a program. Also module declarations, language declarations, control declarations, and statements appear in some definite, but unspecified, order in the ground representation of a program. The only time this order is visible to a programmer is when the predicate `DefinitionInProgram` is called. This predicate returns the list (of representations) of statements in the definition of a proposition or predicate in this order.

A typical meta-program is a debugger. Taking the declarative debugger in [15, page 124] as an example, we see that the debugger switches between manipulating formulas in the bodies of program statements and running goals to the program being debugged. The manipulation of the formulas takes place in the flat language of the appropriate module of the program. The running of a goal takes place in the flat language of the program.

The module `Programs` imports the module `Syntax`. It also declares the following bases.

BASE   Program, ModulePart, Condition.

`Program` is the type of a term representing (the flat form of) a program. `ModulePart` is the type of constants representing the keywords `EXPORT`, `LOCAL`, `CLOSED`, and `MODULE`. Thus there are four constants of type `ModulePart` with declarations as follows.

CONSTANT   Export, Local, Closed, Module : ModulePart.

---

[2]A language and its corresponding flat version can be thought of as simply different presentations (using different conventions for naming symbols) for the same (underlying) language.

Condition is the type of a term representing a condition in a DELAY declaration.

We now discuss in some detail a representative selection of predicates provided by Programs, the complete export part of which is given in Chapter 13. The first of these predicates is TermInProgram, which has the following declaration.

```
PREDICATE  TermInProgram : Program  * VarTyping * Term * Type *
                           VarTyping.
```

TermInProgram is true when its first argument is the representation of a program, the second argument is the representation of a variable typing in the flat language of this program, its third argument is the representation of a term in this language, the fourth is the representation of the type of this term with respect to this variable typing, and the fifth is the representation of the variable typing obtained by combining the variable typing in the second argument with the types of all free variables occurring in the term.

The next collection of predicates in Programs is concerned with the representation of types, terms, and formulas.

```
PREDICATE  StringToProgramType : Program * String * String * List(Type);
           StringToProgramTerm : Program * String * String * List(Term);
           StringToProgramFormula : Program * String * String *
                                    List(Formula).
```

StringToProgramType is true when its first argument is the representation of a program, its second argument is the name of a module in this program, its third argument is a string, and its fourth argument is the list (in a definite order) of representations of types in the flat language of this module in this program whose string representation is the third argument. There may be more than one such type due to overloading. Thus the call StringToProgramType(P, M, "List(Integer)", x), where P is a term representing a program, M is the name of a module in this program, and the constructor List and the base Integer are in the language of M in P, would bind x to the list consisting of the term representing the type List(Integer) (assuming no overloading). Similarly, StringToProgramTerm is true when its first argument is the representation of a program, its second argument is the name of a module in this program, its third argument is a string, and its fourth argument is the list (in a definite order) of representations of terms in the flat language of this module in this program whose string representation is the third argument. Thus the call StringToProgramTerm(P, M, "v1", x), where P is a term representing a program and M is the name of a module in this program, would bind x to the list consisting of the term representing the variable v1. Note that the ground representation represents actual names of variables, which can be recovered by calling the companion predicate ProgramTermToString (see Chapter 13) with the first argument instantiated to a term representing a program, the second argument to the name of a module in this program, the third argument instantiated to the term representing the variable whose name is to be recovered, and the fourth argument a variable. `StringToProgramFormula` is true when its first argument is the representation of a program, its second argument is the name of a module in this program, its third argument is string, and its fourth argument is the list (in a definite order) of representations of formulas, which are standard bodies or standard resultants, in the flat language of this module in this program whose string representation is the third argument. `StringToProgramFormula` provides a convenient way of giving a meta-program the representation of a goal to an object program. For example, the call `StringToProgramFormula`($P, M,$`"Append(x,y,[1,2,3])"`,`z`), where P is a term representing a program and M is the name of a module in this program, would bind `z` to the list consisting of the term representing the goal body `Append(x,y,[1,2,3])`.

Of course, facilities for creating the representation of object programs have also to be provided. Since object programs are usually of a substantial size, Gödel handles the creation of their representation differently from the representation of types, terms, and so on. The discussion of how this is done is postponed to the next section.

The next collection of predicates is concerned with modules and accessing statements in open modules.

```
PREDICATE   OpenModule : Program * String;
            DeclaredInOpenModule : Program * String * Formula;
            StatementInModule : Program * String * Formula;
            StatementMatchAtom : Program * String * Formula * Formula.
```

`OpenModule` is true when its first argument is the representation of a program and its second argument is the name of an open module in this program. `DeclaredInOpenModule` is true when its first argument is the representation of a program, its second argument is the name of an open module in this program, and its third argument is the representation of an atom in the flat language of this program whose proposition or predicate is declared in this module. `StatementInModule` is true when its first argument is the representation of a program, its second argument is the name of an open module in this program, and its third argument is the representation of a statement in this module. `StatementMatchAtom` is true when its first argument is the representation of a program, its second argument is the name of an open module in this program, its third argument is the representation of an atom in the flat language of this program, and its fourth argument is the representation of a statement in this module whose proposition or predicate in the head is the same as the proposition or predicate in this atom.

For the sake of uniformity, a statement that is an atom is represented as a formula with top-level connective `<-` whose left-hand argument is the atom and whose right-hand argument is the empty formula. Thus, to access the head or body of a statement, `StatementInModule` or `StatementMatchAtom` is first used to access the statement and then `IsImpliedBy` from `Syntax` is used to access the head or body. An empty body can be checked for using `EmptyFormula` from `Syntax`.

The next three predicates are concerned with language and import declarations in a program.

```
PREDICATE   ConstructorInModule : Program * String * ModulePart * Name *
                                  Integer * String;
            ConstantInModule : Program * String * ModulePart * Name *
                               Type * String;
            ImportInModule : Program * String * ModulePart * String.
```

`ConstructorInModule` is true when its first argument is the representation of a program, its second argument is the name of a module in this program, its third argument is the representation of a part keyword of this module which cannot be `LOCAL` if this module is closed, its fourth argument is the representation of the flat name of a constructor accessible to this part of this module, its fifth argument is the arity of this constructor, and its sixth argument is the name of the module in which the constructor is declared. Thus the call `ConstructorInModule(`P`, "M6", Module, `N`, 1, "Lists")`, where P is the term representing the program {`M6, M5, Lists, Integers`} and N is the term representing the flat name of `List`, would succeed. `ConstantInModule` is true when its first argument is the representation of a program, its second argument is the name of a module in this program, its third argument is the representation of a part keyword of this module which cannot be `LOCAL` if this module is closed, its fourth argument is the representation of the flat name of a constant accessible to this part of this module, its fifth argument is the representation of the type of this constant, and its sixth argument is the name of the module in which the constant is declared. `ImportInModule` is true when its first argument is the representation of a program, its second argument is the name of a module in this program, its third argument is the representation of a part keyword of this module which cannot be `LOCAL` if this module is closed, and its fourth argument is the name of a module appearing in an `IMPORT` declaration in this part of this module. Note that none of these predicates gives access to declarations or statements in the local part of a closed module.

The next two predicates are needed for dynamic meta-programming.

```
PREDICATE   InsertProgramBase : Program * String * ModulePart * Name *
                                Program;
            DeleteStatement : Program * String * Formula * Program.
```

InsertProgramBase is true when its first argument is the representation of a program, its second argument is the name of an open user module in this program, its third argument is the representation of a part keyword of this module, its fourth argument is the representation of the flat name of a base not declared in this part of this module, and its fifth argument is the representation of a program which differs from the program in the first argument only in that it also contains the declaration of this base in this part of this module. DeleteStatement is true when its first argument is the representation of a program, its second argument is the name of an open user module in this program, its third argument is the representation of a statement in the flat language of this module in this program appearing in this module, and its fourth argument is the representation of a program which differs from the program in the first argument only in that it does not contain this statement in this module.

The final two predicates are concerned with running goals for a program.

```
PREDICATE   Succeed : Program * Formula * TermSubst;
            Fail : Program * Formula.
```

Succeed is true when its first argument is the representation of a program, its second argument is the representation of the body of a goal in the flat language of this program, and its third argument is the representation of a computed answer for this goal and the flat form of this program. The predicate Succeed is the Gödel equivalent of the standard *demo* predicate. Note that, in particular, Succeed can be used to run goals containing predicates declared in the export parts of closed modules. Fail is true when its first argument is the representation of a program and its second argument is the representation of the body of a goal in the flat language of this program such that this goal and the flat form of this program have a finitely failed search tree. Note that Succeed and Fail (and their companions SucceedAll, Compute, and ComputeAll) are the only predicates in Programs which have access to statements in closed modules.

As an illustration of the use of the modules Syntax and Programs, we now give a demo-style interpreter (due to Corin Gurr). This interpreter works for definite programs and goals (without commits), and is perhaps the simplest interpreter one could write in this style. However, it makes an excellent starting point for various extensions such as handling negation or providing more sophisticated computation rules. The key to this kind of interpreter is the use of the predicate Resolve from the Syntax module. Essentially, Resolve takes an atom and a statement and does a resolution step using the atom and the head of the statement. To make the predicate more useful, an input substitution, which normally corresponds to the answer computed so far, can be given. Furthermore, two integer arguments provide a simple way of standardizing apart. (The detailed description of Resolve is given in Chapter 13.) A module very similar to the

`TestInterpreter` module in Section 10.5 can be used to provide a convenient way to run the interpreter. As explained in [8], interpreters using `Resolve` (and its companion `ResolveAll`) in this way are particularly amenable to partial evaluation. A different style of interpreter which replaces `Resolve` by explicit standardization apart, derivation, and composition steps is given in Section 10.5.

```
EXPORT    Demo.

IMPORT    Programs.

PREDICATE Demo :

  Program      % Representation of a definite program.
* Formula      % Representation of the body of a definite goal.
* TermSubst.   % Representation of a computed answer for this goal and
               % program using SLD-resolution.
```

```
LOCAL Demo.

% PREDICATE Demo : Program * Formula * TermSubst.

Demo(program, goal, answer) <-
    FormulaMaxVarIndex([goal], initial_index) &
    EmptyTermSubst(empty_subst) &
    Demo1(program, goal, initial_index, _, empty_subst, subst) &
    RestrictSubstToFormula(goal, subst, answer).


PREDICATE Demo1 :

  Program      % Representation of a definite program.
* Formula      % Representation of the body of a definite goal whose
               % variables have indexes smaller than the third argument.
* Integer      % A non-negative integer.
```

```
    * Integer      % A non-negative integer greater than or equal to the
                   % third argument.
    * TermSubst    % Representation of a term substitution.
    * TermSubst.   % Representation of the term substitution obtained by
                   % composing the term substitution in the fifth argument
                   % and the computed answer for the goal whose body is the
                   % second argument with the term substitution in the fifth
                   % argument applied and this program.

Demo1(_, empty_goal, index, index, subst, subst) <-
    EmptyFormula(empty_goal).

Demo1(program, atom, index, new_index, subst, new_subst) <-
    Atom(atom) &
    StatementMatchAtom(program, _, atom, statement) &
    Resolve(atom, statement, index, index1, subst, subst1, new_goal) &
    Demo1(program, new_goal, index1, new_index, subst1, new_subst).

Demo1(program, goal, index, new_index, subst, new_subst) <-
    And(left, right, goal) &
    Demo1(program, left, index, index1, subst, subst1) &
    Demo1(program, right, index1, new_index, subst1, new_subst).
```

As an example of the use of the module **Programs** for dynamic meta-programming, we give below a module containing the predicate **RemoveAll**, which removes statements whose heads unify with a given atom.

9.3 ProgramsIO

So that a meta-program can read and write terms representing programs, Gödel provides a system module, called **ProgramsIO**, the export part of which is given below. **ProgramsIO** imports IO so that the predicates there can be used to open and close files. The predicate **GetProgram** is called with its first argument ground and instantiates the second argument (which is normally a variable) to the term representing the program in the file with extension .prm corresponding to the input stream in the first argument. The predicate **PutProgram** is called with both arguments ground. It puts the term in the

---

EXPORT   Dynamic.

IMPORT   Programs.

PREDICATE   RemoveAll :

  Program   % The representation of a program P.
* String   % The name of an open module in P.
* Formula   % The representation of an atom in the flat language of
                % this module wrt P.
* Program.   % The representation of the program obtained from P by
                % deleting all statements in this module whose heads
                % unify with this atom (after standardization apart).

DELAY   RemoveAll(x,y,z,_) UNTIL GROUND(x) & GROUND(y) & GROUND(z).

PREDICATE   Remove :

  Program   % The representation of a program P.
* String   % The name of an open module in P.
* Formula   % The representation of an atom in the flat language of
                % this module wrt P.
* Program.   % The representation of the program obtained from P by
                % deleting a statement in this module whose head unifies
                % with this atom (after standardization apart).

DELAY   Remove(x,y,z,_) UNTIL GROUND(x) & GROUND(y) & GROUND(z).

```
LOCAL       Dynamic.

% PREDICATE    RemoveAll : Program * String * Formula * Program.

RemoveAll(program,module,atom,new_program) <-
          IF SOME [program1] Remove(program,module,atom,program1)
          THEN
             RemoveAll(program1,module,atom,new_program)
          ELSE
             new_program = program.


% PREDICATE    Remove : Program * String * Formula * Program.

Remove(program,module,atom,new_program) <-
          StatementMatchAtom(program,module,atom,statement) &
          IsImpliedBy(head,_,statement) &
          RenameFormulas([head],[atom],[renamed_atom]) &
          EmptyTermSubst(empty_subst) &
          UnifyAtoms(head,renamed_atom,empty_subst,_) &
          DeleteStatement(program,module,statement,new_program).
```

---

second argument into the file with extension .prm corresponding to the output stream in the first argument. The predicate ProgramCompile is called with its first argument the name of the main module of a program and produces in its second argument the ground representation of this program. The predicate ProgramDecompile is called with its argument containing the ground representation of a program and writes the files containing the user modules of this program.

Note that ProgramsIO is an input/output module so it should be handled like the module IO. In particular, it is preferable to arrange the module structure of the meta-program so that only its main module depends upon ProgramsIO.

As an alternative to the predicates ProgramCompile and ProgramDecompile used inside meta-programs, Gödel provides two utilities, program-compile and program-decompile, for producing the ground representation of an object program and for producing an object program from its ground representation. The command

---

EXPORT   ProgramsIO.

IMPORT   IO, Programs.

PREDICATE   GetProgram : InputStream * Program;
              PutProgram : OutputStream * Program;
              ProgramCompile : String * Program;
              ProgramDecompile : Program.

`program-compile` *Name*

takes the program with main module *Name*, produces the ground representation of this program, which is a term of type `Program`, and writes this term into a file called *Name*.prm. The command

`program-decompile` *"File"*

finds the file *File*.prm which contains a term of type `Program` representing an object program, creates the user modules of this object program, and produces files containing these modules.

9.4 Scripts

The module `Scripts` discussed in this section is a rather specialized meta-programming module whose main purpose is to support partial evaluation. We begin by explaining the need for such a module.

Partial evaluation and module systems do not fit easily together. The reason for this is that the partial evaluation process naturally "promotes" symbols to a module higher in the module hierarchy than where they are accessible and thus the module system is broken. A natural solution to this problem is to flatten out the module structure of a program before any partial evaluation takes place. We are thus led to the concept of a script which is essentially the flat form of a program with the module structure removed. We now turn to the appropriate definitions.

A *regular script* is what is obtained by removing all module declarations from the flat form of a program and concatenating what remains of the modules making up the program. The program from which the script is obtained is called the *associated pro-*

gram and the script is called the *associated script* (for this program). The predicate `ProgramToScript` discussed below performs this operation. More generally, a *script* is what is obtained from a regular script by a (possibly empty) sequence of applications of the insert and delete predicates in the module `Scripts` (which we discuss below). Thus scripts do not have a fully independent existence but instead can only be created initially from a program and then can only be modified in the restricted ways allowed by the insert and delete predicates. Note also that scripts do not have a textual format as programs do – they only exist in "flattened" form.

A script is divided into two parts. The *closed part* of a script consists of (the flattened forms of) all language declarations, control declarations, and statements which appeared in the local parts of the closed modules of the associated program from which the script was originally constructed. The *open part* of a script is the complement in the script of the closed part. Note that only the open part of a script can be modified.

There are several languages associated with a script. The *language of a script* is the polymorphic many-sorted language given by all the language declarations in the script. The language of a script is naturally "flat", but we omit this qualifier since scripts do not exist in non-flattened form. The *open language of a script* is the sublanguage of the language of the script given by the declarations which appear in the open part of the script. The *goal language* of a regular script is the (flattened form of) the goal language of the associated program. For a script in general, the *goal language* is modified as follows. Any symbol inserted into the script is added to the goal language of the script. If a symbol which appears in the goal language is deleted from the script, then this symbol is also deleted from the goal language.

Now let us turn to the module `Scripts` itself. First, `Scripts` imports `Programs` into its export part. Next, we describe a representative collection of predicates in `Scripts`.

The first predicate `ProgramToScript` has the following declaration.

PREDICATE ProgramToScript : Program * Script.

`ProgramToScript` is true when its first argument is the representation of a program and its second argument is the representation of the associated script obtained from this program. This predicate has a `DELAY` declaration which requires the first argument be given, so that it can only be used to construct the associated script from the given program (or check a given script is associated with the given program). Typically, `ProgramToScript` would be used during the running of a partial evaluator to produce a regular script from the program to be partially evaluated. The appropriate resultants would be produced by the partial evaluator which would then replace (some of) the statements in the regular script. This modified script is now the partially evaluated form of the program and can be script-compiled by the system and run (analogously to the way programs are compiled and run). Legal goals to the script are goals whose flattened form is a formula in the goal language of the script.

The next two predicates are concerned with accessing the declarations of symbols and statements in a script.

```
PREDICATE   BaseInScript : Script * Name;
            StatementInScript : Script * Formula.
```

BaseInScript is true when its first argument is the representation of a script and its second argument is the representation of the flat name of a base in the open language of the script. StatementInScript is true when its first argument is the representation of a script and its second argument is the representation of a statement in the open part of this script.

Finally, we give two predicates needed for dynamic meta-programming.

```
PREDICATE   DeleteScriptProposition : Script * Name * Script;
            InsertStatement : Script * Formula * Script.
```

DeleteScriptProposition is true when its first argument is the representation of a script, its second argument is the representation of the flat name of a proposition whose module name component is not the name of a closed module and which is declared in the open part of this script, and its third argument is the representation of a script which differs from the script in the first argument only in that it does not contain the declaration of this proposition in its open part. InsertStatement is true when its first argument is the representation of a script, its second argument is the representation of a statement in the open language of this script, and its third argument is the representation of a script which differs from the script in the first argument only in that it also contains this statement in the open part of the script.

For a more detailed description of the use of the meta-programming modules, including Scripts, for partial evaluation, the reader is referred to [8] and [9]. Many important issues relevant to partial evaluation, such as the use of the ground representation and self-applicability, are discussed in these two papers.

9.5   ScriptsIO

To allow a meta-program to read and write terms representing scripts, Gödel provides a system module, called ScriptsIO. The predicate GetScript is called with its first argument ground and instantiates the second argument to the term representing the script in the file with extension .scr corresponding to the input stream in the first argument. The predicate `PutScript` is called with both arguments ground. It puts the term representing the script in the second argument into the file with extension `.scr` corresponding to the output stream in the first argument.

EXPORT   ScriptsIO.

IMPORT   IO, Scripts.

PREDICATE   GetScript : InputStream * Script;
                PutScript : OutputStream * Script.

9.6   Theories

The ground representation in this section is a scheme for representing object (polymorphic many-sorted) theories, theorems, declarations, terms, and so on, as terms in a meta-language. A theory is like the local part of a module having only a local part, except that it does not contain conditionals, commits, or control declarations, and it contains arbitrary first order formulas instead of statements. A theory begins with a declaration of the form

THEORY   *Name.*

where *Name* is the name of the theory. A theory can import system modules.

A typical application for the system module **Theories** would be a program synthesis system. For such a system, the specification for a program would be expressed as a theory, which perhaps imported some system modules. Then a meta-program would perform transformation on this theory until it took the form of (essentially) a module. After further modification (for example, adding control information and/or employing conditionals), the synthesized program would result.

Before we turn to the details of the module **Theories**, we give some definitions. The *language* of a theory is the polymorphic many-sorted language given by the language declarations of all symbols accessible to the theory. The *flat form* of a theory T is the "theory" obtained from T by replacing each occurrence of the declared name of a symbol in T by the flat name of the symbol. The *flat language* of a theory is the polymorphic many-sorted language obtained from the language of the theory by replacing the declared name of each symbol appearing in a declaration by its flat name.

The module **Theories** imports the module **Syntax**. It also declares the following base.

BASE   Theory.

Theory is the type of a term representing (the flat form of) an (object) theory.

We now discuss in some detail a representative selection of predicates provided by **Theories**. The complete export part of **Theories** is given in Chapter 13. The first of the predicates provided by **Theories** which we discuss here is **TermInTheory**, which has the following declaration.

PREDICATE TermInTheory : Theory * VarTyping * Term * Type * VarTyping.

TermInTheory is true when its first argument is the representation of a theory, its second argument is the representation of a variable typing in the flat language of this theory, its third argument is the representation of a term in this language, its fourth is the representation of the type of this term with respect to this variable typing, and its fifth is the representation of the variable typing obtained by combining the variable typing in the second argument with the types of all variables occurring in the term.

The next collection of predicates in **Theories** is concerned with the representation of types and formulas.

PREDICATE StringToTheoryType : Theory * String * List(Type);
           StringToTheoryFormula : Theory * String * List(Formula).

StringToTheoryType is true when its first argument is the representation of a theory, its second argument is a string, and its third argument is the list (in a definite order) of representations of types in the flat language of this theory whose string representation is the second argument. Thus the call **StringToTheoryType**(T,"Pair(Person)",x), where T is a term representing a theory, and the constructor **Pair** and the base **Person** are in the language of T, would bind x to the list consisting of the term representing the type **Pair(Person)** (assuming no overloading). **StringToTheoryFormula** is true when its first argument is the representation of a theory, its second argument is a string, and its third argument is the list (in a definite order) of representations of formulas in the flat language of this theory whose string representation is the second argument.

The following predicate is concerned with accessing axioms in theories.

PREDICATE AxiomInTheory : Theory * Formula.

AxiomInTheory is true when its first argument is the representation of a theory and its second argument is the representation of an axiom in this theory.

The next two predicates are concerned with language declarations in a theory.

```
PREDICATE  ConstructorInTheory : Theory * Name * Integer * String;
           ConstantInTheory : Program * Name * Type * String.
```

ConstructorInTheory is true when its first argument is the representation of a theory, its second argument is the representation of the flat name of a constructor accessible to this theory, its third argument is the arity of this constructor, and its fourth argument is the name of the theory or the system module in which this constructor is declared. **ConstantInTheory** is true when its first argument is the representation of a theory, its second argument is the representation of the flat name of a constant accessible to this theory, its third argument is the representation of the type of this constant, and its fourth argument is the name of the theory or the system module in which this constant is declared.

The next two predicates are needed for dynamic meta-programming.

```
PREDICATE  InsertTheoryBase : Theory * Name * Theory;
           DeleteAxiom : Theory * Formula * Theory.
```

InsertTheoryBase is true when its first argument is the representation of a theory, its second argument is the representation of the flat name of a base not declared in this theory, and its third argument is the representation of a theory which differs from the theory in the first argument only in that it also contains the declaration of this base. **DeleteAxiom** is true when its first argument is the representation of a theory, its second argument is the representation of a formula which is an axiom in this theory, and its third argument is the representation of a theory which differs from the theory in the first argument only in that it does not contain this formula as an axiom.

The final predicate is concerned with proving theorems.

```
PREDICATE  Prove : Theory * Formula.
```

Prove is true when the first argument is the representation of a theory and its second argument is the representation of a theorem of this theory.

9.7 TheoriesIO

So that a meta-program can read and write terms representing theories, Gödel provides a system module, called **TheoriesIO**. The module **TheoriesIO** imports **IO** so that the predicates there can be used to open and close files. The predicate **GetTheory** is called with its first argument ground and instantiates the second argument to the term representing the theory in the file with extension .thy corresponding to the input stream in the first argument. The predicate **PutTheory** is called with both arguments ground. It puts the term representing a theory in the second argument into the file with extension .thy corresponding to the output stream in the first argument. The predicate TheoryCompile is called with its first argument the name of a theory and produces in its second argument the ground representation of this theory. The predicate TheoryDecompile is called with its argument containing the ground representation of a theory and writes a file containing this theory.

```
EXPORT        TheoriesIO.

IMPORT        IO, Theories.

PREDICATE     GetTheory : InputStream * Theory;
              PutTheory : OutputStream * Theory;
              TheoryCompile : String * Theory;
              TheoryDecompile : Theory.
```

As an alternative to the predicates TheoryCompile and TheoryDecompile used inside meta-programs, Gödel provides two utilities, theory-compile and theory-decompile, for producing the ground representation of an object theory and producing an object theory from its ground representation. The command

theory-compile *Name*

takes the theory *Name*, produces the ground representation of this theory, which is a term of type Theory, and writes this term into a file called *Name*.thy. The command

theory-decompile "*File*"

finds the file *File*.thy which contains a term of type Theory representing a theory, creates the corresponding theory, and produces a file containing this theory.

10 Example Programs

In this chapter, we give programs to illustrate further the Gödel programming style.

10.1 Fibonacci

The first example program is an iterative Fibonacci program. Given the first argument, Fib finds the Fibonacci number having rank equal to the first argument. Fib can be run in reverse to determine whether or not a number is a Fibonacci number and, if it is, find its rank. It can also be run with both arguments variables to generate all Fibonacci numbers and their ranks. For example, the goal

```
<- Fib(235,y).
```

gives the answer

```
y = 57890920688648205273383724828921139822249794889765
```

the goal

```
<- Fib(x,57890920688648205273383724828921139822249794889765).
```

gives the answer

```
x = 235
```

and the goal

```
<- Fib(x,y).
```

gives the answers

```
x = 0
y = 0

x = 1
y = 1

x = 2
y = 1

x = 3
y = 2
```

and so on.

```
MODULE    Fibonacci.

IMPORT    Integers.


PREDICATE Fib : Integer * Integer.

% Fib(k,n) <-> n is the Fibonacci number F_{k} of rank k.

Fib(0,0).
Fib(1,1).
Fib(k,n) <-
        k > 1 &
        FibIt(k-2,1,1,n).


PREDICATE FibIt : Integer * Integer * Integer * Integer.

% FibIt(k,f,g,n) <-> n  =  F_{k} * f  +  F_{k+1} * g.

FibIt(0,_,g,g).
FibIt(k,f,g,n) <-
        k > 0 &
        g < n &
        FibIt(k-1,g,f+g,n).
```

10.2 WolfGoatCabbage

The next program illustrates the use of extensional set terms. It is a solution of the well-known wolf-goat-cabbage problem, also discussed in [20, pages 285–287]. The problem is as follows. A farmer has a wolf, a goat, and a cabbage on the left bank of a river. He also has a boat that can carry at most one of the three, as well as himself, and he wishes to transport all three to the right bank. However, he cannot leave the wolf alone with the goat (as wolves love to eat goats) or the goat alone with the cabbage (as goats love to eat cabbages). The problem is to find a method to safely transport all three to the right bank so that the goat isn't eaten by the wolf and the cabbage isn't eaten by the goat.

The module **Search** provides a depth-first state-transition search framework for problem solving, similar to the one in [20, page 285] and adapted here for the wolf-goat-cabbage problem.

The program is invoked with the goal

```
<- Run(x).
```

and produces the answers

```
x =
[LeftToRight({Farmer,Goat}),RightToLeft({Farmer}),
LeftToRight({Cabbage,Farmer}),RightToLeft({Farmer,Goat}),
LeftToRight({Farmer,Wolf}),RightToLeft({Farmer}),
LeftToRight({Farmer,Goat})]

x =
[LeftToRight({Farmer,Goat}),RightToLeft({Farmer}),
LeftToRight({Farmer,Wolf}),RightToLeft({Farmer,Goat}),
LeftToRight({Cabbage,Farmer}),RightToLeft({Farmer}),
LeftToRight({Farmer,Goat})].
```

```
MODULE          Search.


% A depth-first state-transition search framework for problem solving,
% similar to the one on page 285 of Sterling and Shapiro, The Art of
% Prolog. It is used here to solve the wolf-goat-cabbage problem, also
% described in Sterling and Shapiro, pages 285-287.


IMPORT          Lists, WolfGoatCabbage.



PREDICATE       Solve : State * List(State) * List(Move).

Solve(current_state, _, []) <-
                Final(current_state).
Solve(current_state, history, [move|moves]) <-
                Applicable(move, current_state) &
                ApplyMove(move, current_state, new_state) &
                Legal(new_state) &
                NoLoops(new_state, history) &
                Solve(new_state, [new_state|history], moves).



PREDICATE   NoLoops : State * List(State).

NoLoops(_, []).
NoLoops(state, [first_state|rest]) <-
                state ~= first_state &
                NoLoops(state, rest).



PREDICATE       Run : List(Move).

Run(moves) <-
                Initial(initial_state) &
                Solve(initial_state, [initial_state], moves).
```

```
EXPORT      WolfGoatCabbage.

% The wolf-goat-cabbage problem, as described in Sterling and Shapiro,
% The Art of Prolog, pages 285-287.

IMPORT      Lists, Sets.

BASE        Object, State, Move.

CONSTANT    Farmer, Wolf, Goat, Cabbage : Object.

FUNCTION    St : Set(Object) * Set(Object) -> State;
            LeftToRight : Set(Object) -> Move;
            RightToLeft : Set(Object) -> Move.

PREDICATE   Initial, Final : State;
            Applicable : Move * State;
            ApplyMove : Move * State * State;
            Legal : State.
```

```
LOCAL WolfGoatCabbage.


% PREDICATE   Initial : State.

Initial(St({Farmer,Wolf,Goat,Cabbage}, {})).


% PREDICATE   Final : State.

Final(St({}, {Farmer,Wolf,Goat,Cabbage})).
```

```
% PREDICATE  Applicable : Move * State.

Applicable(LeftToRight({Farmer}), St(left,_)) <-
                Farmer In left.

Applicable(RightToLeft({Farmer}), St(_,right)) <-
                Farmer In right.

Applicable(LeftToRight({Farmer,x}), St(left,_)) <-
                {Farmer,x} Subset left &
                x In {Wolf,Goat,Cabbage}.

Applicable(RightToLeft({Farmer,x}), St(_,right)) <-
                {Farmer,x} Subset right &
                x In {Wolf,Goat,Cabbage}.


% PREDICATE  ApplyMove : Move * State * State.

ApplyMove(LeftToRight(cargo), St(left,right), St(left\cargo,right+cargo)).

ApplyMove(RightToLeft(cargo), St(left,right), St(left+cargo,right\cargo)).


% PREDICATE  Legal : State.

Legal(St(left,right)) <-
                ~ Illegal(left) &
                ~ Illegal(right).


PREDICATE Illegal : Set(Object).

Illegal(bank) <-
                ~ Farmer In bank &
                ({Goat,Cabbage} Subset bank \/ {Wolf,Goat} Subset bank).
```

10.3 Tableau

The next program, which is a tableau propositional theorem prover, illustrates the use of the system modules Units and Flocks. In this program, a propositional theory is represented as a flock. For example, the theory

```
(A & B) -> ~~E.
E -> (C & D).
A -> F.
F -> A.
(E \/ ~F) -> D.
```

would appear in a flock as

```
->(&(A,B),~(~(E))).
->(E,&(C,D)).
->(A,F).
->(F,A).
->(\/(E,~(F)),D).
```

This flock would be flock-compiled. Then typical queries to the program could be

```
<- TestProve("theory", "->(B,\\/(C,D))", indicator).
```

to which the answer is

```
indicator = YES
```

and

```
<- TestProve("theory", "&(A,B)", indicator).
```

to which the answer is

```
indicator = NO.
```

We remark on two points of interest in this program. The first is that the theorem prover has been written in a "non-failing" style so that the predicate Prove succeeds whether the formula is a theorem or not. This is achieved by adding an extra argument to Prove which records whether there was a proof or not. This style has some important advantages over the more usual one whereby exceptions of one kind or another are captured by failure. These are that the code which results from the "non-failing" style

tends to have a clearer declarative reading and that there is usually much less need for
pruning. For example, in the following program, no pruning is needed at all.

The other point is that the use of abstract data types means that all the heads of the
statements in the predicate `Apply` are most general and it is only in the body by using
`UnitParts` that we determine which case applies. Having such general heads could mean
that no indexing could be done which leads to inefficiencies when the program is run.
However, partial evaluation of the calls to `UnitParts` can be used to push the structure
of the first argument of `Apply` back into the head. This process can be made invisible to
the programmer so that we end up with the advantages of using abstract data types and
also the efficiency obtained from having as much structure in the heads of statements as
possible.

```
MODULE      TestTableau.

IMPORT      FlocksIO, Tableau.


PREDICATE  TestProve :

   String        % The name of a file (without the .flk extension)
                 % containing the flock representation of a propositional
                 % theory.
 * String        % The string representation of a propositional formula.
 * Indicator.    % YES, if the formula is a theorem, and NO, if it is not.

TestProve(theory_string, formula_string, indicator) <-
    FindInput(theory_string ++ ".flk", In(stream)) &
    GetFlock(stream, theory) &
    EndInput(stream) &
    StringToUnit(formula_string, formula) &
    Prove(theory, formula, indicator).

DELAY       TestProve(x,y,_) UNTIL GROUND(x) & GROUND(y).
```

EXPORT   Tableau.

% This module contains an implementation of a tableau propositional
% theorem prover as described, for example, in "Logic for Computer
% Science", S. Reeves and M. Clarke, Addison-Wesley, 1990, pages 64-75.
% The connectives admitted are &, \/, ->, and ~.

IMPORT   Flocks.

BASE   Indicator.
%
% The type of the constants YES, indicating a formula is a theorem of
% a theory, and NO, indicating that it is not.

CONSTANT   YES, NO : Indicator.

PREDICATE   Prove :

  Flock   % A propositional theory.
* Unit   % A propositional formula.
* Indicator.   % YES, if the formula is a theorem of the theory,
                   % and NO, if it is not.

DELAY   Prove(x,y,_) UNTIL GROUND(x) & GROUND(y).

LOCAL   Tableau.

IMPORT   Sets.

BASE   Leaf, Node, Tableau.

FUNCTION   Nd :

  Integer   % A pointer.
* Unit   % The propositional formula in the node pointed to by
                   % this pointer.
-> Node.

FUNCTION   Lf :

  Integer   % A pointer to an open leaf node. (A leaf node is open
                   % if it is at the end of a non-closed branch in a
                   % tableau.)
* Set(Integer)   % The set of pointers to the ancestors of this node
                   % plus the pointer to the node itself.
-> Leaf.

FUNCTION   Tb :

  Set(Leaf)   % The set of open leaf nodes in a tableau.
* Set(Node)   % The set of all nodes in this tableau.
* Set(Integer)   % The set of pointers to nodes in this tableau which
                   % have yet to be expanded and lie on non-closed
                   % branches.
* Integer   % The maximum value of pointers in this tableau.
-> Tableau.

```
% PREDICATE  Prove : Flock * Unit * Indicator.

Prove(theory, theorem, indicator) <-
    UnitParts(neg_thm, "~", [theorem]) &
    (IF Literal(neg_thm) THEN exp = {} ELSE exp = {1}) &
    InitialiseTableau(theory,Tb({Lf(1,{1})},{Nd(1,neg_thm)},exp,1),
                                                        tableau) &
    Unsatisfiable(tableau, indicator).


PREDICATE  InitialiseTableau :

  Flock             % A propositional theory.
* Tableau           % A tableau containing only the negation of the
                    % formula to be proved.
* Tableau.          % The tableau containing just the axioms in this
                    % theory and the negation of the formula to be proved.

InitialiseTableau(theory, Tb(leaves,nodes,exp,max), tableau) <-
    IF SOME [f,n] UnitInFlock(theory, f, n)
    THEN
      DeleteUnit(theory, f, n, new_theory) &
      Lf(max,anc) In leaves &
      (IF Closed(f,anc,nodes)
       THEN
         tableau = Tb({},{},{},0)             % Tableau is closed.
       ELSE
         (IF Literal(f) THEN e = {} ELSE e = {max+1}) &
         InitialiseTableau(new_theory,
         Tb({Lf(max+1,anc+{max+1})},nodes+{Nd(max+1,f)},exp+e,max+1),
         tableau)
      )
    ELSE
      tableau = Tb(leaves,nodes,exp,max).


PREDICATE  Unsatisfiable :
```

```
   Tableau          % A tableau.
 * Indicator.       % YES, if the tableau can be expanded to an
                    % unsatisfiable one, and NO, otherwise.

Unsatisfiable(Tb({},_,_,_), YES).

Unsatisfiable(Tb(leaves,nodes,exp,max), indicator) <-
    leaves ~= {} &
    IF  SOME [n] n In exp
    THEN
      new_exp = exp\{n} &
      Nd(n,f) In nodes &
      leaf_ptrs = {m : SOME [anc] ((Lf(m,anc) In leaves) & (n In anc))} &
      (IF leaf_ptrs = {}
       THEN
         tableau = Tb(leaves,nodes,new_exp,max)
       ELSE
         Apply(f, leaf_ptrs, Tb(leaves,nodes,new_exp,max), tableau)
      ) &
      Unsatisfiable(tableau, indicator)
    ELSE
      indicator = NO.


PREDICATE  Closed :

   Unit             % A formula closed wrt to the formulas in the nodes
                    % in the third argument.
 * Set(Integer)     % A set of pointers to nodes.
 * Set(Node).       % A set of nodes.

Closed(f, ptrs, nodes) <-
    m In ptrs &
    Nd(m,f1) In nodes &
    (UnitParts(f, "~", [f1]) \/ UnitParts(f1, "~", [f])).


PREDICATE  Literal :
```

```
    Unit.          % A propositional formula which is a literal.

Literal(f) <-
    UnitParts(f, _, []).

Literal(f) <-
    UnitParts(f, "~", [f1]) &
    UnitParts(f1, _, []).


PREDICATE  Apply :

    Unit          % A propositional formula which is not a literal.
*  Set(Integer)   % A set of pointers to open leaf nodes.
*  Tableau        % A tableau containing these open leaf nodes.
*  Tableau.       % The tableau obtained by extending this tableau
                  % at each of these open leaf nodes according to this
                  % formula.

Apply(f, leaf_ptrs, Tb(leaves,nodes,exp,max), tableau) <-
    UnitParts(f, "\\/", [f1, f2]) &              % f = f1 \/ f2
    ExpandOr(f1,f2,leaf_ptrs,Tb(leaves,nodes,exp,max),tableau).

Apply(f, leaf_ptrs, Tb(leaves,nodes,exp,max), tableau) <-
    UnitParts(f, "->", [f1, f2]) &               % f = f1 -> f2
    UnitParts(notf1, "~", [f1]) &
    ExpandOr(notf1,f2,leaf_ptrs,Tb(leaves,nodes,exp,max),tableau).

Apply(f, leaf_ptrs, Tb(leaves,nodes,exp,max), tableau) <-
    UnitParts(f, "&", [f1, f2]) &                % f = f1 & f2
    ExpandAnd(f1,f2,leaf_ptrs,Tb(leaves,nodes,exp,max),tableau).

Apply(f, leaf_ptrs, Tb(leaves,nodes,exp,max), tableau) <-
    UnitParts(f, "~", [f1]) &
    UnitParts(f1, "&", [f2, f3]) &               % f = ~(f2 & f3)
    UnitParts(notf2, "~", [f2]) &
    UnitParts(notf3, "~", [f3]) &
```

```
    ExpandOr(notf2,notf3,leaf_ptrs,Tb(leaves,nodes,exp,max),tableau).

Apply(f, leaf_ptrs, Tb(leaves,nodes,exp,max), tableau) <-
    UnitParts(f, "~", [f1]) &
    UnitParts(f1, "\\/", [f2, f3]) &              % f = ~(f2 \/ f3)
    UnitParts(notf2, "~", [f2]) &
    UnitParts(notf3, "~", [f3]) &
    ExpandAnd(notf2,notf3,leaf_ptrs,Tb(leaves,nodes,exp,max),tableau).

Apply(f, leaf_ptrs, Tb(leaves,nodes,exp,max), tableau) <-
    UnitParts(f, "~", [f1]) &
    UnitParts(f1, "->", [f2, f3]) &               % f = ~(f2 -> f3)
    UnitParts(notf3, "~", [f3]) &
    ExpandAnd(f2,notf3,leaf_ptrs,Tb(leaves,nodes,exp,max),tableau).

Apply(f, leaf_ptrs, Tb(leaves,nodes,exp,max), tableau) <-
    UnitParts(f, "~", [f1]) &
    UnitParts(f1, "~", [f2]) &                    % f = ~~f2
    ExpandNegNeg(f2,leaf_ptrs,Tb(leaves,nodes,exp,max),tableau).


PREDICATE  ExpandOr :

  Unit            % A propositional formula.
* Unit            % A propositional formula.
* Set(Integer)    % A set of pointers to open leaf nodes.
* Tableau         % A tableau containing these open leaf nodes.
* Tableau.        % The tableau obtained by extending this tableau at
                  % each of these open leaf nodes with two "or"
                  % children corresponding to each of these formulas.

ExpandOr(f1,f2,leaf_ptrs,Tb(leaves,nodes,exp,max),new_tableau) <-
    IF SOME [n]  n In leaf_ptrs
    THEN
      Lf(n,anc) In leaves &
      max1 = max + 1 &
      max2 = max + 2 &
      (IF Literal(f1) THEN e1 = {} ELSE e1 = {max1}) &
```

```
        (IF Literal(f2) THEN e2 = {} ELSE e2 = {max2}) &
        (IF Closed(f1,anc,nodes) THEN lf1 = {} ELSE
                                        lf1 = {Lf(max1,anc+{max1})}) &
        (IF Closed(f2,anc,nodes) THEN lf2 = {} ELSE
                                        lf2 = {Lf(max2,anc+{max2})}) &
        ExpandOr(f1, f2, leaf_ptrs\{n},
           Tb((leaves\{Lf(n,anc)})+lf1+lf2,
               nodes+{Nd(max1,f1),Nd(max2,f2)}, exp+e1+e2,max2),
           new_tableau)
     ELSE
        new_tableau = Tb(leaves,nodes,exp,max).


PREDICATE  ExpandAnd :

  Unit            % A propositional formula.
* Unit            % A propositional formula.
* Set(Integer)    % A set of pointers to open leaf nodes.
* Tableau         % A tableau containing these open leaf nodes.
* Tableau.        % The tableau obtained by extending this tableau at
                  % each of these open leaf nodes with two "and"
                  % children corresponding to each of these formulas.

ExpandAnd(f1,f2,leaf_ptrs,Tb(leaves,nodes,exp,max),new_tableau) <-
     IF SOME [n]  n In leaf_ptrs
     THEN
       Lf(n,anc) In leaves &
       max1 = max + 1 &
       max2 = max + 2 &
       (IF Literal(f1) THEN e1 = {} ELSE e1 = {max1}) &
       (IF Literal(f2) THEN e2 = {} ELSE e2 = {max2}) &
       (IF (Closed(f1,anc,nodes) \/
                        Closed(f2,anc+{max1},nodes+{Nd(max1,f1)}))
        THEN lf2 = {} ELSE lf2 = {Lf(max2,anc+{max1,max2})}) &
       ExpandAnd(f1, f2, leaf_ptrs\{n},
          Tb((leaves\{Lf(n,anc)})+lf2,
              nodes+{Nd(max1,f1),Nd(max2,f2)}, exp+e1+e2,max2),
          new_tableau)
```

```
    ELSE
      new_tableau = Tb(leaves,nodes,exp,max).


PREDICATE  ExpandNegNeg :

  Unit              % A propositional formula.
* Set(Integer)      % A set of pointers to open leaf nodes.
* Tableau           % A tableau containing these open leaf nodes.
* Tableau.          % The tableau obtained by extending this tableau at
                    % each of these open leaf nodes with a node
                    % containing this formula.

ExpandNegNeg(f1,leaf_ptrs,Tb(leaves,nodes,exp,max),new_tableau) <-
    IF SOME [n]  n In leaf_ptrs
    THEN
      Lf(n,anc) In leaves &
      max1 = max + 1 &
      (IF Literal(f1) THEN e1 = {} ELSE e1 = {max1}) &
      (IF Closed(f1,anc,nodes) THEN lf1 = {} ELSE
                                        lf1 = {Lf(max1,anc+{max1})}) &
      ExpandNegNeg(f1, leaf_ptrs\{n},
         Tb((leaves\{Lf(n,anc)})+lf1, nodes+{Nd(max1,f1)}, exp+e1, max1),
         new_tableau)
    ELSE
      new_tableau = Tb(leaves,nodes,exp,max).
```

10.4   Vanilla

The module **Vanilla** below contains an interpreter written using a non-ground representation. For this example, the object program is the program consisting of the module M2 (with some added control on **Append**).

We adopt the convention that an object level symbol is represented by a meta-level symbol with a name that consists of the name of the object level symbol prefixed by an O (for object). In the non-ground representation, parameters at the object level are represented by parameters at the meta-level, bases by bases, constructors by constructors, variables by variables, constants by constants, functions by functions, propositions by constants, predicates by functions, and connectives by functions. The type **OFormula** is used for the type of meta-level terms representing object-level formulas. The connective & is represented by the function **And**, the connective ~ is represented by the function **Not**, and the connective <- is represented by the function **If**. Note that object level predicates are represented by meta-level *functions*, so that, for example, the predicate **Append** is represented by the function **OAppend** with declaration

FUNCTION   OAppend : OList(ODay) * OList(ODay) * OList(ODay) -> OFormula.

Statements in the object program M2 are represented in OM2 using the predicate **Statement** and the constant **Empty**, which is used to represent the empty body.

Note how control at the object level can be pushed to the meta-level. In M2, we assume that there is a **DELAY** declaration for **Append** as follows.

DELAY   Append(x,_,z) UNTIL NONVAR(x) \/ NONVAR(z).

This **DELAY** declaration is represented by the **DELAY** declaration for **Statement** given in module OM2. Then a goal of the form

<- Solve(OAppend3(r',s',t')).

where r', s', and t' are the representations of r, s, and t, respectively, will run with the same control as the object level goal

<- Append3(r,s,t).

For example, the goal

<- Solve(OAppend3(x, y, z, OCons(OMonday,OCons(OTuesday,ONil)))).

produces the six expected answers and then terminates.

Note that a programmer has to provide the non-ground representation of object level modules, as there is no utility provided to do this. Also there are limitations on what can be represented. For example, it is not possible to use the non-ground representation of a module containing a polymorphic predicate (for example, **Append** in module **M3**). The reason is that the function which represents such a polymorphic predicate has a non-transparent language declaration. Furthermore, there is no way in the non-ground representation to represent quantifiers.

The program {Vanilla, OM2} shows that it is possible to use Gödel to illustrate the basics of the non-ground representation and to write the vanilla interpreter and simple extensions of it, as given in standard Prolog textbooks. However, as we pointed out above, there are restrictions on what can be represented and, in any case, it is not possible to do serious meta-programming in a declarative way with the non-ground representation. These are the main reasons why Gödel does not provide any special support for the non-ground representation, but, instead, provides considerable support for the ground representation.

```
MODULE          Vanilla.

IMPORT          OM2.

PREDICATE       Solve : OFormula.
DELAY           Solve(x) UNTIL NONVAR(x).

Solve(Empty).

Solve(x And y) <-
                Solve(x) &
                Solve(y).

Solve(Not x) <-
                ~ Solve(x).

Solve(x) <-
                Statement(x If y) &
                Solve(y).
```

```
EXPORT        OM2.

BASE          OFormula, ODay.
CONSTRUCTOR   OList/1.

CONSTANT      Empty : OFormula;
              ONil : OList(ODay);
              OMonday, OTuesday, OWednesday, OThursday, OFriday,
              OSaturday, OSunday : ODay.

FUNCTION      And : xFy(110) : OFormula * OFormula -> OFormula;
              Not : Fy(120) : OFormula -> OFormula;
              If : xFx(100) : OFormula * OFormula -> OFormula;
              OCons : ODay * OList(ODay) -> OList(ODay);
              OAppend : OList(ODay) * OList(ODay) * OList(ODay) ->
                        OFormula;
              OAppend3 : OList(ODay) * OList(ODay) * OList(ODay) *
                        OList(ODay) -> OFormula.

PREDICATE     Statement : OFormula.

DELAY         Statement(OAppend(x,_,z) If _) UNTIL NONVAR(x) \/ NONVAR(z).
```

```
LOCAL         OM2.

Statement(OAppend(ONil,x,x) If Empty).
Statement(OAppend(OCons(u,x),y,OCons(u,z)) If OAppend(x,y,z)).
Statement(OAppend3(x,y,z,u) If OAppend(x,y,w) And OAppend(w,z,u)).
```

10.5 Interpreter

The next program shows how a programmer might make use of predicates provided by
Programs and **ProgramsIO**. The module **TestInterpreter** contains the definition of the
predicate **Go1** which, given the name of a file containing the ground representation of an
object program and the string representation of the body of a goal, returns a computed
answer for that program and goal, and the predicate **Go2**, which succeeds if that goal has
a finitely failed SLDNF-tree for that program. **TestInterpreter** imports **ProgramsIO**,
Interpreter, and **Answers**. The module **Answers** (written by Antony Bowers) contains
a predicate for displaying answers as a string. The module **Interpreter** contains the
definitions of the predicates **MySucceed** and **MyFail**. **MySucceed** is intended to be true if
and only if its first argument is the representation of a normal program (without commits
or conditionals), its second argument is the representation of the body of a normal goal to
this program, and its third argument is the representation of a computed answer for this
goal and program using SLDNF-resolution. **MyFail** is intended to be true if and only if its
first argument is the representation of a normal program and its second argument is the
representation of the body of a normal goal in the flat language of the program which
has a finitely failed SLDNF-tree with respect to this program. The predicate **Select**
implements the safe "leftmost literal" computation rule. **Select** is intended to be true
if and only if its first argument represents a non-empty conjunction of literals Q in this
language, its second argument represents the conjunction of literals of Q which is the
largest prefix of Q containing only non-ground negative literals, its third argument is of
the form $\text{Pos}(E)$ or $\text{Neg}(E)$, where E represents the first atom or ground negative literal
appearing in Q (and where **Pos** indicates that it is a positive literal and **Neg** indicates
that it is a ground negative literal), and its fourth argument represents the conjunction
of literals in Q to the right E.

To run the interpreter, a goal such as

```
<- Go1("M4", "Append([Monday, Tuesday], [Wednesday], x)", answer).
```

could be used. This would produce the answer

```
answer = "{x/[Monday,Tuesday,Wednesday]}".
```

Similarly, a goal such as

```
<- Go2("M4", "Append([Monday, Tuesday], [Wednesday], [])").
```

gives the answer

```
Yes.
```

Note the use **Interpreter** makes of the system predicates **Succeed** and **Fail** in **Programs** for running literals whose proposition or predicate is not defined in an open module. The code in **Interpreter** could be used as the basis for an interpreter which required a more sophisticated computation rule using coroutining, for example.

Not surprisingly, **Interpreter** runs rather slowly (in fact, around 2 orders of magnitude slower than running the object program directly). However, it is important to appreciate that, by rewriting parts of the interpreter and employing partial evaluation techniques, it is possible to significantly improve its speed. A similar approach can be applied to other meta-programs. The details of this may be found in [8] and [9].

```
MODULE    TestInterpreter.

IMPORT    Interpreter, ProgramsIO, Answers.


PREDICATE Go1 : String * String * String.

Go1(prog_string, goal_string, answer_string) <-
    FindInput(prog_string ++ ".prm", In(stream)) &
    GetProgram(stream, program) &
    EndInput(stream) &
    MainModuleInProgram(program, module) &
    StringToProgramFormula(program, module, goal_string, [goal]) &
    NormalBody(goal) &
    CommitFreeFormula(goal) &
    MySucceed(program, goal, answer) &
    RestrictSubstToFormula(goal, answer, computed_answer) &
    AnswerString(program, module, computed_answer, answer_string).


PREDICATE Go2 : String * String.

Go2(prog_string, goal_string) <-
    FindInput(prog_string ++ ".prm", In(stream)) &
    GetProgram(stream, program) &
    EndInput(stream) &
    MainModuleInProgram(program, module) &
    StringToProgramFormula(program, module, goal_string, [goal]) &
    NormalBody(goal) &
    CommitFreeFormula(goal) &
    MyFail(program, goal).
```

EXPORT   Answers.

IMPORT   Programs.

PREDICATE   AnswerString : Program * String * TermSubst * String.

LOCAL   Answers.

% PREDICATE   AnswerString : Program * String * TermSubst * String.

```
AnswerString(program, module, answer, "{" ++ string ++ "}") <-
    AnswerString1(program, module, answer, string).
```

PREDICATE   AnswerString1 : Program * String * TermSubst * String.

```
AnswerString1(program, module, answer, string) <-
    {IF SOME [var, term, answer1]
         DelBindingInTermSubst(answer, var, term, answer1)
     THEN
       ProgramTermToString(program, module, var, var_string) &
       ProgramTermToString(program, module, term, term_string) &
       AnswerString2(program, module, answer1,
                              var_string ++ "/" ++ term_string, string)
     ELSE
       string = ""
    }.
```

PREDICATE   AnswerString2 : Program * String * TermSubst * String *
                            String.

```
AnswerString2(program, module, answer, so_far, string) <-
    {IF SOME [var, term, answer1]
         DelBindingInTermSubst(answer, var, term, answer1)
```

```
THEN
  ProgramTermToString(program, module, var, var_string) &
  ProgramTermToString(program, module, term, term_string) &
  AnswerString2(program, module, answer1,
    so_far ++ "," ++ var_string ++ "/" ++ term_string, string)
ELSE
  string = so_far
}.
```

EXPORT   Interpreter.

% This module implements an interpreter for SLDNF-resolution using the
% ground representation. The computation rule employed is the safe
% "leftmost literal" one, that is, the selected literal is the leftmost
% literal which is either an atom or a ground negative literal. This
% module assumes the existence of one above it which handles the
% conversion of goals and answers between their string representation
% and their ground representation.

IMPORT   Programs.

PREDICATE   MySucceed :

   Program   % Representation of a normal program (excluding commits
                    % and conditionals).
 * Formula   % Representation of the body of a normal goal to this
                    % program.
 * TermSubst.   % Representation of a computed answer for this goal
                    % and program using SLDNF-resolution and the safe
                    % leftmost literal computation rule.

DELAY   MySucceed(x,y,_) UNTIL GROUND(x) & GROUND(y).

PREDICATE   MyFail :

   Program   % Representation of a normal program (excluding commits
                    % and conditionals).
 * Formula.   % Representation of the body of a normal goal to this
                    % program such that this goal and this program have a
                    % finitely failed SLDNF-tree using the safe leftmost
                    % literal computation rule.

DELAY   MyFail(x,y) UNTIL GROUND(x) & GROUND(y).

LOCAL   Interpreter.

BASE   SignedFormula.

FUNCTION   Pos, Neg : Formula -> SignedFormula.

% PREDICATE   MySucceed : Program * Formula * TermSubst.

MySucceed(program, body, computed_answer) <-
    EmptyTermSubst(empty_subst) &
    IF EmptyFormula(body)
    THEN
      computed_answer = empty_subst
    ELSE
      Select(body, left, selected, right) &
      MySucceed1(program, body, left, selected, right, empty_subst,
                                                        answer) &
      RestrictSubstToFormula(body, answer, computed_answer).

PREDICATE MySucceed1 :

  Program   % Representation of a normal program.
* Formula   % Representation of the head of a resultant.
* Formula   % Representation of the body of the resultant to the
                     % left of the selected literal.
* SignedFormula   % Representation of the selected literal in the body.
* Formula   % Representation of the body of the resultant to the
                     % right of the selected literal.
* TermSubst   % Representation of a term substitution.
* TermSubst.   % Representation of the term substitution obtained
                     % by composing the term substitution in the sixth
                     % argument with the computed answer obtained for this
                     % program and resultant.

```
MySucceed1(program, head, left, Pos(selected), right, answer_so_far,
                                                          answer) <-
    (IF SOME [module] DeclaredInOpenModule(program, module, selected)
     THEN
        StatementMatchAtom(program, module, selected, stat) &
        RenameFormulas([head,left,selected,right], [stat], [new_stat]) &
        Derive(head, left, selected, right, new_stat, mgu,
                                                  new_resultant) &
        ComposeTermSubsts(answer_so_far, mgu, new_answer) &
        IsImpliedBy(new_head, new_body, new_resultant)
     ELSE
        FormulaMaxVarIndex([head,left,selected,right],varindex) &
        EmptyTermSubst(empty) &
        Compute(program, selected, varindex, _, empty, subst,
                                                    last_goal) &
        EmptyFormula(last_goal) &
        ApplySubstToFormula(head, subst, new_head) &
        AndWithEmpty(left, right, body1) &
        ApplySubstToFormula(body1, subst, new_body) &
        ComposeTermSubsts(answer_so_far, subst, new_answer)
    ) &
    IF EmptyFormula(new_body)
    THEN
        answer = new_answer
    ELSE
        Select(new_body, new_left, new_selected, new_right) &
        MySucceed1(program, new_head, new_left, new_selected, new_right,
                                            new_answer, answer).

MySucceed1(program, head, left, Neg(selected), right, answer_so_far,
                                                          answer) <-
    (IF DeclaredInOpenModule(program, _, selected)
     THEN
        EmptyFormula(empty_formula) &
        MyFail1(program, empty_formula, Pos(selected), empty_formula)
     ELSE
```

```
          Fail(program, selected)
      ) &
      AndWithEmpty(left, right, new_body) &
      IF EmptyFormula(new_body)
      THEN
        answer = answer_so_far
      ELSE
        Select(new_body, new_left, new_selected, new_right) &
        MySucceed1(program, head, new_left, new_selected, new_right,
                                              answer_so_far, answer).


% PREDICATE    MyFail : Program  * Formula.

MyFail(program, body) <-
    Select(body, left, selected, right) &
    MyFail1(program, left, selected, right).


PREDICATE   MyFail1 :

   Program         % Representation of a normal program for which there
                   % exists a finitely failed SLDNF-tree for a goal,
                   % using the safe "leftmost literal" computation rule.
 * Formula         % Representation of the body of the goal to the left
                   % of the selected literal.
 * SignedFormula   % Representation of the selected literal in the body
                   % of the goal.
 * Formula.        % Representation of the body of the goal to the right
                   % of the selected literal.

MyFail1(program, left, Pos(selected), right) <-
    EmptyFormula(empty_formula) &
    IF SOME [module] DeclaredInOpenModule(program, module, selected)
    THEN
      ALL [new_body]
        (SOME [l, s, r] (Select(new_body, l, s, r) &
                                    MyFail1(program, l, s, r))
```

```
        <-
            SOME [stat, new_stat, new_goal]
            (StatementMatchAtom(program, module, selected, stat) &
             RenameFormulas([left,selected,right], [stat], [new_stat]) &
             Derive(empty_formula, left, selected, right, new_stat, _,
                                                              new_goal) &
             IsImpliedBy(empty_formula, new_body, new_goal)
            )
        )
    ELSE
      IF Fail(program, selected)
      THEN
        True
      ELSE
        FormulaMaxVarIndex([left,selected,right],varindex) &
        EmptyTermSubst(empty) &
        Compute(program, selected, varindex, _, empty, subst,
                                                        last_goal) &
        EmptyFormula(last_goal) &
        AndWithEmpty(left, right, body1) &
        ApplySubstToFormula(body1, subst, new_body) &
        Select(new_body, new_left, new_selected, new_right) &
        MyFail1(program, new_left, new_selected, new_right).


MyFail1(program, _, Neg(selected), _) <-
    EmptyFormula(empty_formula) &
    EmptyTermSubst(empty_subst) &
    MySucceed1(program, selected, empty_formula, Pos(selected),
                                    empty_formula, empty_subst, _) |.

MyFail1(program, left, Neg(selected), right) <-
    EmptyFormula(empty_formula) &
    MyFail1(program, empty_formula, Pos(selected), empty_formula) |
    AndWithEmpty(left, right, new_body) &
    Select(new_body, new_left, new_selected, new_right) &
    MyFail1(program, new_left, new_selected, new_right).
```

```
PREDICATE  Select :

   Formula            % Representation of a (non-empty) conjunction of
                      % literals.
 * Formula            % Representation of the conjunction of literals to
                      % the left of the selected literal.
 * SignedFormula      % Term with function Pos or Neg at the top-level
                      % and containing the representation of the atom in
                      % the selected literal (according to the safe
                      % "leftmost literal" computation rule and where Pos
                      % is used if the selected literal is an atom and
                      % Neg otherwise).
 * Formula.           % Representation of the conjunction of literals to
                      % the right of the selected literal.

Select(atom, empty_formula, Pos(atom), empty_formula) <-
    Atom(atom) &
    EmptyFormula(empty_formula).

Select(negative_literal, empty_formula, Neg(atom), empty_formula) <-
    Not(atom, negative_literal) &
    GroundAtom(atom) &
    EmptyFormula(empty_formula).

Select(body, left, selected, right) <-
    And(l, r, body) &
    IF SOME [l1, s1, r1] Select(l, l1, s1, r1)
    THEN
      left = l1 &
      selected = s1 &
      AndWithEmpty(r1, r, right)
    ELSE
      Select(r, l1, selected, right) &
      AndWithEmpty(l, l1, left).
```

10.6   ThreeWiseMen

The next program implements a solution to the three wise men puzzle. The meta-level architecture chosen is a simple one that captures the reasoning of the third wise man in a way which is semantically defensible. However, the main purpose of the program is not to make a contribution to the study of meta-reasoning, but rather to illustrate how dynamic meta-programming can be done in a declarative way.

The three wise men puzzle is as follows. A king, wishing to find out which of his three wise men is the wisest, puts a hat on each of their heads, and tells them that each hat is either black or white and at least one of the hats is white. The king does this in such a way that each wise man can see the hats of the other wise men, but not his own. In fact, each wise man has a white hat on. The king then successively asks each one of wise men whether he knows the colour of his own hat. The first wise man answers "I don't know", as does the second. Then the third announces that his hat is white.

The reasoning of the third wise man is as follows. "Suppose my hat is black. Then the second wise man would see a black hat and a white hat, and would reason that, if his hat is black, the first wise man would see two black hats and hence would conclude that his hat is white on the basis of the king's assurance that at least one of the hats is white. But the second wise man said he didn't know the colour of his hat. Hence my hat must be white."

The program directly simulates the reasoning of the third wise man. The module WiseMan3KB contains the knowledge of the third wise man. The module Reasoner contains two reasoning procedures in the form of the two statements for the predicate Solve. The first statement embodies the principle: "If I can see the other two hats are black, then mine must be white". The second embodies a proof by contradiction: "If I assume my hat is a particular colour and thereby derive a contradiction of the fact that one of the other wise men didn't know the colour of his hat, then my hat must be the other colour".

The program is run by giving it the goal

```
<- Go(colour).
```

for which the answer is

```
colour = White.
```

```
MODULE ThreeWiseMen.

% This program solves the three wise men puzzle.
%
% The module WiseMan3KB needs to be program-compiled first.
%
% Goal:  <- Go(colour).

IMPORT ProgramsIO, Reasoner.

PREDICATE  Go : Colour.

Go(colour) <-
  FindInput("WiseMan3KB.prm", In(stream)) &
  GetProgram(stream, wiseman3_kb) &
  EndInput(stream) &
  Solve(W3,wiseman3_kb, colour).
```

EXPORT   Reasoner.

% This module contains the two reasoning procedures for the three
% wise men puzzle.

IMPORT   Programs.

BASE   Wiseman, Colour.

CONSTANT   W1, W2, W3 : Wiseman;
              Black, White : Colour.

PREDICATE Solve :

  Wiseman   % A wise man.
* Program   % The knowledge known, or assumed to be known, to
                       % this wise man by the third wise man, W3.
* Colour.   % The colour of this wise man's hat.

LOCAL   Reasoner.

IMPORT   Sets.

% PREDICATE   Solve : Wiseman * Program * Colour.

Solve(wiseman, kb, White) <-
      {Enumerate(wiseman, next_wiseman, last_wiseman)} &
      FormBodyString1(wiseman, next_wiseman, Black, body2_string) &
      FormBodyString1(wiseman, last_wiseman, Black, body3_string) &
      Prove(kb, body2_string) &
      Prove(kb, body3_string).

```
Solve(wiseman, kb, colour) <-
     Enumerate(wiseman, next_wiseman, last_wiseman) &
     FormBodyString2(wiseman, next_wiseman, body_string) &
     Prove(kb, body_string)  &
     AssumeHatColour(wiseman, next_wiseman, Black, kb, kb2) &
     AssumeHatColour(wiseman, last_wiseman, Black, kb2, new_kb) &
     IF Solve(next_wiseman, new_kb, _)
     THEN colour = White
     ELSE
         AssumeHatColour(wiseman, next_wiseman, White, kb, kb3) &
         AssumeHatColour(wiseman, last_wiseman, White, kb3, newer_kb) &
         Solve(next_wiseman, newer_kb, _) &
         colour = Black.


PREDICATE    Enumerate :

  Wiseman            % A wise man.
* Wiseman            % A wise man different from the previous one.
* Wiseman.           % The remaining wise man.

Enumerate(x, y, z) <-
     x In {W1, W2, W3} &
     y In {W1, W2, W3}\{x} &
     z In {W1, W2, W3}\{x,y}.


PREDICATE    AssumeHatColour :

  Wiseman            % A wise man.
* Wiseman            % Another wise man.
* Colour             % A colour.
* Program            % A knowledge base.
* Program.           % The knowledge base obtained from this knowledge
                     % base by adding the fact that the second wise man
                     % knows that this colour is the colour of the first
                     % wise man's hat.
```

```
AssumeHatColour(wiseman, other_wiseman, colour, kb, new_kb) <-
    MainModuleInProgram(kb,module) &
    FormBodyString1(other_wiseman, wiseman, colour, string) &
    StringToProgramFormula(kb, module, string, [atom]) &
    EmptyFormula(empty_formula) &
    IsImpliedBy(atom, empty_formula, fact) &
    InsertStatement(kb, module, fact, new_kb).
```

```
PREDICATE    Prove :

  Program            % A knowledge base.
* String.            % The string representation of the body of a goal
                     % which succeeds for this knowledge base.
```

```
Prove(kb,body_string) <-
    MainModuleInProgram(kb,module) &
    StringToProgramFormula(kb, module, body_string, [body]) &
    Succeed(kb,body,_).
```

```
PREDICATE    FormBodyString1 :

  Wiseman            % A wise man.
* Wiseman            % Another wise man.
* Colour             % A colour.
* String.            % The string representation of the body of the fact
                     % that the first wise man knows that this is the
                     % colour of the hat of the second wise man.
```

```
FormBodyString1(W1, W2, White, "Knows(W1, Hat(W2, White))").
FormBodyString1(W1, W3, White, "Knows(W1, Hat(W3, White))").
FormBodyString1(W2, W1, White, "Knows(W2, Hat(W1, White))").
FormBodyString1(W2, W3, White, "Knows(W2, Hat(W3, White))").
FormBodyString1(W3, W1, White, "Knows(W3, Hat(W1, White))").
FormBodyString1(W3, W2, White, "Knows(W3, Hat(W2, White))").
FormBodyString1(W1, W2, Black, "Knows(W1, Hat(W2, Black))").
FormBodyString1(W1, W3, Black, "Knows(W1, Hat(W3, Black))").
```

```
FormBodyString1(W2, W1, Black, "Knows(W2, Hat(W1, Black))").
FormBodyString1(W2, W3, Black, "Knows(W2, Hat(W3, Black))").
FormBodyString1(W3, W1, Black, "Knows(W3, Hat(W1, Black))").
FormBodyString1(W3, W2, Black, "Knows(W3, Hat(W2, Black))").


PREDICATE    FormBodyString2 :

  Wiseman              % A wise man.
* Wiseman              % Another wise man.
* String.              % The string representation of the body of the fact
                       % that the first wise man knows that the second
                       % wise man doesn't know the colour of his own hat.

FormBodyString2(W1, W2, "Knows(W1, DoesntKnow(W2))").
FormBodyString2(W1, W3, "Knows(W1, DoesntKnow(W3))").
FormBodyString2(W2, W1, "Knows(W2, DoesntKnow(W1))").
FormBodyString2(W2, W3, "Knows(W2, DoesntKnow(W3))").
FormBodyString2(W3, W1, "Knows(W3, DoesntKnow(W1))").
FormBodyString2(W3, W2, "Knows(W3, DoesntKnow(W2))").
```

MODULE   WiseMan3KB.

% The knowledge base of the third wise man, W3.

BASE   Wiseman, Colour, Fact.

CONSTANT   W1, W2, W3 : Wiseman;
                Black, White : Colour.

FUNCTION   DoesntKnow : Wiseman -> Fact;
                Hat : Wiseman * Colour -> Fact.

PREDICATE   Knows :

  Wiseman   % A wise man.
* Fact.   % Some knowledge which W3 knows to be known to
                    % this wise man.

Knows(W3, DoesntKnow(W1)).
Knows(W3, DoesntKnow(W2)).
Knows(W3, Hat(W1,White)).
Knows(W3, Hat(W2,White)).
Knows(W2, DoesntKnow(W1)).
Knows(W2, Hat(W1,White)).
Knows(W1, Hat(W2,White)).

II DEFINITION OF GÖDEL

11 Syntax

In this chapter, we present the syntax of Gödel. Our main objective is to define precisely the concepts of program, goal, theory, and flock.

11.1 Notation

We first describe the notation in which the grammar is defined. A grammar rule takes the following form:

$$\text{non-terminal} \quad \longrightarrow \quad \text{sequence of terminals and non-terminals}$$

There may be more than one way of decomposing a non-terminal, in which case the alternatives are separated by |. A terminal is distinguished from a non-terminal by being placed within angle-brackets $< >$. Some non-terminals have arguments: a lower case letter indicates that the argument is a variable. A sequence X of terminals and non-terminals may be enclosed in brackets:

$\{X\}$ means 0 or more occurrences of X.
$\{X\}^{(n)}$ means exactly n occurrences of X.
$[X]$ means 0 or 1 occurrence of X.

For some rules, extra *conditions* determine whether a particular rule can be applied. These conditions are given in italic text following the rule to which they apply.

11.2 Tokens

A program, theory, and so on, can be regarded as text consisting of a string of characters. This string is parsed and substrings of characters are identified as *tokens*. Thus the text is first transformed to a sequence of these tokens. It is this sequence of tokens and not the original text that will be used in the grammars given in subsequent sections. The text includes special sequences of characters, called *layout items*, which improve the layout and readability of the text. In addition, these layout items are used, where necessary, to indicate the separation of tokens. As a guide to the use of layout items, note that if a sequence of characters would form a token but the sequence is included in a larger sequence which would also form a token, then the larger token is preferred. The layout items are not tokens but, so that they can be included in the text, we define the grammar rules for them as well.

The terminals of this grammar are the individual characters of the text. Note that the token Identifier appears only in the grammar for flocks.

Token	$\longrightarrow$	BigName | LittleName | GraphicName | String | Bracket | Comma | Semicolon | Underscore | Terminator | Number | Float | Identifier
BigName	$\longrightarrow$	BigLetter {NameCharacter}
LittleName	$\longrightarrow$	LittleLetter {NameCharacter}
GraphicName	$\longrightarrow$	GraphicCharacter {GraphicCharacter}
String	$\longrightarrow$	< " > {StringCharacter} < " >
Bracket	$\longrightarrow$	<{> | <}> [<_> Label] | <(> | <)> | <[> | <]>
Comma	$\longrightarrow$	<,>
Semicolon	$\longrightarrow$	<;>
Underscore	$\longrightarrow$	<_>
Terminator	$\longrightarrow$	<.>
Number	$\longrightarrow$	Zero {Zero} | PositiveNumber
Float	$\longrightarrow$	Decimal | Decimal < E > <+> Number | Decimal < E > <-> Number
Decimal	$\longrightarrow$	Number < . > Number
Label	$\longrightarrow$	PositiveNumber
NameCharacter	$\longrightarrow$	BigLetter | LittleLetter | Digit | Underscore
GraphicCharacter	$\longrightarrow$	<\> | NonBSGraphicChar
NonBSGraphicChar	$\longrightarrow$	<+> | <-> | <*> |</> | <^> | <#> | <<> | <>> | <=> | <~> | <&> | <?> | <'> | <@> | <!> | <$>

		$|$ `<:>` $|$ `<|>` $|$ `<'>`

BigLetter	$\longrightarrow$	`<A>` $\mid$ `<B>` $\mid$ `<C>` $\mid$ `<D>` $\mid$ `<E>` $\mid$ `<F>` $\mid$ `<G>` $\mid$ `<H>`
		$\mid$ `<I>` $\mid$ `<J>` $\mid$ `<K>` $\mid$ `<L>` $\mid$ `<M>` $\mid$ `<N>` $\mid$ `<O>` $\mid$ `<P>`
		$\mid$ `<Q>` $\mid$ `<R>` $\mid$ `<S>` $\mid$ `<T>` $\mid$ `<U>` $\mid$ `<V>` $\mid$ `<W>` $\mid$ `<X>`
		$\mid$ `<Y>` $\mid$ `<Z>`

LittleLetter	$\longrightarrow$	`<a>` $\mid$ `<b>` $\mid$ `<c>` $\mid$ `<d>` $\mid$ `<e>` $\mid$ `<f>` $\mid$ `<g>` $\mid$ `<h>`
		$\mid$ `<i>` $\mid$ `<j>` $\mid$ `<k>` $\mid$ `<l>` $\mid$ `<m>` $\mid$ `<n>` $\mid$ `<o>` $\mid$ `<p>`
		$\mid$ `<q>` $\mid$ `<r>` $\mid$ `<s>` $\mid$ `<t>` $\mid$ `<u>` $\mid$ `<v>` $\mid$ `<w>` $\mid$ `<x>`
		$\mid$ `<y>` $\mid$ `<z>`

| PositiveNumber | $\longrightarrow$ | {Zero} NonZero {Digit} |

| Digit | $\longrightarrow$ | Zero $\mid$ NonZero |

| NonZero | $\longrightarrow$ | `<1>` $\mid$ `<2>` $\mid$ `<3>` $\mid$ `<4>` $\mid$ `<5>` $\mid$ `<6>` $\mid$ `<7>` $\mid$ `<8>` |
| | | $\mid$ `<9>` |

| Zero | $\longrightarrow$ | `<0>` |

| StringCharacter | $\longrightarrow$ | `<\>` `<\>` $\mid$ `<\>` `<">` $\mid$ [`<\>`] OrdinaryCharacter |

| LayoutItem | $\longrightarrow$ | LayoutCharacter $\mid$ Comment |

| LayoutCharacter | $\longrightarrow$ | $<$ *space* $>$ $\mid$ $<$ *tab* $>$ $\mid$ $<$ *newline* $>$ |

| Comment | $\longrightarrow$ | `<%>` {Character} |

Condition: The sequence {Character} *does not contain a newline, but is followed by a newline.*

| Character | $\longrightarrow$ | `<\>` $\mid$ `<">` $\mid$ OrdinaryCharacter |

OrdinaryCharacter	$\longrightarrow$	LayoutCharacter $\mid$ NonBSGraphicChar $\mid$ NameCharacter
		$\mid$ Semicolon $\mid$ Comma $\mid$ Terminator $\mid$ `<%>` $\mid$ `<{>` $\mid$ `<}>`
		$\mid$ `<(>` $\mid$ `<)>` $\mid$ `<[>` $\mid$ `<]>`

Identifier $\longrightarrow$ QuotedIdent | DbleQuotedIdent | OrdinaryIdent

QuotedIdent $\longrightarrow$ <'> {QuoteChar} <'>

QuoteChar $\longrightarrow$ <'><'> | Character
    Condition: Character *may not be* '.

DbleQuotedIdent $\longrightarrow$ <"> {DbleQuoteChar} <">

DbleQuoteChar $\longrightarrow$ <"><"> | Character
    Condition: Character *may not be* ".

OrdinaryIdent $\longrightarrow$ OrdinaryChar {OrdinaryChar}

OrdinaryChar $\longrightarrow$ NameCharacter | GraphicCharacter | Semicolon
                                     | Terminator | <[> | <]> | <{> | <}>
    Condition: GraphicCharacter *may not be* '.

11.3 Programs

The terminals of the grammars in this and subsequent sections are the tokens defined previously. For some rules it is necessary to know, not just the name of the token, but also the internal structure of the token. In this case, the internal structure is given in place of the token name. For example: if, in a rule, the token 'Number' has to be a positive number, then this is denoted by <PositiveNumber>. If the token has to include a particular string of terminals from the previous grammar, then this string is enclosed in single quotes. For example: <'BASE'> indicates that the token is a BigName consisting of the string 'BASE'. Similarly, <'}' ['_' Label]> indicates that the token is a Bracket consisting of '}' followed by an optional '_' Label. The token name is easily inferred from the given structure.

Program $\longrightarrow$ Module {Module}

Module $\longrightarrow$ ExportPart LocalPart
                                     | ExportPart
                                     | LocalPart

Condition: If a module has a LocalPart *and an* ExportPart, *then the* Module-Name *of each part must be the same.*

ExportPart   ⟶   ExportKind ModuleName <Terminator> {ExportItem}

LocalPart   ⟶   LocalKind ModuleName <Terminator> {LocalItem}

Condition: The LocalPart *of a module has the* LocalKind MODULE *if and only if the module has no* ExportPart.

ExportKind   ⟶   <'EXPORT'> | <'CLOSED'>

LocalKind   ⟶   <'LOCAL'> | <'MODULE'>

ModuleName   ⟶   UserBigName

Condition: ModuleName *for a user module cannot be any of* Integers, Rationals, Floats, Numbers, Lists, Sets, Strings, Tables, Units, Flocks, Syntax, Programs, Scripts, Theories, IO, NumbersIO, FlocksIO, ProgramsIO, ScriptsIO, *or* TheoriesIO.

ExportItem   ⟶   ImportDecl <Terminator>
                             | LanguageDecl <Terminator>
                             | ControlDecl <Terminator>

LocalItem   ⟶   ImportDecl <Terminator>
                             | LiftDecl <Terminator>
                             | LanguageDecl <Terminator>
                             | ControlDecl <Terminator>
                             | Statement <Terminator>

ImportDecl   ⟶   <'IMPORT'> ModuleName {<Comma> ModuleName}

LiftDecl   ⟶   <'LIFT'> ModuleName {<Comma> ModuleName}

Condition: A LIFT *declaration can only appear in the local part of a module which has an export part.*

At this stage, the overall module structure of a (potential) program can be discerned. To explain this, we introduce the following definitions.

A part of a module *refers to* a module N if it contains a declaration of the form

IMPORT N.

or (in the case of a local part)

LIFT N.

A module M *refers to* a module N if either the local or export part of M refers to N.

The relation *depends upon* between modules is defined to be the transitive closure of the relation refers to.

Then the (potential) program must consist of a set $\{M_i\}_{i=0}^n$ of modules with the property that $\{M_i\}_{i=1}^n$ is the set of modules upon which the distinguished module M_0 depends. We say M_0 is the *main module* of the program.

Furthermore, the following module condition can now be checked.

M1: No module may depend upon itself.

Language Declarations

LanguageDecl	$\longrightarrow$	BaseDecl
		| ConstructorDecl
		| ConstantDecl
		| FunctionDecl
		| PropositionDecl
		| PredicateDecl

| BaseDecl | $\longrightarrow$ | <'BASE'> UserNameSeq |

| ConstructorDecl | $\longrightarrow$ | <'CONSTRUCTOR'> ConstrDecl {<Comma> ConstrDecl} |

| ConstrDecl | $\longrightarrow$ | UserName <'/'> <PositiveNumber> |

| ConstantDecl | $\longrightarrow$ | <'CONSTANT'> ConstDecl {<Semicolon> ConstDecl} |

| ConstDecl | $\longrightarrow$ | UserNameSeq <':'> Type |

Note that the declaration of integer, floating-point, and string constants is handled in a different manner by the system.

| FunctionDecl | $\longrightarrow$ | <'FUNCTION'> FuncDecl {<Semicolon> FuncDecl} |

FuncDecl $\longrightarrow$ UserNameSeq

[<‘:’> FunctionSpec(n) <‘(’> <PositiveNumber> <‘)’>]

<‘:’> Type $\{$<‘*’> Type$\}^{(n-1)}$ <‘->’> Type

Condition: The declaration must be transparent, *that is, every parameter appearing in the declaration must also appear in the range type.*

FunctionSpec(1) $\longrightarrow$ <‘Fx’> | <‘Fy’> | <‘xF’> | <‘yF’>

FunctionSpec(2) $\longrightarrow$ <‘xFx’> | <‘xFy’> | <‘yFx’>

PropositionDecl $\longrightarrow$ <‘PROPOSITION’> UserNameSeq

PredicateDecl $\longrightarrow$ <‘PREDICATE’> PredDecl $\{$<Semicolon> PredDecl$\}$

PredDecl $\longrightarrow$ UserNameSeq [<‘:’> PredicateSpec(n)]

<‘:’> Type $\{$<‘*’> Type$\}^{(n-1)}$

PredicateSpec(1) $\longrightarrow$ <‘Pz’> | <‘zP’>

PredicateSpec(2) $\longrightarrow$ <‘zPz’>

UserNameSeq $\longrightarrow$ UserName $\{$< Comma > UserName$\}$

UserName $\longrightarrow$ UserBigName | UserGraphicName

UserBigName $\longrightarrow$ < BigName >

Condition: BigName *is not one of the reserved words:* EXPORT, CLOSED, LOCAL, MODULE, IMPORT, LIFT, THEORY, BASE, CONSTRUCTOR, CONSTANT, FUNCTION, PROPOSITION, PREDICATE, DELAY, UNTIL, GROUND, NONVAR, TRUE, ALL, SOME, IF, THEN, *or* ELSE.

UserGraphicName $\longrightarrow$ < GraphicName>

Condition: GraphicName *is not one of the reserved words:*   :, <-, ->, <->, &, ~, \/, |.

At this point, the symbols which have been declared in, or imported into, the various modules can be determined. We now give the appropriate definitions.

A *symbol* is a base, constructor, constant, function, proposition, or predicate.

A *type symbol* is a base or constructor. Other symbols are *non-type symbols*.

The local part of a module M *1-imports* a symbol S *via* a module N if S has a declaration in the export part of N and the local part of M refers to N.

The export part of a module M *1-imports* a symbol S *via* a module N if S has a declaration in the export part of N and either (i) the export part of M refers to N, or (ii) the local part of M refers to N by means of a LIFT declaration, S is a type symbol, and there is a declaration for S in the export part of M. In the latter case, the export part of M also *1-redeclares* S.

The local part of a module M *n-imports*, $n > 1$, a symbol S *via* a module N if there is a module L such that the export part of L $(n-1)$-imports S via N and the local part of M refers to L.

The export part of a module M *n-imports*, $n > 1$, a symbol S *via* a module N if there is a module L such that the export part of L $(n-1)$-imports S via N and either (i) the export part of M refers to L, or (ii) the local part of M refers to L by means of a LIFT declaration, S is a type symbol, and there is a declaration for S in the export part of M. In the latter case, the export part of M also *n-redeclares* S.

A part of a module M *imports* a symbol S *via* a module N if the part of M n-imports S via N, for some $n \geq 1$.

A module M *imports* a symbol S *via* a module N if either the local or export part of M imports S via N.

The export part of a module *redeclares* a type symbol S if it n-redeclares S, for some $n \geq 1$.

The export part of a module *declares* a type symbol if it contains a declaration for, but does not redeclare, the symbol. It *declares* a non-type symbol if it contains a declaration for the symbol.

The local part of a module *declares* a symbol if it contains a declaration for the symbol.

A module *declares* a symbol if either the local or export part of the module declares the symbol.

A part of a module M *imports* a symbol S *from* a module N if the part of M imports S via N and the export part of N declares S.

A module M *imports* a symbol S *from* a module N if either the local or export part of M imports S from N.

A symbol is *accessible to* the local (resp., export) part of a module if it is either declared in, or imported into, the module (resp., export part of the module).

A module *exports* a symbol if the symbol is accessible to the export part of the module.

The following module conditions can now be checked.

M2: For every name appearing in a part of a module, there must be a symbol having that name accessible to that part.

M3: Distinct symbols cannot be declared in the same module with the same category, name, and arity.

Types

Type	$\longrightarrow$	Parameter
		| Base
		| Constructor(n) <'('> TypeSeq(n) <')'>

TypeSeq(n)	$\longrightarrow$	Type {<Comma> Type}$^{(n-1)}$

Base	$\longrightarrow$	UserName

Condition: A symbol with name UserName *is declared or imported as a base.*

Constructor(n)	$\longrightarrow$	UserName

Condition: A symbol with name UserName *is declared or imported as a constructor of arity* n.

Parameter	$\longrightarrow$	< LittleName >

The following module condition can now be checked.

M4: In a module, the type in a constant declaration or the range type in a function declaration must be either a base type declared in the module or a type with a top-level constructor declared in the module.

Control Declarations

ControlDecl	$\longrightarrow$	<'DELAY'> ContDecl {<Semicolon> ContDecl}

Condition: A DELAY *declaration for a predicate can only appear in the module in which the predicate is declared.*

ContDecl	$\longrightarrow$	Atom <'UNTIL'> Cond

The following conditions on the heads of DELAY declarations can now be checked.

D1: No pair of *Atom*s in the set of DELAY declarations for a predicate can have a common instance.

D2: An *Atom* in the head of a DELAY declaration must be constraint-free and must not contain repeated variables.

Cond $\longrightarrow$ Cond1
                                    | Cond1 <'&'> AndSeq
                                    | Cond1 <'\/'> OrSeq

Cond1 $\longrightarrow$ <'NONVAR'> <'('> Variable <')'>
                                    | <'GROUND'> <'('> Variable <')'>
                                    | <'TRUE'>
                                    | <'('> Cond <')'>

AndSeq $\longrightarrow$ Cond1 | Cond1 <'&'> AndSeq

OrSeq $\longrightarrow$ Cond1 | Cond1 <'\/'> OrSeq

Statements

At this point, the overall module structure of the (potential) program has been determined, as have the language and control declarations that each module contains. However, before we go on to give the grammar for statements, we must give some more definitions. The reason is that statements are formulas in certain polymorphic many-sorted languages and we need to define these languages first.

A module is *closed* if its export part contains a CLOSED declaration and *open* if it is not closed.

Let M be a module in a (potential) program P.

1. The *language* of M in P is the polymorphic many-sorted language given by the language declarations of all symbols accessible to the local part of M.

2. The *export language* of M in P is the polymorphic many-sorted language given by the language declarations of all symbols accessible to the export part of M.

3. The *goal language* of P is the language of the main module M_0 of P, if M_0 is open, or the export language of M_0, if M_0 is closed.

Statements and goals are written in a language more general in several ways than that considered in the Appendix. They may contain commits. These can be ignored for the purposes of language checking. Conditionals and intensional set terms are handled by replacing each occurrence of them by the formulas which give their meaning. After this preprocessing, statements and goals are now in a suitable form for checking to see if they are in the appropriate language.

Statement $\longrightarrow$ Atom [<'<-'> Body]

    Condition: A Statement *(ignoring any commits) must be a formula in the language of the module in which it occurs.*

    A Statement *must satisfy the* head condition, *that is, the tuple of types of the arguments of the* Atom *in the* Statement *must be a variant of the type declared for the predicate in the* Atom.

Body $\longrightarrow$ [CFormula(f)] <'|'> [CFormula(f1)]
                                   | CFormula(f)

CFormula(0) $\longrightarrow$ <'('> CFormula(f) <')'>
                                   | <'{'> CFormula(f) <'}' ['_' Label]>
CFormula(2) $\longrightarrow$ CFormula(f) <'&'> CFormula(f1)

    Condition: f $\leq$ 1, f1 $\leq$ 2.

CFormula(f) $\longrightarrow$ Formula(f)

Formula(0) $\longrightarrow$ Atom
                                   | RangeFormula
                                   | <'('> Formula(f) <')'>
Formula(1) $\longrightarrow$ <'~'> Formula(f)
                                   | <'SOME'> <'['> VariableSeq <']'> Formula(f)
                                   | <'ALL'> <'['> VariableSeq <']'> Formula(f)

    Condition: f $\leq$ 1.

Formula(2) $\longrightarrow$ Formula(f) <'&'> Formula(f1)
                                   | <'IF'> [<'SOME'> <'['> VariableSeq <']'>] Formula(f2)
                                   <'THEN'> ThenPart [<'ELSE'> Formula(f1)]

    Condition: f $\leq$ 1, f1 $\leq$ 2.

Formula(3) $\longrightarrow$ Formula(f) <'\/'> Formula(f1)

    Condition: f $\leq$ 2, f1 $\leq$ 3.

Formula(4) $\longrightarrow$ Formula(f) <'<-'> Formula(f1)
                                   | Formula(f) <'->'> Formula(f1)
                                   | Formula(f) <'<->'> Formula(f)

Condition: f $\leq$ 3, f1 $\leq$ 4.

ThenPart $\longrightarrow$ Formula(f)
| Formula(f) <'**&**'> ThenPart
| <'**IF**'> Formula(f1) <'**THEN**'> ThenPart

Condition: f $\leq$ 1.

Atom $\longrightarrow$ Proposition
| PredicateNoInd(n)
<'('> Term {<Comma> Term}$^{(n-1)}$ <')'>
| PredicateInd(1,'**Pz**') Term
| Term PredicateInd(1,'**zP**')
| Term PredicateInd(2,'**zPz**') Term

RangeFormula $\longrightarrow$ Term Comparator Term Comparator Term

Comparator $\longrightarrow$ <'**<**'> | <'**=<**'>

Term $\longrightarrow$ Term(p)

Term(∞) $\longrightarrow$ Variable
| Constant
| < Number >
| < Float >
| < String >
| List
| Set
| <'('> Term <')'>
| FunctionNoInd(n)
<'('> Term {<Comma> Term}$^{(n-1)}$ <')'>

Term(p) $\longrightarrow$ FunctionInd(1,'**Fx**',p) Term(q)
| FunctionInd(1,'**Fy**',p) Term(r)
| Term(q) FunctionInd(1,'**xF**',p)
| Term(r) FunctionInd(1,'**yF**',p)
| Term(q) FunctionInd(2,'**xFx**',p) Term(q1)
| Term(q) FunctionInd(2,'**xFy**',p) Term(r)

$$| \text{Term(r) FunctionInd}(2, \text{'yFx'}, \text{p}) \text{ Term(q)}$$

Condition: $p < q$, $p < q1$, *and* $p \leq r$.

Constant $\longrightarrow$ UserName

Condition: A symbol with name UserName *is declared or imported as a constant.*

FunctionInd(n,i,p) $\longrightarrow$ UserName

Condition: A symbol with name UserName *is declared or imported as a function with arity* n *and indicator* i(p).

FunctionNoInd(n) $\longrightarrow$ UserName

Condition: A symbol with name UserName *is declared or imported as a function with arity* n *and no indicator.*

Proposition $\longrightarrow$ UserName

Condition: Either (i) a symbol with name UserName *is declared or imported as a proposition, or (ii)* UserName *is* **True** *or* **False**.

PredicateInd(n,i) $\longrightarrow$ UserName

Condition: Either (i) a symbol with name UserName *is declared or imported as a predicate with arity* n *and indicator* i, *or (ii)* UserName *is* = *or* $\sim$=, n *is* 2, *and* i *is* **zPz**.

PredicateNoInd(n) $\longrightarrow$ UserName

Condition: A symbol with name UserName *is declared or imported as a predicate with arity* n *and no indicator.*

List $\longrightarrow$ $<$'['$>$ [ListExpr] $<$']'$>$

ListExpr $\longrightarrow$ Term
| Term $<$Comma$>$ ListExpr
| Term $<$'|'$>$ List
| Term $<$'|'$>$ Variable

Set $\longrightarrow$ <'{'> [SetExpr] <'}' >
                                            | <'{'> Term <':'> Formula(f) <'}' >

SetExpr $\longrightarrow$ Term
                                            | Term <Comma> SetExpr
                                            | Term <'|'> Set
                                            | Term <'|'> Variable

VariableSeq $\longrightarrow$ <LittleName> {<Comma> <LittleName>}

Variable $\longrightarrow$ <LittleName> | <Underscore> [<LittleName>]

The final module condition can now be checked.

M5: A module must declare every proposition or predicate defined in that module.

11.4   Goals

Goal $\longrightarrow$ <'<-'> GoalBody

Condition: A Goal *(ignoring any commits) must be a formula in the goal language of the program.*

GoalBody $\longrightarrow$ Body
                                            | <':'> Body
                                            | VariableSeq <':'> Body

Condition: Each variable in VariableSeq *must occur in* Body.

11.5   Theories

Theory $\longrightarrow$ <'THEORY'> TheoryName <Terminator> {TheoryItem}

TheoryName $\longrightarrow$ <UserBigName>

Condition: TheoryName *cannot be any of* Integers, Rationals, Floats, Numbers, Lists, Sets, Strings, Tables, Units, Flocks, Syntax, Programs, Scripts, Theories, IO, NumbersIO, FlocksIO, ProgramsIO, ScriptsIO, *or* TheoriesIO.

TheoryItem $\longrightarrow$ ImportDecl <Terminator>
                            | LanguageDecl <Terminator>
                            | FirstOrderFormula(f) <Terminator>

Condition: A FirstOrderFormula *must be a formula in the language of the theory, which is the polymorphic many-sorted language given by the language declarations of all symbols accessible to the theory.*

FirstOrderFormula(0) $\longrightarrow$ Atom
                            | <'('> FirstOrderFormula(f) <')'>
FirstOrderFormula(1) $\longrightarrow$ <'~'> FirstOrderFormula(f)
                            | <'SOME'> <'['> VariableSeq <']'> FirstOrderFormula(f)
                            | <'ALL'> <'['> VariableSeq <']'> FirstOrderFormula(f)

Condition: $f \leq 1$.

FirstOrderFormula(2) $\longrightarrow$ FirstOrderFormula(f) <'&'> FirstOrderFormula(f1)

Condition: $f \leq 1$, $f1 \leq 2$.

FirstOrderFormula(3) $\longrightarrow$ FirstOrderFormula(f) <'\/'> FirstOrderFormula(f1)

Condition: $f \leq 2$, $f1 \leq 3$.

FirstOrderFormula(4) $\longrightarrow$ FirstOrderFormula(f) <'<-'> FirstOrderFormula(f1)
                            | FirstOrderFormula(f) <'->'> FirstOrderFormula(f1)
                            | FirstOrderFormula(f) <'<->'> FirstOrderFormula(f)

Condition: $f \leq 3$, $f1 \leq 4$.

11.6 Flocks

Flock $\longrightarrow$ {Unit <Terminator>}

Unit $\longrightarrow$ <Identifier>
                            | <Identifier> <'('> <')'>
                            | <Identifier> <'('> UnitSeq <')'>

UnitSeq $\longrightarrow$ Unit {<Comma> Unit}

11.7 Definitions for the Ground Representation

In this section, we give some auxiliary definitions for the ground representation. These definitions complete the specification of 12 associated predicates in the module **Syntax**. To give these definitions compactly, it is convenient to use a simplified grammar similar to the one previously used to give the syntax of Gödel. In particular, we continue to use | to denote alternatives and [...] to mean zero or one occurrence.

StandardStatement $\longrightarrow$ Atom <- [StandardBody]

NormalStatement $\longrightarrow$ Atom <- [NormalBody]

DefiniteStatement $\longrightarrow$ Atom <- [DefiniteBody]

StandardResultant $\longrightarrow$ [StandardBody] <- [StandardBody]

NormalResultant $\longrightarrow$ [NormalBody] <- [NormalBody]

DefiniteResultant $\longrightarrow$ [DefiniteBody] <- [DefiniteBody]

StandardGoal $\longrightarrow$ <- [StandardBody]

NormalGoal $\longrightarrow$ <- [NormalBody]

DefiniteGoal $\longrightarrow$ <- [DefiniteBody]

StandardBody $\longrightarrow$ StandardFormula
                                           | {StandardBody}_Label
                                           | StandardBody & StandardBody

StandardFormula $\longrightarrow$ Atom
                                           | ~ StandardFormula
                                           | SOME [VariableSeq] StandardFormula
                                           | ALL [VariableSeq] StandardFormula
                                           | StandardFormula & StandardFormula

		| IF StandardFormula **THEN** StandardFormula

		| IF StandardFormula **THEN** StandardFormula
		[**ELSE** StandardFormula]
		| StandardFormula \\/ StandardFormula
		| StandardFormula <- StandardFormula
		| StandardFormula -> StandardFormula
		| StandardFormula <-> StandardFormula
NormalBody	$\longrightarrow$	NormalFormula
		| {NormalBody}_Label
		| NormalBody & NormalBody
NormalFormula	$\longrightarrow$	Atom
		| ~ Atom
		| NormalFormula & NormalFormula
		| IF NormalFormula **THEN** NormalFormula
		[**ELSE** NormalFormula]
DefiniteBody	$\longrightarrow$	DefiniteFormula
		| {DefiniteBody}_Label
		| DefiniteBody & DefiniteBody
DefiniteFormula	$\longrightarrow$	Atom
		| DefiniteFormula & DefiniteFormula

12 Semantics

In this chapter, we define the declarative and procedural semantics of Gödel programs. Before getting started on this, we remark that declared names of symbols do not generally uniquely identify symbols in the context of a program. Thus, throughout this chapter, we make the assumption without further comment that symbols are given suitable unique names and are referred to by these names. For example, the flat names discussed in Chapter 9 will serve this purpose.

12.1   Declarative Semantics

Our main aim in this section is to give the definition of a correct answer for a program[1] and goal. For that, we must first associate with each program its completion which is a polymorphic many-sorted theory (in the sense of the Appendix).

There are two main things that have to be done in preparation for the definition of the completion of a program. The first is that we must remove all commits, replace conditionals and intensional set terms by the formulas giving their meanings, and so on. The second is that we must deal with the system modules imported into the program. The problem here is that the definition of Gödel only specifies the intended meaning of the symbols exported by the system modules (see Chapter 13) and does not specify the associated code which implements the system predicates. Thus, for the purposes of the definitions of this section, it is convenient to assume that the local parts of all the system modules and the code they contain are explicitly available. These local parts will depend upon the implementation, of course. We also assume that code for system predicates is in the form of statements and that it is appropriate to complete (in the sense of Section A.3) the definitions of these predicates as we will do shortly for user predicates.[2] Of course, this code must be correct with respect to the intended meanings of the symbols exported by the system modules. The definitions of the built-in propositions True and False are included as part of the system code.

The three definitions which follow are assumed to be given in the context of some program.

Definition The *canonical form of a body* of a statement or goal is defined to be the polymorphic many-sorted formula obtained by applying the following transformations to the body:

---

[1]Strictly speaking, we should exclude the input/output modules in the program since these do not have declarative readings.

[2]These assumptions may not be appropriate for some system predicates. For these, it is a simple matter to extend the following definitions by using some appropriate set of axioms to define such a predicate instead of a completed definition.

- Remove all commits.
- Replace all conditionals by the formulas giving their meaning. Thus:

  IF *Condition* THEN *Formula*

  is replaced by

  (*Condition* & *Formula*)   \/   ~ *Condition*.

  IF SOME $[x_1, \ldots, x_n]$ *Condition* THEN *Formula*

  is replaced by

  (SOME $[x_1, \ldots, x_n]$ (*Condition* & *Formula*))   \/   ~ SOME $[x_1, \ldots, x_n]$ *Condition*.

  IF *Condition* THEN *Formula1* ELSE *Formula2*

  is replaced by

  (*Condition* & *Formula1*)   \/   (~*Condition* & *Formula2*).

  IF SOME $[x_1, \ldots, x_n]$ *Condition* THEN *Formula1* ELSE *Formula2*

  is replaced by

  (SOME $[x_1, \ldots, x_n]$ (*Condition* & *Formula1*))   \/

                                                 (~ SOME $[x_1, \ldots, x_n]$ *Condition* & *Formula2*).

- Replace all intensional set terms by the formulas giving their meanings. Thus, suppose {*T* : *W*} is an outermost intensional set term, where *T* has free variables $y_1, \ldots, y_n$, appearing in a literal *L*. Let *L′* be *L* with {*T* : *W*} replaced by a new variable, **s** say. Then *L* is replaced in the body by

  SOME [s] (*L′* & ALL [x] (x In s   <-\>   SOME $[y_1, \ldots, y_n]$ ((x = *T*) & *W*))).

- Replace each occurrence of a variable beginning with an underscore in a body by a new variable existentially quantified at the front of the atom in which it appears. (In preparation for this step, each atom of the form *S* ~= *T* is replaced by ~(*S* = *T*).)
- Replace the colon notation by its meaning. Thus each goal body of the form

  $x_1, \ldots, x_n$: *W*

  is replaced by

  SOME $[y_1, \ldots, y_m]$ *W*,

  where $y_1, \ldots, y_m$ are all the free variables of *W* not in $\{x_1, \ldots, x_n\}$.

Definition The *canonical form of a statement* is defined to be the polymorphic many-sorted formula obtained by applying the following transformations to the head of the statement and then applying the above transformations to the body of the statement:

- Replace all outermost intensional set terms in the head by the formulas giving their meanings. Thus, if T has the free variables $y_1, \ldots, y_n$, then $\{T : W\}$ is replaced by a new variable, s say, and the formula

ALL [x] (x In s <-> SOME [$y_1, \ldots, y_n$] ((x = T) & W))

is added as an additional conjunct to the body of the statement.

• Replace each occurrence of a variable beginning with an underscore in the head of a statement by a new variable.

Definition The *canonical form of a definition* of a proposition or predicate is the collection of canonical forms of the statements in the definition of the proposition or predicate.

Note that the canonical form of a body is a body in the sense of Section A.3, the canonical form of a statement is a statement in the sense of Section A.3, and the canonical form of a definition is a definition in the sense of Section A.3. We denote the canonical form of a body W by $\overline{W}$.

We now want to give the definition of the completion of a program. For all predicates except = and ~=, the completion contains the completion of the canonical form of their definitions, as defined in Section A.3. However, for equality some care is needed, since as we have already explained in Section 4.1, the standard equality theory of "syntactic identity" given in the definition of the completion in Section A.3, is not appropriate for some types. Thus we assume an appropriate equality theory for all system types is given. For types with some user-defined component, we employ the appropriate "syntactic identity" equality axioms, as explained in Sections 4.1 and A.3. Disequality is simply defined as the negation of equality, as explained in Section 4.1. The entire collection of axioms for = and ~= is called the *equality theory* for the program.

Definition The *completion* of a program is the polymorphic many-sorted theory whose language is defined by the language declarations of all symbols in the program[3] and whose axioms are the completed definitions obtained from the canonical forms of all definitions in the program together with the axioms of the equality theory of the program.

Now we can give the definition of the key declarative concept of a correct answer. Recall that $\forall(W)$ denotes the universal closure of the formula W.

---

[3]We make the assumption here, as we may, that the polymorphic many-sorted logic of the appendix is equipped to handle operators and their declarations.

Definition Let P be a program, G a goal $<-W$, and θ an answer for $P \cup \{G\}$. We say θ is a *correct answer* for $P \cup \{G\}$ if $\forall(\overline{W\theta})$ is a logical consequence of the completion of P.

12.2   Procedural Semantics

The precise details of the procedural semantics of Gödel are not specified. Instead, we only specify what properties an implementation of certain key aspects of the procedural semantics must satisfy. These aspects are the DELAY declarations and the commit. In addition, an implementation must be sound in the sense that computed answers must be correct. Thus, in this section, we describe how DELAY declarations affect the computation rule and how commits prune search trees. We also give the definition of a computed answer.

The description of the procedural semantics is given for goals and statements in their source form, except for the bar and one-solution commits which are assumed to be preprocessed away as follows. A body of the form $V \mid W$ (resp., $V \mid$, $\mid W$, $\mid$) is replaced by $\{V\}\_n$ & W (resp., $\{V\}\_n$, $\{\text{True}\}\_n$ & W, $\{\text{True}\}\_n$), for a suitable positive integer n. If the bar commit is in the body of a goal, then n must be different from any other label in the goal. For bar commits appearing in a definition, n must be the same for all bar commits in the definition and different from the label of any other commits in the definition. Finally, any one-solution commits are given a label unique to the goal or definition in which they appear. After this preprocessing, all bodies contain only commits of the form $\{W\}\_n$, where W is a non-empty formula.

We now give a suitably abstract definition of a search tree for a program and goal.

Definition Let P be a program and G a goal. A *search tree* for $P \cup \{G\}$ is a finite tree whose nodes are labelled by goals, the root node being labelled by G. Each child of a node in a search tree corresponds to a child created by an extension step as defined below.

In the following, we identify a node in a search tree with its label. A search tree is created by applying a sequence of extension steps and pruning steps. Initially the search tree consists of just the original goal G. If a search tree has a (non-empty) leaf node, an extension step at this node, called the *current goal*, adds the children of this node to the tree. A pruning step removes a subtree from the search tree. We first describe in more detail an extension step and then a pruning step. An extension step uses a subformula selected by a computation rule, which we define next.

Definition In the context of a search tree, a *computation rule* selects some subformula in the body of the current goal. The subformula selected must be a commit-free, top-level conjunct of the body of the goal (but which may be in the scope of some commits, of course).

There are four different kinds of *extension step*. These are expansion, replacement, elimination, and splitting step, and are defined next.

Definition Suppose <- W is the current goal in a search tree for a program P.

- An *expansion step* requires the selected subformula to be an atom $R(s_1, \ldots, s_n)$, for some R and $n \geq 0$. Suppose that $R(t_{11}, \ldots, t_{1n})$ <- B_1, $\ldots$, $R(t_{k1}, \ldots, t_{kn})$ <- B_k are all the statements (standardized apart so that they have no variables or commit labels which already appear in the tree) in the definition of R in P. This step adds the children <- W_1, $\ldots$, <- W_k, where W_i is obtained from W by replacing the atom $R(s_1, \ldots, s_n)$ by B'_i and where B'_i is obtained from B_i by adding $s_1 = t_{i1}$ & $\ldots$ & $s_n = t_{in}$ as a top-level conjunct to B_i inside the scope of every commit in B_i, for $i \in \{1, \ldots, k\}$.

- A *replacement step* adds the child <- $W_1\theta$, where W_1 is obtained from W by replacing the selected subformula V by a commit-free formula V_1 such that the canonical form of $\forall(V\theta$ <-> $V_1\theta)$ is a logical consequence of the completion of P, for some substitution θ.

- An *elimination step* requires the selected subformula to have the form $\exists x_1 \ldots \exists x_n V$. This step adds the child <- W_1, where W_1 is obtained from W by replacing the selected subformula by V.

- A *splitting step* requires the selected subformula to have the form $V_1 \ \backslash\!/ \ V_2$. This step adds the children <- W_1 and <- W_2, where W_i is obtained from W by replacing the selected subformula by V_i, for $i \in \{1, 2\}$.

Extension steps other than expansion steps include negation as failure calls, calls to conditionals, "evaluation" of intensional set terms, solving of constraints, and transformations which reduce a body to normal form [15]. Needless to say, there are many opportunities to optimize the implementation of an extension step, as described above. Associated with each (non-root) node in a branch of a search tree, there is a substitution which depends on the extension step used to obtain the node. For expansion, elimination and splitting steps, this substitution is the identity. For a replacement step, it is the substitution θ described in this step.

Now let us turn to the meaning of the DELAY declaration. In the grammar for *Cond* given in Chapter 11, the reserved word & stands for conjunction, \/ stands for disjunction, TRUE stands for the truth value true, NONVAR is true if and only if its argument is a nonvariable term, and GROUND is true if and only if its argument is a ground term. Now suppose an atom A is an instance by a substitution θ of an *Atom* (that is, $A = Atom\,\theta$) in a DELAY declaration. Then we say A *satisfies* the corresponding condition *Cond* in this DELAY declaration if, when θ is applied to the variables in *Cond*, the resulting condition has truth value true using the above meanings given to the various reserved words. Otherwise, we say A does *not satisfy* the corresponding condition.

DELAY declarations cause atoms to be delayed according to the following rules:

- An atom in a goal is delayed if it has a common instance with some *Atom* in a DELAY declaration but is not an instance of this *Atom*.
- An atom in a goal is delayed if it is an instance of an *Atom* in a DELAY declaration but does not satisfy the corresponding condition *Cond*.

An implementation must ensure that if a delayed atom is selected from the current goal, then it is not used by an expansion step. Furthermore, it is understood that DELAY declarations must be similarly respected for any computation which goes on inside a replacement step. For example, a replacement step may be a negation as failure computation, which requires the building of a subsidiary finitely failed tree. Expansion steps used in the building of this tree must also respect any relevant DELAY declarations. Thus DELAY declarations give programmers some influence over the computation rule and can be used to ensure that atoms will not be selected for an expansion step until they are sufficiently instantiated.

We now explain when pruning steps can take place and which subtrees may be pruned.

Definition Let T be a search tree, G_0 a non-leaf node in T, and G_1 a child of G_0. Then G_1 is an *l-child* of G_0 if **either**

1. G_0 contains a commit labelled l and the selected subformula in G_0 is in the scope of this commit, **or**

2. G_1 is derived from G_0 in an expansion step using a statement which contains a commit labelled l (after standardization apart of the commit labels).

Definition Let S be a search tree. We say that the search tree S' is obtained from S by a *pruning step* in S at G_0 if the following conditions are satisfied.

1. S has a node G_0 with distinct l-children G_1 and G_2, and there is a node G_2' in S which is either equal to or below G_2 and does not contain a commit with label l.

2. S' is obtained from S by removing the subtree of S rooted at G_1.

Definition Let P be a program and G a goal. A *computed answer* for $P \cup \{G\}$ is obtained by restricting to the free variables in the body of G a substitution obtained by composing in order the successive substitutions associated with each (non-root) node on a branch ending in the empty goal of a search tree for $P \cup \{G\}$ constructed by an implementation employing the above semantics for **DELAY** declarations and the commit.

It can be shown that every computed answer is a correct answer, that is, an implementation which gives computed answers according to the above definition is sound.

13 System Modules and Utilities

The system modules `Integers`, `Rationals`, `Floats`, `Lists`, `Sets`, `Strings`, `Numbers`, `Tables`, `Units`, `Flocks`, `Syntax`, `Programs`, `Scripts`, `Theories`, `IO`, `NumbersIO`, `FlocksIO`, `ProgramsIO`, `ScriptsIO`, and `TheoriesIO` are provided by Gödel. The export parts of these are given in this chapter. The figure over the page shows the relationships between the system modules. An arrow from one module to another means the first module refers to the second.

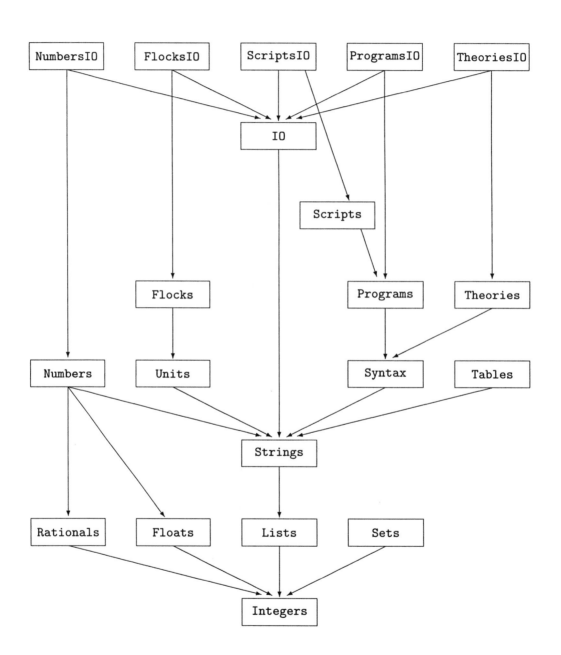

13.1 Integers

EXPORT   Integers.

% Module providing the integers and some standard functions and
% predicates with integer arguments.
%
% This module conforms to the standard for the data type Integer in
% Version 4.0 (August 1992) of the Language Independent Arithmetic
% Standard (LIAS) ISO/IEC CD 10967-1:1992 (JTC1/SC22/WG11 N318, ANSI
% X3T2 92-064).
%
% The intended interpretation of the symbols in this module is as
% follows.
%
% The domain of the intended interpretation is the integers Z. The
% constant 0 is interpreted as the integer 0, the constant 1 is
% interpreted as the integer 1, and so on. The various functions, such
% as +, -, etc., have their usual interpetation as mappings from Z x Z
% (or Z, as appropriate) into Z. Similarly, the various predicates, such
% as >, <, etc., have their usual interpretation on Z x Z. The details
% are given below.
%
% The LIAS boolean bounded is false. Thus infinite precision integer
% arithmetic is provided.

BASE   Integer.
%
% Type of the integers.

% CONSTANT   0, 1, 2, ... : Integer.

FUNCTION   ^ : yFx(540) : Integer * Integer -> Integer.
%
% Exponentiation.
%

```
% ^ is defined by
%           x^y  = x raised to the power y,      if y >= 0
%                = 0,                             if y < 0.
%
% The function ^ is defined to be 0 when y < 0 to make it a total
% function. This result will never be used. If exponentiation with
% y < 0 is attempted, the computation will halt with an error message.


FUNCTION      - : Fy(530) : Integer -> Integer.
%
% Unary minus.
%
% The function - corresponds to the LIAS function neg.


FUNCTION      * : yFx(520) : Integer * Integer -> Integer.
%
% Multiplication.
%
% The function * corresponds to the LIAS function mul.


FUNCTION      Div : yFx(520) : Integer * Integer -> Integer.
%
% Integer division.
%
% Div is defined by
%     x Div y = Rnd(x/y),   if y ~= 0
%             = 0,          if y = 0
% where Rnd is the LIAS rounding function "round towards zero".
%
% The function Div corresponds to the LIAS function div. Div is
% defined to be 0 when y = 0 to make it a total function. This result
% will never be used.  If division by 0 is attempted, the computation
% will halt with an error message.


FUNCTION      Mod : yFx(520) : Integer * Integer -> Integer.
%
```

```
% Modulus.
%
% Mod is defined by
%      x Mod y = x - (x Div y) * y,   if y ~= 0
%              = 0,                    if y = 0
%
% The function Mod corresponds to the LIAS function rem.  Mod is
% defined to be 0 when y = 0 to make it a total function. This result
% will never be used.  If division by 0 is attempted, the computation
% will halt with an error message.


FUNCTION     Rem : yFx(520) : Integer * Integer -> Integer.
%
% Remainder after integer division.
%
% Rem is defined by
%      x Rem y = x - [x/y] * y,   if y ~= 0
%              = 0,               if y = 0
% where the rounding function [] is the floor function.
%
% The function Rem corresponds to the LIAS function mod^1.  Rem is
% defined to be 0 when y = 0 to make it a total function. This result
% will never be used.  If division by 0 is attempted, the computation
% will halt with an error message.


FUNCTION     + : yFx(510) : Integer * Integer -> Integer.
%
% Addition.
%
% The function + corresponds to the LIAS function add.


FUNCTION     - : yFx(510) : Integer * Integer -> Integer.
%
% Subtraction.
%
% The function - corresponds to the LIAS function sub.
```

```
FUNCTION      Abs : Integer -> Integer.
%
% Absolute value.
%
% The function Abs corresponds to the LIAS function abs.

FUNCTION      Sign : Integer -> Integer.
%
% Sign of an integer.
%
% Sign is defined by
%     Sign(x) =  1,   if x > 0
%             =  0,   if x = 0
%             = -1,   if x < 0

FUNCTION      Max : Integer * Integer -> Integer.
%
% Maximum.

FUNCTION      Min : Integer * Integer -> Integer.
%
% Minimum.

PREDICATE    > : zPz :

  Integer        % An integer greater than the integer in the second
                 % argument.
* Integer.       % An integer.

% The predicate > corresponds to the LIAS predicate gtr.

PREDICATE    < : zPz :

  Integer        % An integer less than the integer in the second argument.
* Integer.       % An integer.

% The predicate < corresponds to the LIAS predicate lss.
```

PREDICATE   >= : zPz :

  Integer   % An integer greater than or equal to the integer in the
                 % second argument.
* Integer.   % An integer.

% The predicate >= corresponds to the LIAS predicate geq.

PREDICATE   =< : zPz :

  Integer   % An integer less than or equal to the integer in the
                 % second argument.
* Integer.   % An integer.

% The predicate =< corresponds to the LIAS predicate leq.

PREDICATE   Interval :

  Integer   % An integer less than or equal to the integer in the
                 % second argument.
* Integer   % An integer less than or equal to the integer in the
                 % third argument.
* Integer.   % An integer.

DELAY   Interval(x,_,z) UNTIL GROUND(x) & GROUND(z).

13.2   Rationals

EXPORT   Rationals.

% Module providing the rationals and some standard functions and
% predicates with rational arguments.
%
% The intended interpretation of the symbols in this module is as
% follows.
%
% The intended domain is the rationals Q. The various functions, such as
% +, -, etc., have their usual interpetation as mappings from Q x Q (or
% Q, as appropriate) into Q. Similarly, the various predicates, such as
% >, <, etc., have their usual interpretation on Q x Q. The details are
% given below.
%
% Note that infinite precision rational arithmetic is provided.

IMPORT   Integers.

BASE   Rational.
%
% Type of the rationals.

FUNCTION   // : yFx(520) : Integer * Integer -> Rational.
%
% For integers x and y, x//y is the rational obtained from the quotient
% of x by y.
%
% Note that // gives conversion from Integer to Rational in that x//1
% is the rational corresponding to the integer x. Conversion from
% Rational to Integer can be achieved with a call of the form x//1 = y,
% where y is a rational (reducible to) N/1, for some integer N.
%
% // is defined to be 0 when the second argument is 0 to make it a
% total function. This result will never be used. If // is called with

% the second argument 0, the computation will halt with an error
% message.

FUNCTION   ^ : yFx(540) : Rational * Integer -> Rational.
%
% Exponentiation.
%
% ^ is defined to be 0 when the first argument is 0 and the second
% argument is negative to make it a total function. This result will
% never be used. If such an exponentiation is attempted, the
% computation will halt with an error message.

FUNCTION   - : Fy(530) : Rational -> Rational.
%
% Unary minus.

FUNCTION   * : yFx(520) : Rational * Rational -> Rational.
%
% Multiplication.

FUNCTION   / : yFx(520) : Rational * Rational -> Rational.
%
% Division.
%
% / is defined to be 0 when the second argument is 0 to make it a total
% function. This result will never be used. If division by 0 is
% attempted, the computation will halt with an error message.

FUNCTION   + : yFx(510) : Rational * Rational -> Rational.
%
% Addition.

FUNCTION   - : yFx(510) : Rational * Rational -> Rational.
%
% Subtraction.

```
FUNCTION      Abs : Rational -> Rational.
%
% Absolute value.


FUNCTION      Sign : Rational -> Rational.
%
% Sign of a rational.
%
% Sign is defined by
%     Sign(x) =  1,    if x > 0
%             =  0,    if x = 0
%             = -1,    if x < 0


FUNCTION      Max : Rational * Rational -> Rational.
%
% Maximum.


FUNCTION      Min : Rational * Rational -> Rational.
%
% Minimum.


PREDICATE    > : zPz :

   Rational        % A rational greater than the rational in the second
                   % argument.
 * Rational.       % A rational.


PREDICATE    < : zPz :

   Rational        % A rational less than the rational in the second
                   % argument.
 * Rational.       % A rational.
```

PREDICATE   >= : zPz :

  Rational   % A rational greater than or equal to the rational in
                 % the second argument.
* Rational.   % A rational.

PREDICATE   =< : zPz :

  Rational   % A rational less than or equal to the rational in the
                 % second argument.
* Rational.   % A rational.

PREDICATE   StandardRational :

  Rational   % A rational.
* Integer   % The numerator of the standard form of this rational.
* Integer.   % The denominator of the standard form of this rational.

DELAY   StandardRational(x,_,_) UNTIL GROUND(x).

13.3   Floats

EXPORT   Floats.

% Module providing floating-point numbers and some standard functions
% and predicates with floating-point arguments.
%
% This module conforms to the standard for the data type Floating-Point
% in Version 4.0 (August 1992) of the Language Independent Arithmetic
% Standard (LIAS) ISO/IEC CD 10967-1:1992 (JTC1/SC22/WG11 N318, ANSI
% X3T2 92-064). It also conforms to the ANSI/IEEE Standard for Binary
% Floating-Point Arithmetic 754-1985.
%
% The four IEEE Standard 754-1985 rounding functions (round toward
% nearest, round toward plus infinity, round toward minus infinity, and
% round toward zero) are provided by compiler options. The default
% rounding function is round toward nearest.
%
% The intended interpretation of the symbols in this module is as
% follows.
%
% The domain of the intended interpretation is the finite set F of
% floating-point numbers characterised by a fixed radix, a fixed
% precision, and fixed smallest and largest exponent. Thus F is the
% finite set of numbers of the form either 0 or s0.f1...fp * r^e, where
% r is the radix, p is the precision, e is the exponent, s is either +
% or -, and each fi satisfies 0 =< fi < r. Note that the LIAS boolean
% denorm is true. Thus denormalised floating-point numbers are provided.
%
% The language contains finitely many constants, exactly one
% corresponding to each floating-point number in F. However, for the
% convenience of the user, there is some syntactic sugar used instead
% of the names of these constants. This is the usual decimal number
% notation, with or without an exponent. Typical decimal numbers without
% exponent are 3.1416 and 0, and typical decimal numbers with exponent
% are -2.345619E-12 and 674328.89E+2. Such decimal numbers are converted

% (according to the ANSI/IEEE standard 754-1985) by the system to
% floating-point numbers in the form above. Then the convention is
% that a decimal number is syntactic sugar for the constant whose
% interpretation is the floating-point number obtained from the decimal
% number. This means that there is more than one way of denoting each of
% these constants. For example, both 3.1416 and 314.16E-2 denote the
% same constant. Similarly, when answers are displayed by the system,
% floating-point numbers are converted back to a more convenient
% decimal form.
%
% The various functions, such as +, -, etc., have their usual
% interpretation as mappings from F x F (or F, as appropriate) into F.
% Similarly, the various predicates, such as >, <, etc., have their
% usual interpretation on F x F. The details are given below.

IMPORT   Integers.

BASE   Float.
%
% Type of the floating-point numbers.

% CONSTANT   Finitely many constants, one for each number in the finite
% set F of floating-point numbers determined by the radix, precision,
% and smallest and largest exponent.

FUNCTION   ^ : yFx(540) : Float * Float -> Float.
%
% Exponentiation.
%
% ^ is defined by
%   x^y = Exp(y*Log(x)),   if x>0 and no underflow or overflow occurs
%   = 0,   otherwise.
% The function ^ is defined to be 0 when x =< 0 or underflow or overflow
% occurs to make it a total function. This result will never be used. If
% exponentiation is attempted with x =< 0 or underflow or overflow
% occurs, the computation will halt with an appropriate error message.

```
FUNCTION     - : Fy(530) : Float -> Float.
%
% Unary minus.
%
% The function - corresponds to the LIAS function neg.


FUNCTION     * : yFx(520) : Float * Float -> Float.
%
% Multiplication.
%
% * can overflow or underflow. In either case, the multiplication is
% defined to be 0 to make * total. Such a result will never be used. If
% a multiplication leads to an underflow or overflow, the computation
% will halt with an appropriate error message.
%
% The function * corresponds to the LIAS function mul.


FUNCTION     / : yFx(520) : Float * Float -> Float.
%
% Division.
%
% / can overflow, underflow, or have a zero divisor. In all such cases,
% the division is defined to be 0 to make / total. Such a result will
% never be used. If a division leads to an underflow, overflow, or a
% zero divisor, the computation will halt with an appropriate error
% message.
%
% The function / corresponds to the LIAS function div.


FUNCTION     + : yFx(510) : Float * Float -> Float.
%
% Addition.
%
% + can overflow or underflow. In either case, the addition is defined
% to be 0 to make + total. Such a result will never be used. If an
% addition leads to an underflow or overflow, the computation will halt
% with an appropriate error message.
```

```
%
% The function + corresponds to the LIAS function add. The LIAS
% approximate addition function add* is true (exact) addition.

FUNCTION      - : yFx(510) : Float * Float -> Float.
%
% Subtraction.
%
% - can overflow or underflow. In either case, the subtraction is
% defined to be 0 to make - total. Such a result will never be used.
% If a subtraction leads to an underflow or overflow, the computation
% will halt with an appropriate error message.
%
% The function - corresponds to the LIAS function sub.


FUNCTION      Abs : Float -> Float.
%
% Absolute value.
%
% The function Abs corresponds to the LIAS function abs.


FUNCTION      Max : Float * Float -> Float.
%
% Maximum.


FUNCTION      Min : Float * Float -> Float.
%
% Minimum.


FUNCTION      Sqrt : Float -> Float.
%
% Square root.
%
% Sqrt is defined to be 0 when its argument is negative to make it
% total. Such a result will never be used. In such a case, the
% computation will halt with an appropriate error message.
```

```
FUNCTION      Sign : Float -> Float.
%
% Sign(x) = 1,    if x>0
%         = 0,    if x=0
%           -1,   if x<0
%
% The function Sign corresponds to the LIAS function sign.


FUNCTION      Fraction : Float -> Float.
%
% The fraction part s0.f1...fp of a non-zero floating-point number
% s0.f1...fp * r^e (normalized so that f1 ~= 0, if necessary) or 0
% for the floating-point number 0.
%
% The function Fraction corresponds to the LIAS function fraction.


FUNCTION      Scale : Float * Integer -> Float.
%
% Scale scales a floating-point number in the first argument by an
% integer power of the radix, where the integer is in the second
% argument. Scale is defined to be 0 when underflow or overflow occurs
% to make it a total function. Such a result will never be used. If
% underflow or overflow occurs, the computation will halt with an
% error message.
%
% The function Scale corresponds to the LIAS function scale.


FUNCTION      Successor : Float -> Float.
%
% Successor returns the closest number in F greater than its argument.
% Successor is defined to be 0 when overflow occurs to make it a total
% function. Such a result will never be used. If overflow occurs, the
% computation will halt with an error message.
%
% The function Successor corresponds to the LIAS function succ.
```

FUNCTION   Predecessor : Float -> Float.
%
% Predecessor returns the closest number in F less than its argument.
% Predecessor is defined to be 0 when overflow occurs to make it a
% total function. Such a result will never be used. If overflow occurs,
% the computation will halt with an error message.
%
% The function Predecessor corresponds to the LIAS function pred.

FUNCTION   UnitInLastPlace : Float -> Float.
%
% UnitInLastPlace gives the weight of the least significant digit of
% a non-zero argument. UnitInLastPlace is defined to be 0 when its
% argument is 0 or underflow occurs to make it a total function. Such
% a result will never be used. If its argument is 0 or underflow
% occurs, the computation will halt with an error message.
%
% The function UnitInLastPlace corresponds to the LIAS function ulp.

FUNCTION   Truncate : Float * Integer -> Float.
%
% Truncate zeros out the low (p - n) digits of its first argument, where
% p is the precision and n is the second argument. If n =< 0, then 0
% is returned and if n >= p, the first argument is returned.
%
% The function Truncate corresponds to the LIAS function trunc.

FUNCTION   Round : Float * Integer -> Float.
%
% Round rounds its first argument to n significant digits. That is,
% the nearest n-digit floating-point value is returned. Values exactly
% half-way between two adjacent n-digit floating-point numbers round
% away from zero. Round is defined to be 0 when overflow occurs to
% make it a total function. Such a result will never be used. If
% overflow occurs, the computation will halt with an error message.
%
% The function Round corresponds to the LIAS function round.

```
FUNCTION      IntegerPart : Float -> Float.
%
% IntegerPart returns (in floating-point form) the integer part of a
% floating point number.
%
% The function IntegerPart corresponds to the LIAS function intpart.


FUNCTION      FractionalPart : Float -> Float.
%
% FractionalPart returns the value of its argument minus its integer
% part.
%
% The function FractionalPart corresponds to the LIAS function
% fractpart.


FUNCTION      Sin : Float -> Float.
%
% Sine.


FUNCTION      Cos : Float -> Float.
%
% Cosine.


FUNCTION      Tan : Float -> Float.
%
% Tangent.
%
% Tan is defined to be 0 when overflow occurs to make it total. Such
% a result will never be used.  If overflow occurs, the computation
% will halt with an error message.


FUNCTION      ArcSin : Float -> Float.
%
% ArcSine.
%
% ArcSin is defined to be 0 when its argument is outside the range
```

% [-1,1] to make it total. Such a result will never be used. If
% ArcSin is called with such an argument, the computation will halt
% with an error message.

FUNCTION   ArcCos : Float -> Float.
%
% ArcCosine.
%
% ArcCos is defined to be 0 when its argument is outside the range
% [-1,1] to make it total. Such a result will never be used. If
% ArcCos is called with such an argument, the computation will halt
% with an error message.

FUNCTION   ArcTan : Float -> Float.
%
% ArcTangent.

FUNCTION   Exp : Float -> Float.
%
% Exponential.
%
% Exponential is defined to be 0 when underflow or overflow occurs to
% make it total. Such a result will never be used. If underflow or
% overflow occurs, the computation will halt with an error message.

FUNCTION   Log : Float -> Float.
%
% Natural logarithm.
%
% Log is defined to be 0 when its argument is not greater than 0 or
% underflow or overflow occurs to make it total. Such a result will
% never be used. In such cases, the computation will halt with an error
% message.

```
FUNCTION      Log10 : Float -> Float.
%
% Base 10 logarithm.
%
% Log10 is defined to be 0 when its argument is not greater than 0 or
% underflow or overflow occurs to make it total. Such a result will
% never be used. In such cases, the computation will halt with an error
% message.


PREDICATE     IntegerToFloat :

   Integer      % An integer.
 * Float.       % The floating-point number resulting from the conversion
                % of this integer.

DELAY         IntegerToFloat(x,_) UNTIL GROUND(x).

% The predicate IntegerToFloat corresponds to the LIAS function
% cvt_{I->F}.


PREDICATE     TruncateToInteger :

   Float        % A floating-point number.
 * Integer.     % The integer resulting from the conversion of this
                % floating-point number using the function
                % x -> sign(x).[|x|], where sign gives the sign of its
                % argument, [] is the floor function, and . is
                % multiplication.

DELAY         TruncateToInteger(x,_) UNTIL GROUND(x).

% The predicate TruncateToInteger corresponds to an LIAS function
% cvt_{F->I}.


PREDICATE     RoundToInteger :

   Float        % A floating-point number.
```

* Integer.   % The integer resulting from the conversion of this
                % floating-point number using the function
                % x -> sign(x).[|x| + 1/2], where sign gives the sign of
                % its argument, [] is the floor function, and . is
                % multiplication.

DELAY   RoundToInteger(x,_) UNTIL GROUND(x).

% The predicate Nearest corresponds to an LIAS function cvt_{F->I}.

PREDICATE   Floor :

  Float   % A floating-point number.
* Integer.   % The integer resulting from the conversion of this
                % floating-point number using the floor function.

DELAY   Floor(x,_) UNTIL GROUND(x).

% The predicate Floor corresponds to an LIAS function cvt_{F->I}.

PREDICATE   Ceiling :

  Float   % A floating-point number.
* Integer.   % The integer resulting from the conversion of this
                % floating-point number using the ceiling function.

DELAY   Ceiling(x,_) UNTIL GROUND(x).

% The predicate Ceiling corresponds to an LIAS function cvt_{F->I}.

PREDICATE   Exponent :

  Float   % A (non-zero) floating-point number s0.f1...fp * r^e
                % (normalized so that f1 ~= 0, if necessary).
* Integer.   % The exponent e of this number.

DELAY   Exponent(x,_) UNTIL GROUND(x).

% The predicate Exponent corresponds to the LIAS function exponent.

PREDICATE   Radix :

   Integer.   % The radix 2 used in the representation of
                % floating-point numbers.

% The predicate Radix gives the LIAS parameter r.

PREDICATE   Precision :

   Integer.   % The maximum number 24 of radix digits allowed in the
                % representation of floating-point numbers.

% The predicate Precision gives the LIAS parameter p.

PREDICATE   MaxExponent :

   Integer.   % The maximum exponent 128 allowed in the representation
                % of floating-point numbers.

% The predicate MaxExponent gives the LIAS parameter emax.

PREDICATE   MinExponent :

   Integer.   % The minimum exponent -125 allowed in the representation
                % of floating-point numbers.

% The predicate MinExponent gives the LIAS parameter emin.

PREDICATE   MaxFloat :

   Float.   % The largest floating-point number 3.402823466E+38
                % (approx.).

% The predicate MaxFloat gives the LIAS constant fmax.

PREDICATE   MinNormFloat :

  Float.   % The normalised floating-point number 1.175494351E-38
                % (approx.) with the smallest magnitude.

% The predicate MinNormFloat gives the LIAS constant fmin_{N}.

PREDICATE   MinFloat :

  Float.   % The denormalised floating-point number 1.401298464E-45
                % (approx.) with the smallest magnitude.

% The predicate MinNormFloat gives the LIAS constant fmin_{D}.

PREDICATE   Epsilon :

  Float.   % Maximum relative spacing 1.192092896E-7 (approx.) in F.

% The predicate Epsilon gives the LIAS constant epsilon.

PREDICATE   > : zPz :

  Float   % A floating-point number greater than the number in the
              % second argument.
* Float.   % A floating-point number.

DELAY   x > y UNTIL GROUND(x) & GROUND(y).

% The predicate > corresponds to the LIAS predicate gtr.

PREDICATE   < : zPz :

  Float   % A floating-point number less than the number in the
              % second argument.
* Float.   % A floating-point number.

DELAY   x < y UNTIL GROUND(x) & GROUND(y).

% The predicate < corresponds to the LIAS predicate lss.

PREDICATE   >= : zPz :

   Float   % A floating-point number greater than or equal to the
                  % number in the second argument.
 * Float.   % A floating-point number.

DELAY   x >= y UNTIL GROUND(x) & GROUND(y).

% The predicate >= corresponds to the LIAS predicate geq.

PREDICATE   =< : zPz :

   Float   % A floating-point number less than or equal to the
                  % number in the second argument.
 * Float.   % A floating-point number.

DELAY   x =< y UNTIL GROUND(x) & GROUND(y).

% The predicate =< corresponds to the LIAS predicate leq.

13.4   Lists

EXPORT   Lists.

% Module providing a collection of standard list processing predicates.

IMPORT   Integers.

CONSTRUCTOR   List/1.
%
% List constructor.

CONSTANT   Nil : List(a).
%
% Empty list.

FUNCTION   Cons : a * List(a) -> List(a).
%
% Cons function.

PREDICATE   Member :

    a   % An element.
  * List(a).   % A list containing this element.

DELAY   Member(_,y) UNTIL NONVAR(y).

PREDICATE   MemberCheck :

    a   % An element.
  * List(a).   % A list containing this element.
                        %
                        % MemberCheck is a version of Member which
                        % efficiently checks whether a given element is a
                        % member of a given list. It prunes the search

```
                    % space so that MemberCheck succeeds at most once.
                    %
                    % If a call to Member with the same arguments has
                    % at most one answer, then the call to MemberCheck
                    % has a declarative reading.  (In particular, if
                    % the call to MemberCheck is ground, this
                    % condition is automatically satisfied.)

DELAY           MemberCheck(_, []) UNTIL TRUE;
                MemberCheck(x, [y|_]) UNTIL NONVAR(x) & NONVAR(y).

PREDICATE       Append :

  List(a)           % A list.
* List(a)           % A list.
* List(a).          % The list obtained by appending the list in the
                    % second argument to the end of the list in the
                    % first argument.

DELAY           Append(x,_,z) UNTIL NONVAR(x) \/ NONVAR(z).

PREDICATE       Permutation :

  List(a)           % A list.
* List(a).          % A list which is a permutation of the list in the
                    % first argument.

DELAY           Permutation(x,y) UNTIL NONVAR(x) \/ NONVAR(y).

PREDICATE       Delete :

  a                 % An element.
* List(a)           % A list containing this element.
* List(a).          % A list which differs from the list in the second
                    % argument only in that exactly one occurrence of
                    % the element in the first argument is missing.

DELAY           Delete(_,y,z) UNTIL NONVAR(y) \/ NONVAR(z).
```

PREDICATE   DeleteFirst :

    a   % An element.
 * List(a)   % A list containing this element.
 * List(a).   % A list which differs from the list in the second
                      % argument only in that the first occurrence of the
                      % element in the first argument is missing.

DELAY   DeleteFirst(x,y,z) UNTIL NONVAR(x) &
                                        (NONVAR(y) \/ NONVAR(z)).

PREDICATE   Reverse :

  List(a)   % A list.
 * List(a).   % The list consisting of the elements of the list
                      % in the first argument in reverse order.

DELAY   Reverse(x,y) UNTIL NONVAR(x) \/ NONVAR(y).

PREDICATE   Prefix :

  List(a)   % A list.
 * Integer   % A non-negative integer less than or equal to the
                      % length of the list in the first argument.
 * List(a).   % The prefix of the list in the first argument
                      % having length equal to the integer in the second
                      % argument.

DELAY   Prefix(x,y,z) UNTIL NONVAR(x) & (NONVAR(y) \/ NONVAR(z)).

PREDICATE   Suffix :

  List(a)   % A list.
 * Integer   % A non-negative integer less than or equal to the
                      % length of the list in the first argument.
 * List(a).   % The suffix of the list in the first argument
                      % having length equal to the integer in the second

```
                        % argument.

DELAY           Suffix(x,y,z) UNTIL NONVAR(x) & (NONVAR(y) \/ NONVAR(z)).


PREDICATE       Length :

  List(a)               % A list.
* Integer.              % The length of the list in the first argument.

DELAY           Length(x,y) UNTIL NONVAR(x) \/ NONVAR(y).


PREDICATE       Sorted :

  List(Integer).    % A list of integers in non-decreasing order.

DELAY           Sorted([]) UNTIL TRUE;
                Sorted([_|x]) UNTIL NONVAR(x).


PREDICATE       Sort :

  List(Integer)       % A list of integers.
* List(Integer).      % The list consisting of the elements of the list
                      % in the first argument in non-decreasing order.

DELAY           Sort(x,_) UNTIL NONVAR(x).


PREDICATE       Merge :

  List(Integer)       % A list of integers.
* List(Integer)       % A list of integers.
* List(Integer).      % The list which is the result of merging the lists
                      % in the first and second arguments.

DELAY           Merge(x,y,z) UNTIL (NONVAR(x) & NONVAR(y)) \/ NONVAR(z).
```

13.5   Sets

EXPORT   Sets.

% Module providing finite sets and a collection of standard set
% processing functions and predicates.
%
% Also provided by this module are intensional set terms which have the
% form
%
% {T : W}
%
% where T is a term with free variables y1,...,yn, say, and W is a
% formula (not involving commits) which has y1,...,yn amongst its free
% variables. The variables y1,...,yn must be local to {T : W}. The free
% variables of {T : W} are the free variables of W other than y1,...,yn.
% (Note that T may itself be an intensional set term and that it is
% possible for n to be 0.)
%
% Informally, {T : W} means "the set of all instances of T
% corresponding to the instances of W which are true".

IMPORT   Integers.

CONSTRUCTOR Set/1.
%
% Set constructor.

CONSTANT   Null : Set(a).
%
% Empty set.

FUNCTION   Inc : a * Set(a) -> Set(a).
%
% The function Inc used to form sets. The intended meaning of Inc is
% the mapping Include such that Include(d,S) = {d} union S, where d is

% an element from the domain of type a and S is a set of elements of
% type a.

```
FUNCTION      *  : yFx(120) : Set(a) * Set(a) -> Set(a).
%
% Set-theoretic intersection.


FUNCTION      +  : yFx(110) : Set(a) * Set(a) -> Set(a).
%
% Set-theoretic union.


FUNCTION      \ : yFx(100) : Set(a) * Set(a) -> Set(a).
%
% Set-theoretic difference.


PREDICATE     In : zPz :

   a              % An element.
 * Set(a).        % A set containing this element.

DELAY           _ In y UNTIL GROUND(y).


PREDICATE     Subset : zPz :

   Set(a)         % A subset of the set in the second argument.
 * Set(a).        % A set.

DELAY           _ Subset y UNTIL GROUND(y).


PREDICATE     StrictSubset : zPz :

   Set(a)         % A strict subset of the set in the second argument.
 * Set(a).        % A set.

DELAY           _ StrictSubset y UNTIL GROUND(y).
```

PREDICATE   Size :

  Set(a)   % A set.
* Integer.   % The number of elements in the set.

DELAY   Size(x,_) UNTIL GROUND(x).

───

13.6   Strings

EXPORT   Strings.

% Module providing strings and a collection of standard string
% processing predicates.

IMPORT   Lists.

BASE   String.
%
% Type of a string.

% CONSTANT Infinitely many constants which are in one-to-one
% correspondence with all possible strings. A constant of the form
% "c1...cn", where each ci is a character, is interpreted as the
% string consisting of the characters c1, ..., cn in that order.

FUNCTION   ++ : yFx(500) : String * String -> String.
%
% String concatenation.

PREDICATE StringInts :

   String   % A string.
 * List(Integer). % The list of ASCII codes of the characters in this
                    % string in the order in which they appear there.

DELAY   StringInts(x,y) UNTIL GROUND(x) \/ GROUND(y).

PREDICATE FirstSubstring :

   String   % A string.
 * Integer   % A non-negative integer n less than or equal to the
                   % length of the string in the first argument.

* String.   % The substring consisting of the first n characters
                   % of the string in the first argument.

DELAY   FirstSubstring(x,y,z) UNTIL GROUND(x) &
                                      (GROUND(y) \/ GROUND(z)).

PREDICATE LastSubstring :

  String   % A string.
* Integer   % A non-negative integer n less than or equal to the
                   % length of this string.
* String.   % The substring consisting of the last n characters
                   % of the string in the first argument.

DELAY   LastSubstring(x,y,z) UNTIL GROUND(x) &
                                      (GROUND(y) \/ GROUND(z)).

PREDICATE Width :

  String   % A string.
* Integer.   % The number of characters in this string.

DELAY   Width(x,_) UNTIL GROUND(x).

PREDICATE > : zPz :

  String   % A string lexically greater than the string in the
                   % second argument.
* String.   % A string.

DELAY   x > y UNTIL GROUND(x) & GROUND(y).

PREDICATE < : zPz :

  String   % A string lexically less than the string in the
                   % second argument.

```
* String.          % A string.

DELAY     x < y UNTIL GROUND(x) & GROUND(y).


PREDICATE  >= : zPz :

  String          % A string lexically greater than or equal to the
                  % string in the second argument.
* String.         % A string.

DELAY     x >= y UNTIL GROUND(x) & GROUND(y).


PREDICATE  =< : zPz :

  String          % A string lexically less than or equal to the string
                  % in the second argument.
* String.         % A string.

DELAY     x =< y UNTIL GROUND(x) & GROUND(y).
```

13.7   Numbers

EXPORT   Numbers.

% Module providing various conversion predicates for integer, rational,
% and floating-point numbers, and strings.

IMPORT   Rationals, Floats, Strings.

PREDICATE   RationalToFloat :

  Rational   % A rational.
 * Float.   % The floating-point number nearest the rational. In the
                % case of a value exactly half-way between two
                % neighbouring values in F, the one selected will be the
                % one with the least significant bit zero. If underflow
                % or overflow occurs, the computation will halt with an
                % error message.

DELAY   RationalToFloat(x,_) UNTIL GROUND(x).

PREDICATE   FloatToRational :

  Float   % A floating-point number.
 * Rational.   % The rational resulting from the exact conversion of
                % this floating-point number.

DELAY   FloatToRational(x,_) UNTIL GROUND(x).

PREDICATE   IntegerString :

  Integer   % An integer.
 * String.   % The string consisting of the characters in the
                % integer.

DELAY   IntegerString(x,y) UNTIL GROUND(x) \/ GROUND(y).

PREDICATE   RationalString :

  Rational   % A rational.
* String.   % The string consisting of the characters in the
                 % (standard form a/b of the) rational.

DELAY   RationalString(x,y) UNTIL GROUND(x) \/ GROUND(y).

PREDICATE   FloatString :

  Float   % A floating-point number.
* String.   % The string consisting of the characters in the
                 % standard form decimal representation of the
                 % floating-point number. (A decimal is in standard
                 % form if it is either 0 or has the form s0.d1...dnEe,
                 % where s is + or - and d1 ~= 0.)

DELAY   FloatString(x,y) UNTIL GROUND(x) \/ GROUND(y).

13.8 Tables

EXPORT   Tables.

% Module providing the abstract data type Table(t) and predicates
% for processing terms of type Table(t), for any type t. A term of
% type Table(t) represents a data structure consisting of an ordered
% collection of nodes, each of which has two components, a key which
% must be a string and a value which must be of type t. The ordering
% is given by the lexical ordering of the keys.

IMPORT   Strings.

CONSTRUCTOR   Table/1.

PREDICATE   EmptyTable :

  Table(a).   % An empty table.

PREDICATE   NodeInTable :

  Table(a)   % A table.
* String   % The key of a node in the table.
* a.   % The value in this node.

DELAY   NodeInTable(x,_,_) UNTIL NONVAR(x).

PREDICATE   InsertNode :

  Table(a)   % A table.
* String   % A key, not in this table.
* a   % A value.
* Table(a).   % A table which differs from the table in the
                         % first argument only in that it also contains a
                         % node with this key and value.

DELAY   InsertNode(x,y,_,_) UNTIL NONVAR(x) & GROUND(y).

```
PREDICATE    DeleteNode :

  Table(a)            % A table.
* String             % A key in this table.
* a                  % A value.
* Table(a).          % A table which differs from the table in the
                     % first argument only in that it does not contain
                     % a node with this key and value.

DELAY        DeleteNode(x,_,_,_) UNTIL NONVAR(x).

PREDICATE    UpdateTable :

  Table(a)            % A table.
* String             % The key of a node in the table.
* a                  % A new value to be associated with the key.
* Table(a)           % The table with the node updated.
* a.                 % The old value that was associated with the key.

DELAY        UpdateTable(x,y,_,_,_) UNTIL NONVAR(x) & GROUND(y).

PREDICATE    AmendTable :

  Table(a)            % A table.
* String             % A key.
* a                  % A (new) value to be associated with the key.
* a                  % A value (a default "old value").
* Table(a)           % The table updated so that the new value is
                     % associated with the key. (If the key is already
                     % present in the table, the associated value will
                     % be updated; otherwise the node with this key
                     % and value will be inserted into the table.)
* a.                 % The old value associated with the key if it was
                     % already present in the table, otherwise the
                     % value in the fourth argument.

DELAY        AmendTable(x,y,_,_,_,_) UNTIL NONVAR(x) & GROUND(y).
```

```
PREDICATE      JoinTables :

  Table(a)              % A table.
* Table(a)              % A table.
* Table(a).             % The table formed from the first argument by
                        % adding to it all the nodes in the second
                        % argument whose keys are not already present in
                        % the first argument.

DELAY          JoinTables(x,y,_) UNTIL NONVAR(x) & NONVAR(y).

PREDICATE      ListTable :

  Table(a)              % A table.
* List(String)          % The lexically ordered list of keys of nodes in
                        % the table.
* List(a).              % The corresponding list of values.

DELAY          ListTable(x,y,z) UNTIL NONVAR(x) \/
                                            (NONVAR(y) & NONVAR(z)).

PREDICATE      FirstNode :

  Table(a)              % A table.
* String                % The key of the node which is lexically first
                        % amongst all keys in the table.
* a.                    % The value in this node.

DELAY          FirstNode(x,_,_) UNTIL NONVAR(x).

PREDICATE      LastNode :

  Table(a)              % A table.
* String                % The key of the node which is lexically last
                        % amongst all keys in the table.
* a.                    % The value in this node.

DELAY          LastNode(x,_,_) UNTIL NONVAR(x).
```

```
PREDICATE     NextNode :

  Table(a)              % A table.
* String              % The key of a node in the table.
* String              % The key of the node which is the lexical
                      % successor of the key in the second argument.
* a.                  % The value in this node.

DELAY         NextNode(x,y,_,_) UNTIL NONVAR(x) & NONVAR(y).


PREDICATE     PreviousNode :

  Table(a)              % A table.
* String              % The key of a node in the table.
* String              % The key of the node which is the lexical
                      % predecessor of the key in the second argument.
* a.                  % The value in this node.

DELAY         PreviousNode(x,y,_,_) UNTIL NONVAR(x) & NONVAR(y).
```

13.9 Units

EXPORT   Units.

% Module providing the abstract data type Unit and predicates for
% processing terms of type Unit. A term of type Unit represents a
% unit which is a term-like structure.

IMPORT   Strings.

BASE   Unit.
%
% Type of a unit.

PREDICATE StringToUnit :

  String   % String representation of a unit.
* Unit.   % This unit.

DELAY   StringToUnit(x,_) UNTIL GROUND(x).

PREDICATE UnitToString :

  Unit   % A unit.
* String.   % String representation in a standard form of
                    % this unit.

DELAY   UnitToString(x,_) UNTIL GROUND(x).

PREDICATE UnitParts :

  Unit   % A unit.
* String   % String representation of the top-level identifier
                    % of this unit.
* List(Unit).   % List of top-level subunits of this unit. (The list
                    % is empty if the unit is just an identifier.)

```
PREDICATE  UnitArgument :

   Unit                % A unit.
 * Integer             % A positive integer n.
 * Unit.               % The nth top-level subunit of this unit.

DELAY      UnitArgument(x,_,_) UNTIL NONVAR(x).
```

13.10   Flocks

EXPORT   Flocks.

% Module providing the abstract data type Flock and predicates for
% processing terms of type Flock. A term of type Flock represents
% a flock which is an ordered collection of units.

IMPORT   Units.

BASE   Flock.
%
% Type of a flock.

PREDICATE   EmptyFlock :

   Flock.   % An empty flock.

PREDICATE   Extent :

   Flock   % A flock.
 * Integer.   % The number of units in this flock.

DELAY   Extent(x,_) UNTIL GROUND(x).

PREDICATE   UnitInFlock :

   Flock   % A flock.
 * Unit   % A unit in this flock.
 * Integer.   % Position of this unit in this flock.

DELAY   UnitInFlock(x,_,_) UNTIL GROUND(x).

```
PREDICATE  UnitWithIdentifier :

  Flock             % A flock.
* String            % String representation of an identifier.
* Unit              % A unit in this flock whose top-level identifier is
                    % the identifier in the second argument.
* Integer.          % Position of this unit in this flock.

DELAY      UnitWithIdentifier(x,_,_,_) UNTIL GROUND(x).


PREDICATE  InsertUnit :

  Flock             % A flock.
* Unit              % A unit.
* Integer           % A positive integer n.
* Flock.            % A flock which differs from the flock in the first
                    % argument only in that it also contains this unit in
                    % the nth position.

DELAY      InsertUnit(x,y,z,_) UNTIL GROUND(x) & GROUND(y) & GROUND(z).


PREDICATE  DeleteUnit :

  Flock             % A flock.
* Unit              % A unit in this flock.
* Integer           % The position of this unit in this flock.
* Flock.            % A flock which differs from the flock in the first
                    % argument only in that it does not contain this unit
                    % in this position.

DELAY      DeleteUnit(x,_,_,_) UNTIL GROUND(x).
```

13.11   Syntax

EXPORT   Syntax.

% Module providing a number of abstract data types for representing
% object-level expressions (using a ground representation) and
% predicates for processing terms of these types.

IMPORT   Strings.

BASE   Name,   % Type of a term representing the name of
                               % a symbol.
            Type,   % Type of a term representing a type.
            Term,   % Type of a term representing a term.
            Formula,   % Type of a term representing a formula.
            TypeSubst,   % Type of a term representing a type
                               % substitution.
            TermSubst,   % Type of a term representing a term
                               % substitution.
            FunctionInd,   % Type of a term representing a function
                               % indicator.
            PredicateInd,   % Type of a term representing a predicate
                               % indicator.
            VarTyping.   % Type of a term representing a variable
                               % typing.

CONSTANT   NoPredInd : PredicateInd.
%
% Constant stating that a predicate has no indicator.

CONSTANT   ZPZ, ZP, PZ : PredicateInd.
%
% Constants representing the predicate indicators zPz, zP, and Pz
% (resp.).

CONSTANT   NoFunctInd : FunctionInd.

```
%
% Constant stating that a function has no indicator.

FUNCTION   XFX, XFY, YFX, XF, FX, YF, FY : Integer -> FunctionInd.
%
% Functions representing the function indicators xFx, xFy, yFx, xF, Fx,
% yF, and Fy (resp.).


PREDICATE  And :

   Formula          % Representation of a formula W.
 * Formula          % Representation of a formula V.
 * Formula.         % Representation of the formula  W & V.


PREDICATE  AndWithEmpty :

   Formula          % Representation of possibly empty formula W.
 * Formula          % Representation of possibly empty formula V.
 * Formula.         % Representation of W & V, if W and V are non-empty;
                    % W, if V is the empty formula; and V, if W is the
                    % empty formula.

DELAY      AndWithEmpty(x,y,_) UNTIL GROUND(x) & GROUND(y).


PREDICATE  Or :

   Formula          % Representation of a formula W.
 * Formula          % Representation of a formula V.
 * Formula.         % Representation of the formula W \/ V.


PREDICATE  Not :

   Formula          % Representation of a formula W.
 * Formula.         % Representation of the formula ~ W.
```

PREDICATE Implies :

```
  Formula           % Representation of a formula W.
* Formula           % Representation of a formula V.
* Formula.          % Representation of the formula W -> V.
```

PREDICATE IsImpliedBy :

```
  Formula           % Representation of a formula W.
* Formula           % Representation of a formula V.
* Formula.          % Representation of the formula W <- V.
```

PREDICATE Equivalent :

```
  Formula           % Representation of a formula W.
* Formula           % Representation of a formula V.
* Formula.          % Representation of the formula W <-> V.
```

PREDICATE Some :

```
  List(Term)        % List of representations of variables.
* Formula           % Representation of a formula.
* Formula.          % Representation of the formula obtained by taking
                    % the existential quantification over the set of
                    % variables in the first argument of the formula in
                    % the second argument.
```

PREDICATE All :

```
  List(Term)        % List of representations of variables.
* Formula           % Representation of a formula.
* Formula.          % Representation of the formula obtained by taking
                    % the universal quantification over the set of
                    % variables in the first argument of the formula in
                    % the second argument.
```

PREDICATE   IfThen :

```
   Formula          % Representation of a formula, Condition.
 * Formula          % Representation of a formula, Formula.
 * Formula.         % Representation of the IF-THEN construct which has
                    % the form IF Condition THEN Formula.
```

PREDICATE   IfSomeThen :

```
   List(Term)       % List of representations of variables, v1,...,vn.
 * Formula          % Representation of a formula, Condition.
 * Formula          % Representation of a formula, Formula.
 * Formula.         % Representation of the IF-THEN construct which has
                    % the form IF SOME [v1,...,vn] Condition THEN Formula.
```

PREDICATE   IfThenElse :

```
   Formula          % Representation of a formula, Condition.
 * Formula          % Representation of a formula, Formula1.
 * Formula          % Representation of a formula, Formula2.
 * Formula.         % Representation of the IF-THEN-ELSE construct which
                    % has the form IF Condition THEN Formula1 ELSE
                    % Formula2.
```

PREDICATE   IfSomeThenElse :

```
   List(Term)       % List of representations of variables, v1,...,vn.
 * Formula          % Representation of a formula, Condition.
 * Formula          % Representation of a formula, Formula1.
 * Formula          % Representation of a formula, Formula2.
 * Formula.         % Representation of the IF-THEN-ELSE construct which
                    % has the form IF SOME [v1,...,vn] Condition THEN
                    % Formula1 ELSE Formula2.
```

PREDICATE   Commit :

```
  Integer             % Commit label.
* Formula             % Representation of a formula.
* Formula.            % Representation of the formula obtained by enclosing
                      % the formula in the second argument using a commit
                      % with this label.
```

PREDICATE IntensionalSet :

```
  Term                % Representation of a term T.
* Formula             % Representation of a formula W.
* Term.               % Representation of the intensional set term {T : W}.
```

PREDICATE Parameter :

```
  Type.               % Representation of a parameter.
```

DELAY   Parameter(x) UNTIL GROUND(x).

PREDICATE ParameterName :

```
  Type                % Representation of a parameter.
* String              % The root of the name of the parameter.
* Integer.            % The index of the parameter.
```

PREDICATE TypeMaxParIndex :

```
  List(Type)          % List of representations of types.
* Integer.            % One more than the maximum index of parameters
                      % appearing in these types. (If there are no such
                      % parameters, this argument is 0.)
```

DELAY   TypeMaxParIndex(x,_) UNTIL GROUND(x).

PREDICATE Variable :

```
  Term.               % Representation of a variable.
```

DELAY   Variable(x) UNTIL GROUND(x).

PREDICATE   VariableName :

  Term   % Representation of a variable.
* String   % The root of the name of the variable.
* Integer.   % The index of the variable.

PREDICATE   TermMaxVarIndex :

  List(Term)   % List of representations of terms.
* Integer.   % One more than the maximum index of variables
                   % appearing in these terms. (If there are no such
                   % variables, this argument is 0.)

DELAY   TermMaxVarIndex(x,_) UNTIL GROUND(x).

PREDICATE   FormulaMaxVarIndex :

  List(Formula)   % List of representations of formulas.
* Integer.   % One more than the maximum index of variables
                   % appearing in these formulas. (If there are no such
                   % variables, this argument is 0.)

DELAY   FormulaMaxVarIndex(x,_) UNTIL GROUND(x).

PREDICATE   TypeParameters :

  Type   % Representation of a type.
* List(Type).   % List (in some order) of the representations of the
                   % parameters occurring in this type.

DELAY   TypeParameters(x,_) UNTIL GROUND(x).

PREDICATE   TermVariables :

  Term   % Representation of a term.
* List(Term).   % List (in some order) of the representations of the

```
                      % (free) variables occurring in this term.

DELAY       TermVariables(x,_) UNTIL GROUND(x).


PREDICATE  FormulaVariables :

  Formula           % Representation of a formula.
* List(Term).       % List (in some order) of the representations of the
                    % free variables occurring in this formula.

DELAY       FormulaVariables(x,_) UNTIL GROUND(x).


PREDICATE  EmptyFormula :

  Formula.          % Representation of the empty formula.


PREDICATE  EmptyTypeSubst :

  TypeSubst.        % Representation of the empty type substitution.


PREDICATE  EmptyTermSubst :

  TermSubst.        % Representation of the empty term substitution.


PREDICATE  EmptyVarTyping :

  VarTyping.        % Representation of the empty variable typing.


PREDICATE  NonParameter :

  Type.             % Representation of a non-parameter type.

DELAY       NonParameter(x) UNTIL GROUND(x).
```

```
PREDICATE  NonVariable :

  Term.           % Representation of a non-variable term.

DELAY      NonVariable(x) UNTIL GROUND(x).


PREDICATE  Atom :

  Formula.        % Representation of an atom.

DELAY      Atom(x) UNTIL GROUND(x).


PREDICATE  ConjunctionOfAtoms :

  Formula.        % Representation of a conjunction of atoms.

DELAY      ConjunctionOfAtoms(x) UNTIL GROUND(x).


PREDICATE  Literal :

  Formula.        % Representation of a literal.

DELAY      Literal(x) UNTIL GROUND(x).


PREDICATE  ConjunctionOfLiterals :

  Formula.        % Representation of a conjunction of literals.

DELAY      ConjunctionOfLiterals(x) UNTIL GROUND(x).


PREDICATE  CommitFreeFormula :

  Formula.        % Representation of a commit-free formula.

DELAY      CommitFreeFormula(x) UNTIL GROUND(x).
```

PREDICATE GroundType :

  Type.   % Representation of a parameter-free type.

DELAY   GroundType(x) UNTIL GROUND(x).

PREDICATE GroundTerm :

  Term.   % Representation of a term with no free variables.

DELAY   GroundTerm(x) UNTIL GROUND(x).

PREDICATE GroundAtom :

  Formula.   % Representation of an atom with no free variables.

DELAY   GroundAtom(x) UNTIL GROUND(x).

PREDICATE ClosedFormula :

  Formula.   % Representation of a formula with no free variables.

DELAY   ClosedFormula(x) UNTIL GROUND(x).

PREDICATE Body :

  Formula.   % Representation of a standard body.

DELAY   Body(x) UNTIL GROUND(x).

PREDICATE NormalBody :

  Formula.   % Representation of a normal body.

DELAY   NormalBody(x) UNTIL GROUND(x).

```
PREDICATE  DefiniteBody :

  Formula.        % Representation of a definite body.

DELAY      DefiniteBody(x) UNTIL GROUND(x).


PREDICATE  Goal :

  Formula.        % Representation of a standard goal.

DELAY      Goal(x) UNTIL GROUND(x).


PREDICATE  NormalGoal :

  Formula.        % Representation of a normal goal.

DELAY      NormalGoal(x) UNTIL GROUND(x).


PREDICATE  DefiniteGoal :

  Formula.        % Representation of a definite goal.

DELAY      DefiniteGoal(x) UNTIL GROUND(x).


PREDICATE  Resultant :

  Formula.        % Representation of a standard resultant.

DELAY      Resultant(x) UNTIL GROUND(x).


PREDICATE  NormalResultant :

  Formula.        % Representation of a normal resultant.

DELAY      NormalResultant(x) UNTIL GROUND(x).
```

```
PREDICATE  DefiniteResultant :

  Formula.         % Representation of a definite resultant.

DELAY      DefiniteResultant(x) UNTIL GROUND(x).

PREDICATE  Statement :

  Formula.         % Representation of a standard statement.

DELAY      Statement(x) UNTIL GROUND(x).

PREDICATE  NormalStatement :

  Formula.         % Representation of a normal statement.

DELAY      NormalStatement(x) UNTIL GROUND(x).

PREDICATE  DefiniteStatement :

  Formula.         % Representation of a definite statement.

DELAY      DefiniteStatement(x) UNTIL GROUND(x).

PREDICATE  BaseType :

  Type             % Representation of a non-opaque base.
* Name.            % Representation of the name of this base.

PREDICATE  ConstructorType :

  Type             % Representation of a non-opaque type with a
                   % constructor at the top level.
* Name             % Representation of the name of this constructor.
* List(Type).      % List of representations of the top-level subtypes
                   % of this type.
```

PREDICATE ConstantTerm :

  Term   % Representation of a non-opaque constant.
* Name.   % Representation of the name of this constant.

PREDICATE FunctionTerm :

  Term   % Representation of a non-opaque term with a function
                   % at the top level.
* Name   % Representation of the name of this function.
* List(Term).   % List of representations of the top-level subterms
                   % of this term.

PREDICATE PropositionAtom :

  Formula   % Representation of a non-opaque proposition.
* Name.   % Representation of the name of this proposition.

PREDICATE PredicateAtom :

  Formula   % Representation of a non-opaque atom with a predicate
                   % at the top level.
* Name   % Representation of the name of this predicate.
* List(Term).   % List of representations of the top-level terms of
                   % this atom.

PREDICATE OpaqueType :

  Type.   % Representation of an opaque type.

DELAY   OpaqueType(x) UNTIL GROUND(x).

PREDICATE OpaqueTerm :

  Term.   % Representation of an opaque term.

DELAY   OpaqueTerm(x) UNTIL GROUND(x).

```
PREDICATE  OpaqueAtom :

  Formula.        % Representation of an opaque atom.

DELAY      OpaqueAtom(x) UNTIL GROUND(x).


PREDICATE  ApplySubstToType :

  Type            % Representation of a type.
* TypeSubst       % Representation of a type substitution.
* Type.           % Representation of the type obtained by applying
                  % this substitution to this type.

DELAY      ApplySubstToType(x,y,_) UNTIL GROUND(x) & GROUND(y).


PREDICATE  ApplySubstToTerm :

  Term            % Representation of a term.
* TermSubst       % Representation of a term substitution.
* Term.           % Representation of the term obtained by applying
                  % this substitution to this term.

DELAY      ApplySubstToTerm(x,y,_) UNTIL GROUND(x) & GROUND(y).


PREDICATE  ApplySubstToFormula :

  Formula         % Representation of a formula.
* TermSubst       % Representation of a term substitution.
* Formula.        % Representation of the formula obtained by applying
                  % this substitution to this formula.

DELAY      ApplySubstToFormula(x,y,_) UNTIL GROUND(x) & GROUND(y).


PREDICATE  ComposeTypeSubsts :

  TypeSubst       % Representation of a type substitution.
```

```
* TypeSubst        % Representation of a type substitution.
* TypeSubst.       % Representation of the substitution obtained by
                   % composing these two substitutions (in the order
                   % that they appear as arguments).

DELAY       ComposeTypeSubsts(x,y,_) UNTIL GROUND(x) & GROUND(y).


PREDICATE   ComposeTermSubsts :

  TermSubst        % Representation of a term substitution.
* TermSubst        % Representation of a term substitution.
* TermSubst.       % Representation of the substitution obtained by
                   % composing these two substitutions (in the order
                   % that they appear as arguments).

DELAY       ComposeTermSubsts(x,y,_) UNTIL GROUND(x) & GROUND(y).


PREDICATE   CombineVarTypings :

  VarTyping        % Representation of a variable typing.
* VarTyping        % Representation of a variable typing.
* VarTyping.       % Representation of the variable typing obtained by
                   % combining these two variable typings.

DELAY       CombineVarTypings(x,y,_) UNTIL GROUND(x) & GROUND(y).


PREDICATE   RestrictSubstToType :

  Type             % Representation of a type.
* TypeSubst        % Representation of a type substitution.
* TypeSubst.       % Representation of the substitution obtained by
                   % restricting this type substitution to the
                   % parameters in this type.

DELAY       RestrictSubstToType(x,y,_) UNTIL GROUND(x) & GROUND(y).
```

PREDICATE RestrictSubstToTerm :

  Term   % Representation of a term.
* TermSubst   % Representation of a term substitution.
* TermSubst.   % Representation of the substitution obtained by
                  % restricting this term substitution to the variables
                  % in this term.

DELAY   RestrictSubstToTerm(x,y,_) UNTIL GROUND(x) & GROUND(y).

PREDICATE RestrictSubstToFormula :

  Formula   % Representation of a formula.
* TermSubst   % Representation of a term substitution.
* TermSubst.   % Representation of the substitution obtained by
                  % restricting this term substitution to the free
                  % variables in this formula.

DELAY   RestrictSubstToFormula(x,y,_) UNTIL GROUND(x) & GROUND(y).

PREDICATE BindingToTypeSubst :

  Type   % Representation of a parameter.
* Type   % Representation of a type.
* TypeSubst.   % Representation of the type substitution containing
                  % just the binding in which this parameter is bound
                  % to this type.

DELAY   BindingToTypeSubst(x,y,_) UNTIL GROUND(x) & GROUND(y).

PREDICATE BindingToTermSubst :

  Term   % Representation of a variable.
* Term   % Representation of a term.
* TermSubst.   % Representation of the term substitution containing
                  % just the binding in which this variable is bound
                  % to this term.

```
DELAY       BindingToTermSubst(x,y,_) UNTIL GROUND(x) & GROUND(y).


PREDICATE  BindingToVarTyping :

  Term              % Representation of a variable.
* Type              % Representation of a type.
* VarTyping.        % Representation of the variable typing containing
                    % just the binding in which this variable is bound
                    % to this type.

DELAY       BindingToVarTyping(x,y,_) UNTIL GROUND(x) & GROUND(y).


PREDICATE  BindingInTypeSubst :

  TypeSubst         % Representation of a type substitution.
* Type              % Representation of a parameter in the first
                    % component of a binding in this substitution.
* Type.             % Representation of the type to which this parameter
                    % is bound in this substitution.

DELAY       BindingInTypeSubst(x,_,_) UNTIL GROUND(x).


PREDICATE  BindingInTermSubst :

  TermSubst         % Representation of a term substitution.
* Term              % Representation of a variable in the first
                    % component of a binding in this substitution.
* Term.             % Representation of the term to which this variable
                    % is bound in this substitution.

DELAY       BindingInTermSubst(x,_,_) UNTIL GROUND(x).


PREDICATE  BindingInVarTyping :

  VarTyping         % Representation of a variable typing.
```

```
* Term               % Representation of a variable in a binding in
                     % this variable typing.
* Type.              % Representation of the type to which this variable
                     % is bound in this variable typing.

DELAY      BindingInVarTyping(x,_,_) UNTIL GROUND(x).


PREDICATE  DelBindingInTypeSubst :

  TypeSubst          % Representation of a type substitution.
* Type               % Representation of a parameter.
* Type               % Representation of a type.
* TypeSubst.         % Representation of the type substitution obtained
                     % from the first argument by deleting the binding of
                     % this parameter to this type.

DELAY      DelBindingInTypeSubst(x,_,_,_) UNTIL GROUND(x).


PREDICATE  DelBindingInTermSubst :

  TermSubst          % Representation of a term substitution.
* Term               % Representation of a variable.
* Term               % Representation of a term.
* TermSubst.         % Representation of the term substitution obtained
                     % from the first argument by deleting the binding of
                     % this variable to this term.

DELAY      DelBindingInTermSubst(x,_,_,_) UNTIL GROUND(x).


PREDICATE  DelBindingInVarTyping :

  VarTyping          % Representation of a variable typing.
* Term               % Representation of a variable.
* Type               % Representation of a type.
* VarTyping.         % Representation of the variable typing obtained
                     % from the first argument by deleting the binding
                     % of this variable to this type.
```

```
DELAY      DelBindingInVarTyping(x,_,_,_) UNTIL GROUND(x).
```

PREDICATE UnifyTypes :

  Type   % Representation of a type.
* Type   % Representation of a type.
* TypeSubst   % Representation of a type substitution.
* TypeSubst.   % Representation of the type substitution obtained by
                    % composing the type substitution in the third
                    % argument with a specific, unique mgu for the types
                    % which are obtained by applying the type substitution
                    % in the third argument to the types in the first two
                    % arguments. (The mgu binds a parameter in the first
                    % argument to a parameter in the second argument, not
                    % the other way around.)

```
DELAY      UnifyTypes(x,y,z,_) UNTIL GROUND(x) & GROUND(y) & GROUND(z).
```

PREDICATE UnifyTerms :

  Term   % Representation of a term.
* Term   % Representation of a term.
* TermSubst   % Representation of a term substitution.
* TermSubst.   % Representation of the term substitution obtained by
                    % composing the term substitution in the third
                    % argument with a specific, unique mgu for the terms
                    % which are obtained by applying the term substitution
                    % in the third argument to the terms in the first two
                    % arguments. (The mgu binds a variable in the first
                    % argument to a variable in the second argument, not
                    % the other way around.)

```
DELAY      UnifyTerms(x,y,z,_) UNTIL GROUND(x) & GROUND(y) & GROUND(z).
```

PREDICATE UnifyAtoms :

```
   Formula            % Representation of an atom.
 * Formula            % Representation of an atom.
 * TermSubst          % Representation of a term substitution.
 * TermSubst.         % Representation of the term substitution obtained by
                      % composing the term substitution in the third
                      % argument with a specific, unique mgu for the atoms
                      % which are obtained by applying the term substitution
                      % in the third argument to the atoms in the first two
                      % arguments. (The mgu binds a variable in the first
                      % argument to a variable in the second argument, not
                      % the other way around.)

 DELAY        UnifyAtoms(x,y,z,_) UNTIL GROUND(x) & GROUND(y) & GROUND(z).


 PREDICATE    RenameTypes :

   List(Type)         % List of representations of types.
 * List(Type)         % List of representations of types.
 * List(Type).        % List of representations of the types obtained by
                      % renaming the parameters of the types in the second
                      % argument by a specific, unique type substitution
                      % such that they become distinct from the parameters
                      % in the types in the first argument.

 DELAY        RenameTypes(x,y,_) UNTIL GROUND(x) & GROUND(y).


 PREDICATE    RenameTerms :

   List(Term)         % List of representations of terms.
 * List(Term)         % List of representations of terms.
 * List(Term).        % List of representations of the terms obtained by
                      % renaming the (free) variables of the terms in the
                      % second argument by a specific, unique term
                      % substitution such that they become distinct from
                      % the (free) variables in the terms in the first
                      % argument.

 DELAY        RenameTerms(x,y,_) UNTIL GROUND(x) & GROUND(y).
```

PREDICATE   RenameFormulas :

  List(Formula)   % List of representations of formulas.
* List(Formula)   % List of representations of formulas.
* List(Formula).   % List of representations of the formulas obtained
                    % by renaming the free variables of the formulas in
                    % the second argument by a specific, unique term
                    % substitution such that they become distinct from
                    % the free variables in the formulas in the first
                    % argument.

DELAY   RenameFormulas(x,y,_) UNTIL GROUND(x) & GROUND(y).

PREDICATE   VariantTypes :

  List(Type)   % List of representation of types.
* List(Type).   % List of representations of types which are variants
                    % of the types in the first argument.

DELAY   VariantTypes(x,y) UNTIL GROUND(x) & GROUND(y).

PREDICATE   VariantTerms :

  List(Term)   % List of representation of terms.
* List(Term).   % List of representations of terms which are variants
                    % of the terms in the first argument.

DELAY   VariantTerms(x,y) UNTIL GROUND(x) & GROUND(y).

PREDICATE   VariantFormulas :

  List(Formula)   % List of representations of formulas.
* List(Formula).   % List of representations of formulas which are
                    % variants of the formulas in the first argument.

DELAY   VariantFormulas(x,y) UNTIL GROUND(x) & GROUND(y).

PREDICATE   StandardiseFormula :

   Formula   % Representation of a formula.
 * Integer   % A non-negative integer.
 * Integer   % A non-negative integer.
 * Formula.   % Representation of the formula obtained by
                   % systematically replacing the variables of the
                   % formula in the first argument by variables with
                   % indexes greater than or equal to the second
                   % argument and strictly less than the third argument.

DELAY   StandardiseFormula(x,y,_,_) UNTIL GROUND(x) & GROUND(y).

PREDICATE   Derive :

   Formula   % Representation of the head of a resultant.
 * Formula   % Representation of the body to the left of the
                   % selected atom of this resultant.
 * Formula   % Representation of the selected atom in this
                   % resultant.
 * Formula   % Representation of the body to the right of the
                   % selected atom of this resultant.
 * Formula   % Representation of a statement whose head unifies
                   % with the selected atom in the resultant.
 * TermSubst   % Representation of a specific, unique mgu of the
                   % head of the selected atom and the head of this
                   % statement. (The mgu binds a variable in the head to
                   % a variable in the selected atom, not the other way
                   % around.)
 * Formula.   % Representation of the derived resultant obtained
                   % from this resultant and this statement using this
                   % mgu.

DELAY   Derive(x,y,z,u,v,_,_) UNTIL GROUND(x) & GROUND(y) &
                                        GROUND(z) & GROUND(u) & GROUND(v).

PREDICATE   Resolve :

```
   Formula            % Representation of an atom.
 * Formula            % Representation of a statement.
 * Integer            % A non-negative integer.
 * Integer            % A non-negative integer.
 * TermSubst          % Representation of a term substitution.
 * TermSubst          % Representation of the substitution obtained by
                      % composing the substitution in the fifth argument
                      % with a specific, unique mgu of the atom in the
                      % first argument with the substitution in the fifth
                      % argument applied and the head of a renamed version
                      % of the statement in the second argument. The
                      % renaming is achieved by systematically replacing
                      % the variables of the statement by variables with
                      % indexes greater than or equal to the third argument
                      % and strictly less than the fourth argument. (The
                      % mgu binds a variable in the head to a variable in
                      % the atom in the first argument with the substitution
                      % applied, not the other way around.)
 * Formula.           % Representation of the formula obtained by applying
                      % the mgu in the sixth argument to the body of the
                      % renamed statement.

DELAY     Resolve(x,y,z,_,u,_,_) UNTIL GROUND(x) & GROUND(y) &
                                          GROUND(z) & GROUND(u).


PREDICATE  ResolveAll :

   Formula            % Representation of an atom.
 * List(Formula)      % List of representations of statements.
 * Integer            % A non-negative integer.
 * Integer            % A non-negative integer.
 * Integer            % A non-negative integer.
 * Integer            % A non-negative integer.
 * TermSubst          % Representation of a term substitution.
 * List(TermSubst)    % List of representations of the substitutions
                      % obtained by composing the substitution in the
                      % seventh argument with a specific, unique mgu of the
```

```
                  % atom in the first argument with the substitution in
                  % the seventh argument applied and the head of a
                  % renamed version of a corresponding statement in the
                  % second argument. The renaming is achieved by
                  % systematically replacing the variables of the
                  % statement by variables with indexes greater than or
                  % equal to the third argument and strictly less than
                  % the fourth argument, and commit labels of the
                  % statement by commit labels greater than or equal
                  % to the fifth argument and strictly less than the
                  % sixth argument. (Each mgu binds a variable in the
                  % head to a variable in the atom in the first
                  % argument with the substitution applied, not the
                  % other way around.)
* List(Formula).  % List of representations of the formulas obtained by
                  % applying the corresponding mgu in the eighth
                  % argument to the body of the corresponding renamed
                  % statement.

DELAY      ResolveAll(x,y,z,_,u,_,v,_,_) UNTIL GROUND(x) & GROUND(y) &
                                    GROUND(z) & GROUND(u) & GROUND(v).
```

13.12   Programs

EXPORT   Programs.

% Module providing the abstract data type Program for representing
% Goedel programs (using a ground representation) and predicates for
% processing terms of type Program.

IMPORT   Syntax.

BASE   Program,   % Type of a term representing (the flat form
                           % of) a program.
           ModulePart,   % Type of constants representing the keywords
                           % EXPORT, LOCAL, CLOSED, and MODULE.
           Condition.   % Type of a term representing a condition
                           % in a DELAY declaration.

CONSTANT   Export, Local, Closed, Module : ModulePart.
%
% Constants representing the keywords EXPORT, LOCAL, CLOSED, and MODULE
% (resp.).

PREDICATE TypeInProgram :

   Program   % Representation of a program.
 * Type.   % Representation of a type in the flat language of
                   % this program.

DELAY   TypeInProgram(x,y) UNTIL GROUND(x) & GROUND(y).

PREDICATE TermInProgram :

   Program   % Representation of a program.
 * VarTyping   % Representation of a variable typing in the flat
                   % language of this program.
 * Term   % Representation of a term in the flat language of

	% this program.
* Type	% Representation of the type of this term with respect
	% to this variable typing.
* VarTyping.	% Representation of the variable typing obtained by
	% combining the variable typing in the second argument
	% with the types of all free variables occurring in the
	% term.

DELAY   TermInProgram(x,y,z,_,_) UNTIL GROUND(x) & GROUND(y) &
                                                        GROUND(z).

PREDICATE   FormulaInProgram :

Program	% Representation of a program.
* VarTyping	% Representation of a variable typing in the flat
	% language of this program.
* Formula	% Representation of a formula, which is a standard
	% body or standard resultant, in the flat language of
	% this program.
* VarTyping.	% Representation of the variable typing obtained by
	% combining the variable typing in the second argument
	% with the types of all free variables occurring in
	% the formula.

DELAY   FormulaInProgram(x,y,z,_) UNTIL GROUND(x) & GROUND(y) &
                                                        GROUND(z).

PREDICATE   TypeInModule :

Program	% Representation of a program.
* String	% Name of a module in this program.
* ModulePart	% Representation of a part keyword of this module.
* Type.	% Representation of a type in the flat language of
	% this module, if the keyword is LOCAL or MODULE, or
	% the flat export language of this module, if the
	% keyword is EXPORT or CLOSED.

```
DELAY       TypeInModule(x,y,z,u) UNTIL GROUND(x) & GROUND(y) &
                                        GROUND(z) & GROUND(u).
```

PREDICATE TermInModule :

```
  Program        % Representation of a program.
* String         % Name of a module in this program.
* ModulePart     % Representation of a part keyword of this module.
* VarTyping      % Representation of a variable typing in the flat
                 % language of this module, if the keyword is LOCAL or
                 % MODULE, or the flat export language of this module,
                 % if the keyword is EXPORT or CLOSED.
* Term           % Representation of a term in the flat language of
                 % this module, if the keyword is LOCAL or MODULE, or
                 % the flat export language of this module, if the
                 % keyword is EXPORT or CLOSED.
* Type           % Representation of the type of this term with
                 % respect to this variable typing.
* VarTyping.     % Representation of the variable typing obtained by
                 % combining the variable typing in the fifth argument
                 % with the types of all variables occurring in the
                 % term.
```

```
DELAY       TermInModule(x,y,z,u,v,_,_) UNTIL GROUND(x) & GROUND(y) &
                               GROUND(z) & GROUND(u) & GROUND(v).
```

PREDICATE FormulaInModule :

```
  Program        % Representation of a program.
* String         % Name of a module in this program.
* ModulePart     % Representation of a part keyword of this module.
* VarTyping      % Representation of a variable typing in the flat
                 % language of this module, if the keyword is LOCAL
                 % or MODULE, or the flat export language of this
                 % module, if the keyword is EXPORT or CLOSED.
* Formula        % Representation of a formula, which is a standard body
                 % or standard resultant, in the flat language of this
```

```
                         % module, if the keyword is LOCAL or MODULE, or the
                         % flat export language of this module, if the keyword
                         % is EXPORT or CLOSED.
* VarTyping.             % Representation of the variable typing obtained by
                         % combining the variable typing in the fourth argument
                         % with the types of all free variables occurring in
                         % the formula.

DELAY      FormulaInModule(x,y,z,u,v,_) UNTIL GROUND(x) & GROUND(y) &
                                        GROUND(z) & GROUND(u) & GROUND(v).


PREDICATE  StringToProgramType :

  Program                % Representation of a program.
* String                 % Name of a module in this program.
* String                 % A string.
* List(Type).            % List (in a definite order) of representations of
                         % types in the flat language of this module wrt this
                         % program whose string representation is the third
                         % argument.

DELAY      StringToProgramType(x,y,z,_) UNTIL GROUND(x) & GROUND(y) &
                                        GROUND(z).


PREDICATE  StringToProgramTerm :

  Program                % Representation of a program.
* String                 % Name of a module in this program.
* String                 % A string.
* List(Term).            % List (in a definite order) of representations of
                         % terms in the flat language of this module wrt this
                         % program whose string representation is the third
                         % argument.

DELAY      StringToProgramTerm(x,y,z,_) UNTIL GROUND(x) & GROUND(y) &
                                        GROUND(z).
```

PREDICATE StringToProgramFormula :

  Program   % Representation of a program.
* String   % Name of a module in this program.
* String   % A string.
* List(Formula).   % List (in a definite order) of representations of
                   % formulas, which are standard bodies or standard
                   % resultants, in the flat language of this module wrt
                   % this program whose string representation is the
                   % third argument.

DELAY   StringToProgramFormula(x,y,z,_) UNTIL GROUND(x) & GROUND(y) &
                                                   GROUND(z).

PREDICATE ProgramTypeToString :

  Program   % Representation of a program.
* String   % Name of a module in this program.
* Type   % Representation of a type.
* String.   % The string representation of this type. (Subtypes
                   % of the type not in the flat language of the module
                   % do not appear.)

DELAY   ProgramTypeToString(x,y,z,_) UNTIL GROUND(x) & GROUND(y) &
                                                 GROUND(z).

PREDICATE ProgramTermToString :

  Program   % Representation of a program.
* String   % Name of a module in this program.
* Term   % Representation of a term.
* String.   % The string representation of this term. (Subterms
                   % of the term not in the flat language of the module
                   % do not appear.)

DELAY   ProgramTermToString(x,y,z,_) UNTIL GROUND(x) & GROUND(y) &
                                                 GROUND(z).

PREDICATE   ProgramFormulaToString :

  Program   % Representation of a program.
* String   % Name of a module in this program.
* Formula   % Representation of a formula, which is a standard
                   % body or standard resultant.
* String.   % The string representation of this formula. (Terms
                   % of the formula not in the flat language of the
                   % module do not appear.)

DELAY   ProgramFormulaToString(x,y,z,_) UNTIL GROUND(x) & GROUND(y) &
                                                              GROUND(z).

PREDICATE   ProgramBaseName :

  Program   % Representation of a program.
* String   % Name of a module in this program.
* String   % Name of a base.
* Name.   % Representation of the corresponding flat name of
                   % this base.

DELAY   ProgramBaseName(x,y,z,u) UNTIL GROUND(x) &
                             ((GROUND(y) & GROUND(z)) \/ GROUND(u)).

PREDICATE   ProgramConstructorName :

  Program   % Representation of a program.
* String   % Name of a module in this program.
* String   % Name of a constructor.
* Integer   % Arity of this constructor.
* Name.   % Representation of the corresponding flat name of
                   % this constructor.

DELAY   ProgramConstructorName(x,y,z,u,v) UNTIL GROUND(x) &
                      ((GROUND(y) & GROUND(z) & GROUND(u)) \/ GROUND(v)).

```
PREDICATE  ProgramConstantName :

   Program          % Representation of a program.
 * String          % Name of a module in this program.
 * String          % Name of a constant.
 * Name.            % Representation of the corresponding flat name of
                    % this constant.

DELAY      ProgramConstantName(x,y,z,u) UNTIL GROUND(x) &
                                ((GROUND(y) & GROUND(z)) \/ GROUND(u)).


PREDICATE  ProgramFunctionName :

   Program          % Representation of a program.
 * String          % Name of a module in this program.
 * String          % Name of a function.
 * Integer         % Arity of this function.
 * Name.            % Representation of the corresponding flat name of
                    % this function.

DELAY      ProgramFunctionName(x,y,z,u,v) UNTIL GROUND(x) &
                    ((GROUND(y) & GROUND(z) & GROUND(u)) \/ GROUND(v)).


PREDICATE  ProgramPropositionName :

   Program          % Representation of a program.
 * String          % Name of a module in this program.
 * String          % Name of a proposition.
 * Name.            % Representation of the corresponding flat name of
                    % this proposition.

DELAY      ProgramPropositionName(x,y,z,u) UNTIL GROUND(x) &
                                ((GROUND(y) & GROUND(z)) \/ GROUND(u)).


PREDICATE  ProgramPredicateName :

   Program          % Representation of a program.
```

```
* String          % Name of a module in this program.
* String          % Name of a predicate.
* Integer         % Arity of this predicate.
* Name.           % Representation of the corresponding flat name of
                  % this predicate.

DELAY      ProgramPredicateName(x,y,z,u,v) UNTIL GROUND(x) &
                 ((GROUND(y) & GROUND(z) & GROUND(u)) \/ GROUND(v)).


PREDICATE  MainModuleInProgram :

  Program         % Representation of a program.
* String.         % Name of the main module in this program.

DELAY      MainModuleInProgram(x,_) UNTIL GROUND(x).


PREDICATE  ModuleInProgram :

  Program         % Representation of a program.
* String.         % Name of a module in this program.

DELAY      ModuleInProgram(x,_) UNTIL GROUND(x).


PREDICATE  OpenModule :

  Program         % Representation of a program.
* String.         % Name of an open module in this program.

DELAY      OpenModule(x,_) UNTIL GROUND(x).


PREDICATE  DeclaredInOpenModule :

  Program         % Representation of a program.
* String          % Name of an open module in this program.
* Formula.        % Representation of an atom in the flat language
                  % of this program whose proposition or predicate is
```

```
                    % declared in this module.

DELAY       DeclaredInOpenModule(x,_,z) UNTIL GROUND(x) & GROUND(z).


PREDICATE   DeclaredInClosedModule :

   Program            % Representation of a program.
 * String             % Name of a closed module in this program.
 * Formula.            % Representation of an atom in the flat language of
                       % this program whose proposition or predicate is
                       % declared in the export part of this module.

DELAY       DeclaredInClosedModule(x,_,z) UNTIL GROUND(x) & GROUND(z).


PREDICATE   StatementInModule :

   Program            % Representation of a program.
 * String             % Name of an open module in this program.
 * Formula.            % Representation of a statement in this module.

DELAY       StatementInModule(x,_,_) UNTIL GROUND(x).


PREDICATE   StatementMatchAtom :

   Program            % Representation of a program.
 * String             % Name of an open module in this program.
 * Formula             % Representation of an atom in the flat language of
                       % this program.
 * Formula.            % Representation of a statement in this module whose
                       % proposition or predicate in the head is the same
                       % as the proposition or predicate in this atom.

DELAY       StatementMatchAtom(x,_,z,_) UNTIL GROUND(x) & GROUND(z).


PREDICATE   DefinitionInProgram :
```

```
   Program            % Representation of a program.
 * String             % Name of an open module in this program.
 * Name               % Representation of the flat name of a proposition
                      % or predicate declared in this module.
 * List(Formula).     % List (in a definite order) of representations of
                      % statements in the definition of this proposition
                      % or predicate.

DELAY      DefinitionInProgram(x,_,_,_) UNTIL GROUND(x).


PREDICATE  ControlInProgram :

   Program            % Representation of a program.
 * String             % Name of an open module in this program.
 * Name               % Representation of the flat name of a predicate
                      % declared in this module.
 * List(Formula)      % List (in a definite order) of representations of
                      % the heads of all DELAY declarations for this
                      % predicate.
 * List(Condition).   % List of representations of the DELAY conditions
                      % corresponding to each head in the fourth argument.

DELAY      ControlInProgram(x,_,_,_,_) UNTIL GROUND(x).


PREDICATE  AndCondition :

   Condition          % Representation of a DELAY declaration condition,
                      % Cond1.
 * Condition          % Representation of a DELAY declaration condition,
                      % Cond2.
 * Condition.         % Representation of the condition Cond1 & Cond2.


PREDICATE  OrCondition :

   Condition          % Representation of a DELAY declaration condition,
                      % Cond1.
 * Condition          % Representation of a DELAY declaration condition,
```

```
                    % Cond2.
* Condition.        % Representation of the condition Cond1 \/ Cond2.


PREDICATE  TrueCondition :

  Condition.        % Representation of the DELAY condition TRUE.


PREDICATE  NonVarCondition :

  Term              % Representation of a variable, var.
* Condition.        % Representation of the DELAY condition NONVAR(var).


PREDICATE  GroundCondition :

  Term              % Representation of a variable, var.
* Condition.        % Representation of the DELAY condition GROUND(var).


PREDICATE  StringToCondition :

  String            % The string representation of a DELAY condition.
* Condition.        % Representation of this condition.

DELAY      StringToCondition(x,_) UNTIL GROUND(x).


PREDICATE  ConditionToString :

  Condition         % Representation of a DELAY condition.
* String.           % The string representation of this condition (in
                    % a canonical form).

DELAY      ConditionToString(x,_) UNTIL GROUND(x).
```

PREDICATE   BaseInModule :

  Program   % Representation of a program.
* String   % Name of a module in this program.
* ModulePart   % Representation of a part keyword of this module
                    % which cannot be LOCAL if this module is closed.
* Name   % Representation of the flat name of a base
                    % accessible to this part of this module.
* String.   % Name of module in which this base is declared.

DELAY   BaseInModule(x,_,_,_,_) UNTIL GROUND(x).

PREDICATE   ConstructorInModule :

  Program   % Representation of a program.
* String   % Name of a module in this program.
* ModulePart   % Representation of a part keyword of this module
                    % which cannot be LOCAL if this module is closed.
* Name   % Representation of the flat name of a constructor
                    % accessible to this part of this module.
* Integer   % Arity of this constructor.
* String.   % Name of module in which this constructor is
                    % declared.

DELAY   ConstructorInModule(x,_,_,_,_,_) UNTIL GROUND(x).

PREDICATE   ConstantInModule :

  Program   % Representation of a program.
* String   % Name of a module in this program.
* ModulePart   % Representation of a part keyword of this module
                    % which cannot be LOCAL if this module is closed.
* Name   % Representation of the flat name of a constant
                    % accessible to this part of this module.
* Type   % Representation of the type of this constant.
* String.   % Name of module in which this constant is declared.

DELAY   ConstantInModule(x,_,_,_,_,_) UNTIL GROUND(x).

```
PREDICATE  FunctionInModule :

  Program          % Representation of a program.
* String           % Name of a module in this program.
* ModulePart       % Representation of a part keyword of this module
                   % which cannot be LOCAL if this module is closed.
* Name             % Representation of the flat name of a function
                   % accessible to this part of this module.
* FunctionInd      % Representation of the indicator for this function.
* List(Type)       % List of the representations of the domain types of
                   % this function.
* Type             % Representation of the range type of this function.
* String.          % Name of module in which this function is declared.

DELAY     FunctionInModule(x,_,_,_,_,_,_,_) UNTIL GROUND(x).


PREDICATE  PropositionInModule :

  Program          % Representation of a program.
* String           % Name of a module in this program.
* ModulePart       % Representation of a part keyword of this module
                   % which cannot be LOCAL if this module is closed.
* Name             % Representation of the flat name of a proposition
                   % accessible to this part of this module.
* String.          % Name of module in which this proposition is
                   % declared.

DELAY     PropositionInModule(x,_,_,_,_) UNTIL GROUND(x).


PREDICATE  PredicateInModule :

  Program          % Representation of a program.
* String           % Name of a module in this program.
* ModulePart       % Representation of a part keyword of this module
                   % which cannot be LOCAL if this module is closed.
* Name             % Representation of the flat name of a predicate
                   % accessible to this part of this module.
```

* PredicateInd   % Representation of the indicator for this predicate.
* List(Type)   % List of the representations of the types for this
                    % predicate.
* String.   % Name of module in which this predicate is declared.

DELAY   PredicateInModule(x,_,_,_,_,_,_) UNTIL GROUND(x).

PREDICATE DelayInModule :

  Program   % Representation of a program.
* String   % Name of a module in this program.
* ModulePart   % Representation of a part keyword of this module
                    % which cannot be LOCAL if this module is closed.
* Formula   % Representation of the Atom part of a DELAY
                    % declaration appearing in this part of this module.
* Condition.   % Representation of the Cond part of this DELAY
                    % declaration.

DELAY   DelayInModule(x,_,_,_,_) UNTIL GROUND(x).

PREDICATE ImportInModule :

  Program   % Representation of a program.
* String   % Name of a module in this program.
* ModulePart   % Representation of a part keyword of this module
                    % which cannot be LOCAL if this module is closed.
* String.   % Name of a module appearing in an IMPORT declaration
                    % in this part of this module.

DELAY   ImportInModule(x,_,_,_) UNTIL GROUND(x).

PREDICATE LiftInModule :

  Program   % Representation of a program.
* String   % Name of an open module in this program.
* String.   % Name of a module appearing in a LIFT declaration
                    % in the local part of this module.

```
DELAY      LiftInModule(x,_,_) UNTIL GROUND(x).
```

```
PREDICATE  NewProgram :
```

```
  String          % A string.
* Program.        % Representation of a program with this string as
                  % the name of the main module. If the name of the
                  % module is that of one of the system modules, then
                  % the program consists of that module and all the
                  % ones upon which it depends. Otherwise, the program
                  % is an empty one and the main module has both a
                  % local and an export part.
```

```
DELAY      NewProgram(x,_) UNTIL GROUND(x).
```

```
PREDICATE  InsertProgramBase :
```

```
  Program         % Representation of a program.
* String          % Name of an open user module in this program.
* ModulePart      % Representation of a part keyword of this module.
* Name            % Representation of the flat name of a base not
                  % declared in this part of this module.
* Program.        % Representation of a program which differs from
                  % the program in the first argument only in that it
                  % also contains the declaration of this base in this
                  % part of this module.
```

```
DELAY      InsertProgramBase(x,y,z,u,_) UNTIL GROUND(x) & GROUND(y) &
                                          GROUND(z) & GROUND(u).
```

```
PREDICATE  DeleteProgramBase :
```

```
  Program         % Representation of a program.
* String          % Name of an open user module in this program.
* ModulePart      % Representation of a part keyword of this module.
* Name            % Representation of the flat name of a base declared
```

```
                     % in this part of this module.
* Program.           % Representation of a program which differs from the
                     % program in the first argument only in that it does
                     % not contain the declaration of this base in this
                     % part of this module.


DELAY      DeleteProgramBase(x,y,z,_,_) UNTIL GROUND(x) & GROUND(y) &
                                                          GROUND(z).



PREDICATE  InsertProgramConstructor :

  Program            % Representation of a program.
* String             % Name of an open user module in this program.
* ModulePart         % Representation of a part keyword of this module.
* Name               % Representation of the flat name of a constructor
                     % not declared in this part of this module.
* Integer            % Arity of this constructor.
* Program.           % Representation of a program which differs from the
                     % program in the first argument only in that it also
                     % contains the declaration of this constructor in
                     % this part of this module.

DELAY      InsertProgramConstructor(x,y,z,u,v,_) UNTIL GROUND(x) &
                     GROUND(y) & GROUND(z) & GROUND(u) & GROUND(v).



PREDICATE  DeleteProgramConstructor :

  Program            % Representation of a program.
* String             % Name of an open user module in this program.
* ModulePart         % Representation of a part keyword of this module.
* Name               % Representation of the flat name of a constructor
                     % declared in this part of this module.
* Integer            % Arity of this constructor.
* Program.           % Representation of a program which differs from the
                     % program in the first argument only in that it does
                     % not contain the declaration of this constructor in
                     % this part of this module.
```

```
DELAY       DeleteProgramConstructor(x,y,z,_,_,_) UNTIL GROUND(x) &
                                              GROUND(y) & GROUND(z).
```

PREDICATE InsertProgramConstant :

Program	% Representation of a program.
* String	% Name of an open user module in this program.
* ModulePart	% Representation of a part keyword of this module.
* Name	% Representation of the flat name of a constant not
	% declared in this part of this module.
* Type	% Representation of the type of this constant.
* Program.	% Representation of a program which differs from the
	% program in the first argument only in that it also
	% contains the declaration of this constant in this
	% part of this module.

```
DELAY       InsertProgramConstant(x,y,z,u,v,_) UNTIL GROUND(x) &
                    GROUND(y) & GROUND(z) & GROUND(u) & GROUND(v).
```

PREDICATE DeleteProgramConstant :

Program	% Representation of a program.
* String	% Name of an open user module in this program.
* ModulePart	% Representation of a part keyword of this module.
* Name	% Representation of the flat name of a constant
	% declared in this part of this module.
* Type	% Representation of the type of this constant.
* Program.	% Representation of a program which differs from the
	% program in the first argument only in that it does
	% not contain the declaration of this constant in this
	% part of this module.

```
DELAY       DeleteProgramConstant(x,y,z,_,_,_) UNTIL GROUND(x) &
                                              GROUND(y) & GROUND(z).
```

PREDICATE   InsertProgramFunction :

  Program   % Representation of a program.
* String   % Name of an open user module in this program.
* ModulePart   % Representation of a part keyword of this module.
* Name   % Representation of the flat name of a function not
                       % declared in this part of this module.
* FunctionInd   % Representation of the indicator for this function.
* List(Type)   % List of the representations of the domain types of
                       % this function.
* Type   % Representation of the range type of this function.
* Program.   % Representation of a program which differs from the
                       % program in the first argument only in that it also
                       % contains the declaration of this function in this
                       % part of this module.

DELAY   InsertProgramFunction(x,y,z,u,v,w,r,_) UNTIL GROUND(x) &
                                  GROUND(y) & GROUND(z) & GROUND(u) &
                                  GROUND(v) & GROUND(w) & GROUND(r).

PREDICATE   DeleteProgramFunction :

  Program   % Representation of a program.
* String   % Name of an open user module in this program.
* ModulePart   % Representation of a part keyword of this module.
* Name   % Representation of the flat name of a function
                       % declared in this part of this module.
* FunctionInd   % Representation of the indicator for this function.
* List(Type)   % List of the representations of the domain types of
                       % this function.
* Type   % Representation of the range type of this function.
* Program.   % Representation of a program which differs from the
                       % program in the first argument only in that it does
                       % not contain the declaration of this function in
                       % this part of this module.

DELAY   DeleteProgramFunction(x,y,z,_,_,_,_,_) UNTIL GROUND(x) &
                                  GROUND(y) & GROUND(z).

PREDICATE InsertProgramProposition :

```
  Program           % Representation of a program.
* String            % Name of an open user module in this program.
* ModulePart        % Representation of a part keyword of this module.
* Name              % Representation of the flat name of a proposition
                    % not declared in this part of this module.
* Program.          % Representation of a program which differs from the
                    % program in the first argument only in that it also
                    % contains the declaration of this proposition in
                    % this part of this module.
```

```
DELAY      InsertProgramProposition(x,y,z,u,_) UNTIL GROUND(x) &
                                GROUND(y) & GROUND(z) & GROUND(u).
```

PREDICATE DeleteProgramProposition :

```
  Program           % Representation of a program.
* String            % Name of an open user module in this program.
* ModulePart        % Representation of a part keyword of this module.
* Name              % Representation of the flat name of a proposition
                    % declared in this part of this module.
* Program.          % Representation of a program which differs from the
                    % program in the first argument only in that it does
                    % not contain the declaration of this proposition in
                    % this part of this module.
```

```
DELAY      DeleteProgramProposition(x,y,z,_,_) UNTIL GROUND(x) &
                                      GROUND(y) & GROUND(z).
```

PREDICATE InsertProgramPredicate :

```
  Program           % Representation of a program.
* String            % Name of an open user module in this program.
* ModulePart        % Representation of a part keyword of this module.
* Name              % Representation of the flat name of a predicate
                    % not declared in this part of this module.
```

* PredicateInd   % Representation of the indicator for this predicate.
* List(Type)   % List of the representations of the types of this
                      % predicate.
* Program.   % Representation of a program which differs from the
                      % program in the first argument only in that it also
                      % contains the declaration of this predicate in this
                      % part of this module.

DELAY   InsertProgramPredicate(x,y,z,u,v,w,_) UNTIL GROUND(x) &
                 GROUND(y) & GROUND(z) & GROUND(u) & GROUND(v) & GROUND(w).

PREDICATE DeleteProgramPredicate :

  Program   % Representation of a program.
* String   % Name of an open user module in this program.
* ModulePart   % Representation of a part keyword of this module.
* Name   % Representation of the flat name of a predicate
                      % declared in this part of this module.
* PredicateInd   % Representation of the indicator for this predicate.
* List(Type)   % List of the representations of the types of this
                      % predicate.
* Program.   % Representation of a program which differs from the
                      % program in the first argument only in that it does
                      % not contain the declaration of this predicate in
                      % this part of this module.

DELAY   DeleteProgramPredicate(x,y,z,_,_,_,_) UNTIL GROUND(x) &
                                              GROUND(y) & GROUND(z).

PREDICATE InsertDelay :

  Program   % Representation of a program.
* String   % Name of an open user module in this program.
* ModulePart   % Representation of a part keyword of this module.
* Formula   % Representation of a DELAY Atom part.
* Condition   % Representation of a DELAY Cond part.
* Program.   % Representation of a program which differs from the

```
                 % program in the first argument only in that it also
                 % contains in this part of this module the DELAY
                 % declaration consisting of the Atom part in the
                 % fourth argument and the Cond part in the fifth
                 % argument.

DELAY       InsertDelay(x,y,z,u,v,_) UNTIL GROUND(x) & GROUND(y) &
                                     GROUND(z) & GROUND(u) & GROUND(v).


PREDICATE  DeleteDelay :

   Program          % Representation of a program.
 * String           % Name of an open user module in this program.
 * ModulePart       % Representation of a part keyword of this module.
 * Formula          % Representation of the Atom part of DELAY
                    % declaration in this part of this module.
 * Condition        % Representation of the Cond part of this DELAY
                    % declaration.
 * Program.         % Representation of a program which differs from the
                    % program in the first argument only in that it does
                    % not contain this DELAY declaration in this part of
                    % this module.

DELAY       DeleteDelay(x,y,z,_,_,_) UNTIL GROUND(x) & GROUND(y) &
                                                       GROUND(z).


PREDICATE  InsertStatement :

   Program          % Representation of a program.
 * String           % Name of an open user module in this program.
 * Formula          % Representation of a statement in the flat language
                    % of this module wrt this program.
 * Program.         % Representation of a program which differs from the
                    % program in the first argument only in that it also
                    % contains this statement in this module.

DELAY       InsertStatement(x,y,z,_) UNTIL GROUND(x) & GROUND(y) &
                                                       GROUND(z).
```

PREDICATE   DeleteStatement :

  Program   % Representation of a program.
* String   % Name of an open user module in this program.
* Formula   % Representation of a statement in the flat language
                   % of this module wrt this program appearing in this
                   % module.
* Program.   % Representation of a program which differs from the
                   % program in the first argument only in that it does
                   % not contain this statement in this module.

DELAY   DeleteStatement(x,y,_,_) UNTIL GROUND(x) & GROUND(y).

PREDICATE   InsertProgramImport :

  Program   % Representation of a program.
* String   % Name of an open user module in this program.
* ModulePart   % Representation of a part keyword of this module.
* String   % Name of a module.
* Program.   % Representation of a program which differs from the
                   % program in the first argument in that it also
                   % contains in this part of this module the IMPORT
                   % declaration importing the module in the fourth
                   % argument.
                   %
                   % If the module named in the IMPORT declaration is not
                   % already in the program and it is not a system module,
                   % then an empty module with that name is added to the
                   % program; if the module named in the IMPORT
                   % declaration is a system module not already in the
                   % program, then the system module is added to the
                   % program.

DELAY   InsertProgramImport(x,y,z,u,_) UNTIL GROUND(x) & GROUND(y) &
                                               GROUND(z) & GROUND(u).

PREDICATE   DeleteProgramImport :

```
   Program         % Representation of a program.
 * String          % Name of an open user module in this program.
 * ModulePart      % Representation of a part keyword of this module.
 * String          % Name of a module.
 * Program.        % Representation of a program which differs from the
                   % program in the first argument in that it contains
                   % one less IMPORT declaration importing the module in
                   % the fourth argument in this part of this module.
                   %
                   % If the IMPORT declaration deleted is the last import
                   % declaration in the program containing the name of a
                   % particular module, then this module is deleted from
                   % the program.

DELAY      DeleteProgramImport(x,y,z,_,_) UNTIL GROUND(x) & GROUND(y) &
                                                         GROUND(z).


PREDICATE  InsertProgramLift :

   Program         % Representation of a program.
 * String          % Name of an open user module in this program.
 * String          % Name of a module.
 * Program.        % Representation of a program which differs from the
                   % program in the first argument in that it also
                   % contains in the local part of this module the LIFT
                   % declaration importing the module in the third
                   % argument.
                   %
                   % If the module named in the LIFT declaration is not
                   % already in the program and it is not a system module,
                   % then an empty module with that name is added to the
                   % program; if the module named in the LIFT declaration
                   % is a system module not already in the program, then
                   % the system module is added to the program.

DELAY      InsertProgramLift(x,y,z,_) UNTIL GROUND(x) & GROUND(y) &
                                                      GROUND(z).
```

PREDICATE   DeleteProgramLift :

   Program   % Representation of a program.
 * String   % Name of an open user module in this program.
 * String   % Name of a module.
 * Program.   % Representation of a program which differs from the
                  % program in the first argument in that it contains
                  % one less LIFT declaration importing the module in
                  % the third argument in the local part of this module.
                  %
                  % If the LIFT declaration deleted is the last import
                  % declaration in the program containing the name of a
                  % particular module, then this module is deleted from
                  % the program.

DELAY   DeleteProgramLift(x,y,_,_) UNTIL GROUND(x) & GROUND(y).

PREDICATE   RunnableAtom :

   Program   % Representation of a program.
 * Formula.   % Representation of an atom in the flat language of
                  % this program which has a user-defined predicate and
                  % is not delayed (according to any DELAY declarations
                  % for the predicate).

DELAY   RunnableAtom(x,y) UNTIL GROUND(x) & GROUND(y).

PREDICATE   Succeed :

   Program   % Representation of a program.
 * Formula   % Representation of the body of a goal in the flat
                  % language of this program.
 * TermSubst.   % Representation of a computed answer for this goal
                  % and the flat form of this program.

DELAY   Succeed(x,y,_) UNTIL GROUND(x) & GROUND(y).

PREDICATE Compute :

```
  Program          % Representation of a program.
* Formula          % Representation of the body of a goal in the flat
                   % language of this program.
* Integer          % A non-negative integer.
* Integer          % A non-negative integer.
* TermSubst        % Representation of a term substitution.
* TermSubst        % Representation of the term substitution obtained by
                   % composing the term substitution in the fifth
                   % argument with a computed answer for the goal whose
                   % body is obtained by applying the term substitution
                   % in the fifth argument to the body in the second
                   % argument and the flat form of this program or, if
                   % the computation flounders, the representation of the
                   % answer computed up to the step at which the
                   % computation floundered. Indexes of any new variables
                   % in the terms to which variables in the goal are bound
                   % in the computed answer are greater than or equal to
                   % the third argument and strictly less than the fourth
                   % argument.
* Formula.         % Representation of the body of the last goal in the
                   % derivation (which is empty if the derivation
                   % succeeded and is non-empty if the derivation
                   % floundered).

DELAY      Compute(x,y,z,_,w,_,_) UNTIL GROUND(x) & GROUND(y) &
                                        GROUND(z) & GROUND(w).
```

PREDICATE SucceedAll :

```
  Program          % Representation of a program.
* Formula          % Representation of the body of a goal in the flat
                   % language of this program.
* List(TermSubst).% List of representations of computed answers for
                   % this goal and the flat form of this program.

DELAY      SucceedAll(x,y,_) UNTIL GROUND(x) & GROUND(y).
```

PREDICATE ComputeAll :

  Program   % Representation of a program.
* Formula   % Representation of the body of a goal in the flat
                     % language of this program.
* Integer   % A non-negative integer.
* Integer   % A non-negative integer.
* TermSubst   % Representation of a term substitution.
* List(TermSubst)   % List of representations of all term substitutions
                     % obtained by composing the term substitution in the
                     % fifth argument with a computed answer for the goal
                     % whose body is obtained by applying the term
                     % substitution in the fifth argument to the body in the
                     % second argument and the flat form of this program or,
                     % for computations which end in a flounder, the
                     % representation of the answer computed up to the step
                     % at which the computation floundered. Indexes of any
                     % new variables in the terms to which variables in the
                     % goal are bound in the computed answers are greater
                     % than or equal to the third argument and strictly less
                     % than the fourth argument.
* List(Formula).   % List of representations of the bodies of the last
                     % goals in each of the corresponding derivations (which
                     % are empty if the derivation succeeded and are
                     % non-empty if the derivation floundered).

DELAY   ComputeAll(x,y,z,_,w,_,_) UNTIL GROUND(x) & GROUND(y) &
                                                 GROUND(z) & GROUND(w).

PREDICATE Fail :

  Program   % Representation of a program.
* Formula.   % Representation of the body of a goal in the flat
                     % language of this program such that this goal and the
                     % flat form of this program have a finitely failed
                     % search tree.

DELAY   Fail(x,y) UNTIL GROUND(x) & GROUND(y).

13.13   Scripts

EXPORT   Scripts.

% Module providing the abstract data type Script for representing
% Goedel scripts (using a ground representation) and predicates for
% processing terms of type Script.

IMPORT   Programs.

BASE   Script.   % Type of a term representing a script.

PREDICATE ProgramToScript :

  Program   % Representation of a program.
* Script.   % Representation of the associated script for this
                    % program.

DELAY   ProgramToScript(x,_) UNTIL GROUND(x).

PREDICATE TypeInScript :

  Script   % Representation of a script.
* Type.   % Representation of a type in the language of this
                    % script.

DELAY   TypeInScript(x,y) UNTIL GROUND(x) & GROUND(y).

PREDICATE TermInScript :

  Script   % Representation of a script.
* VarTyping   % Representation of a variable typing in the language
                    % of this script.
* Term   % Representation of a term in the language of this
                    % script.

```
* Type            % Representation of the type of this term with respect
                  % to this variable typing.
* VarTyping.      % Representation of the variable typing obtained by
                  % combining the variable typing in the second argument
                  % with the types of all variables occurring in the
                  % term.

DELAY      TermInScript(x,y,z,_,_) UNTIL GROUND(x) & GROUND(y) &
                                                        GROUND(z).


PREDICATE  FormulaInScript :

  Script          % Representation of a script.
* VarTyping       % Representation of a variable typing in the language
                  % of this script.
* Formula         % Representation of a formula, which is a standard
                  % body or standard resultant, in the language of this
                  % script.
* VarTyping.      % Representation of the variable typing obtained by
                  % combining the variable typing in the second argument
                  % with the types of all free variables occurring in
                  % the formula.

DELAY      FormulaInScript(x,y,z,_) UNTIL GROUND(x) & GROUND(y) &
                                                        GROUND(z).


PREDICATE  BaseInScript :

  Script          % Representation of a script.
* Name.           % Representation of the flat name of a base in the
                  % open language of this script.

DELAY      BaseInScript(x,_) UNTIL GROUND(x).


PREDICATE  ConstructorInScript :

  Script          % Representation of a script.
```

```
* Name           % Representation of the flat name of a constructor in
                 % the open language of this script.
* Integer.       % Arity of this constructor.

DELAY      ConstructorInScript(x,_,_) UNTIL GROUND(x).


PREDICATE  ConstantInScript :

  Script         % Representation of a script.
* Name           % Representation of the flat name of a constant in
                 % the open language of this script.
* Type.          % Representation of the type of this constant.

DELAY      ConstantInScript(x,_,_) UNTIL GROUND(x).


PREDICATE  FunctionInScript :

  Script         % Representation of a script.
* Name           % Representation of the flat name of a function in
                 % the open language of this script.
* FunctionInd    % Representation of the indicator for this function.
* List(Type)     % List of the representations of the domain types of
                 % this function.
* Type.          % Representation of the range type of this function.

DELAY      FunctionInScript(x,_,_,_,_) UNTIL GROUND(x).


PREDICATE  PropositionInScript :

  Script         % Representation of a script.
* Name.          % Representation of the flat name of a proposition in
                 % the open language of this script.

DELAY      PropositionInScript(x,_) UNTIL GROUND(x).
```

PREDICATE PredicateInScript :

```
  Script          % Representation of a script.
* Name            % Representation of the flat name of a predicate in
                  % the open language of this script.
* PredicateInd    % Representation of the indicator for this predicate.
* List(Type).     % List of the representations of the types for this
                  % predicate.
```

DELAY   PredicateInScript(x,_,_,_) UNTIL GROUND(x).

PREDICATE StatementInScript :

```
  Script          % Representation of a script.
* Formula.        % Representation of a statement in the open part of
                  % this script.
```

DELAY   StatementInScript(x,_) UNTIL GROUND(x).

PREDICATE StatementMatchAtom :

```
  Script          % Representation of a script.
* Formula         % Representation of an atom in the language of this
                  % script, whose proposition or predicate symbol is in
                  % the open language of this script.
* Formula.        % Representation of a statement in the open part of
                  % this script whose proposition or predicate in the
                  % head is the same as the proposition or predicate in
                  % this atom.
```

DELAY   StatementMatchAtom(x,z,_) UNTIL GROUND(x) & GROUND(z).

PREDICATE DefinitionInScript :

```
  Script          % Representation of a script.
* Name            % Representation of the flat name of a proposition or
                  % predicate in the open language of this script.
```

* List(Formula). % List (in a definite order) of representations of
                  % statements in the definition of this proposition or
                  % predicate.

DELAY   DefinitionInScript(x,_,_) UNTIL GROUND(x).

PREDICATE ControlInScript :

  Script   % Representation of a script.
* Name   % Representation of the flat name of a predicate in
                  % the open language of this script.
* List(Formula)   % List (in a definite order) of representations of the
                  % heads of all DELAY declarations for this predicate.
* List(Condition).% List of representations of the DELAY conditions
                  % corresponding to each head in the fourth argument.

DELAY   ControlInScript(x,_,_,_) UNTIL GROUND(x).

PREDICATE DelayInScript :

  Script   % Representation of a script.
* Formula   % Representation of the Atom part of a DELAY
                  % declaration appearing in the open part of this
                  % script.
* Condition.   % Representation of the Cond part of this DELAY
                  % declaration.

DELAY   DelayInScript(x,_,_) UNTIL GROUND(x).

PREDICATE InsertScriptProposition :

  Script   % Representation of a script.
* Name   % Representation of the flat name of a proposition
                  % whose module name component is not the name of a
                  % closed module and which is not declared in this
                  % script.
* Script.   % Representation of a script which differs from the

```
                % script in the first argument only in that it also
                % contains the declaration of this proposition in its
                % open part.

DELAY       InsertScriptProposition(x,y,_) UNTIL GROUND(x) & GROUND(y).


PREDICATE   DeleteScriptProposition :

  Script        % Representation of a script.
* Name          % Representation of the flat name of a proposition
                % whose module name component is not the name of a
                % closed module and which is declared in the open part
                % of this script.
* Script.       % Representation of a script which differs from the
                % script in the first argument only in that it does
                % not contain the declaration of this proposition in
                % its open part.

DELAY       DeleteScriptProposition(x,_,_) UNTIL GROUND(x).


PREDICATE   InsertScriptPredicate :

  Script        % Representation of a script.
* Name          % Representation of the flat name of a predicate whose
                % module name component is not the name of a closed
                % module and which is not declared in this script.
* PredicateInd  % Representation of the indicator for this predicate.
* List(Type)    % List of the representations of the types of this
                % predicate.
* Script.       % Representation of a script which differs from the
                % script in the first argument only in that it also
                % contains the declaration of this predicate in its
                % open part.

DELAY       InsertScriptPredicate(x,y,z,u,_) UNTIL GROUND(x) &
                                GROUND(y) & GROUND(z) & GROUND(u).
```

PREDICATE   DeleteScriptPredicate :

```
  Script            % Representation of a script.
* Name              % Representation of the flat name of a predicate whose
                    % module name component is not the name of a closed
                    % module and which is declared in the open part of
                    % this script.
* PredicateInd      % Representation of the indicator for this predicate.
* List(Type)        % List of the representations of the types of this
                    % predicate.
* Script.           % Representation of a script which differs from the
                    % script in the first argument only in that it does
                    % not contain the declaration of this predicate in its
                    % open part.
```

DELAY   DeleteScriptPredicate(x,_,_,_,_) UNTIL GROUND(x).

PREDICATE   InsertDelay :

```
  Script            % Representation of a script.
* Formula           % Representation of a DELAY Atom part.
* Condition         % Representation of a DELAY Cond part.
* Script.           % Representation of a script which differs from the
                    % script in the first argument only in that it also
                    % contains in its open part the DELAY declaration
                    % consisting of the Atom part in the second argument
                    % and the Cond part in the third argument.
```

DELAY   InsertDelay(x,y,z,_) UNTIL GROUND(x) & GROUND(y) & GROUND(z).

PREDICATE   DeleteDelay :

```
  Script            % Representation of a script.
* Formula           % Representation of the Atom part of a DELAY
                    % declaration in the open part of this script.
* Condition         % Representation of the Cond part of this DELAY
                    % declaration.
```

* Script.   % Representation of a script which differs from the
                     % script in the first argument only in that it does
                     % not contain this DELAY declaration in its open part.

DELAY   DeleteDelay(x,_,_,_) UNTIL GROUND(x).

PREDICATE   InsertStatement :

  Script   % Representation of a script.
* Formula   % Representation of a statement in the open language
                     % of this script.
* Script.   % Representation of a script which differs from the
                     % script in the first argument only in that it also
                     % contains this statement in the open part of the
                     % script.

DELAY   InsertStatement(x,y,_) UNTIL GROUND(x) & GROUND(y).

PREDICATE   DeleteStatement :

  Script   % Representation of a script.
* Formula   % Representation of a statement in the open language
                     % of this script in this script.
* Script.   % Representation of a script which differs from the
                     % script in the first argument only in that it does
                     % not contain this statement in the open part of the
                     % script.

DELAY   DeleteStatement(x,_,_) UNTIL GROUND(x).

13.14   Theories

EXPORT   Theories.

% Module providing the abstract data type Theory for representing
% polymorphic many-sorted theories (using a ground representation)
% and predicates for processing terms of type Theory.

IMPORT   Syntax.

BASE   Theory.   % Type of a term representing a theory.

PREDICATE TypeInTheory :

  Theory   % Representation of a theory.
* Type.   % Representation of a type in the flat language of
                 % this theory.

DELAY   TypeInTheory(x,y) UNTIL GROUND(x) & GROUND(y).

PREDICATE TermInTheory :

  Theory   % Representation of a theory.
* VarTyping   % Representation of a variable typing in the flat
                 % language of this theory.
* Term   % Representation of a term in the flat language of
                 % this theory.
* Type   % Representation of the type of this term with respect
                 % to this variable typing.
* VarTyping.   % Representation of the variable typing obtained by
                 % combining the variable typing in the second argument
                 % with the types of all variables occurring in the
                 % term.

DELAY   TermInTheory(x,y,z,_,_) UNTIL GROUND(x) & GROUND(y) &
                                                  GROUND(z).

PREDICATE   FormulaInTheory :

  Theory   % Representation of a theory.
* VarTyping   % Representation of a variable typing in the flat
                % language of this theory.
* Formula   % Representation of a formula in the flat language of
                % this theory.
* VarTyping.   % Representation of the variable typing obtained by
                % combining the variable typing in the second argument
                % with the types of all free variables occurring in the
                % formula.

DELAY   FormulaInTheory(x,y,z,_) UNTIL GROUND(x) & GROUND(y) &
                                                        GROUND(z).

PREDICATE   StringToTheoryType :

  Theory   % Representation of a theory.
* String   % A string.
* List(Type).   % List (in a definite order) of representations of
                % types in the flat language of this theory whose
                % string representation is the second argument.

DELAY   StringToTheoryType(x,y,_) UNTIL GROUND(x) & GROUND(y).

PREDICATE   StringToTheoryTerm :

  Theory   % Representation of a theory.
* String   % A string.
* List(Term).   % List (in a definite order) of representations of
                % terms in the flat language of this theory whose
                % string representation is the second argument.

DELAY   StringToTheoryTerm(x,y,_) UNTIL GROUND(x) & GROUND(y).

PREDICATE   StringToTheoryFormula :

```
  Theory            % Representation of a theory.
* String            % A string.
* List(Formula).    % List (in a definite order) of representations of
                    % formulas in the flat language of this theory whose
                    % string representation is the second argument.

DELAY      StringToTheoryFormula(x,y,_) UNTIL GROUND(x) & GROUND(y).


PREDICATE  TheoryTypeToString :

  Theory            % Representation of a theory.
* Type              % Representation of a type.
* String.           % The string representation of this type. (Subtypes of
                    % the type not in the flat language of this theory do
                    % not appear.)

DELAY      TheoryTypeToString(x,y,_) UNTIL GROUND(x) & GROUND(y).


PREDICATE  TheoryTermToString :

  Theory            % Representation of a theory.
* Term              % Representation of a term.
* String.           % The string representation of this term. (Subterms of
                    % the term not in the flat language of this theory do
                    % not appear.)

DELAY      TheoryTermToString(x,y,_) UNTIL GROUND(x) & GROUND(y).


PREDICATE  TheoryFormulaToString :

  Theory            % Representation of a theory.
* Formula           % Representation of a formula.
* String.           % The string representation of this formula. (Terms
                    % of the formula not in the flat language of this
                    % theory do not appear.)

DELAY      TheoryFormulaToString(x,y,_) UNTIL GROUND(x) & GROUND(y).
```

PREDICATE   TheoryBaseName :

  Theory   % Representation of a theory.
* String   % Name of this theory.
* String   % Name of a base.
* Name.   % Representation of the corresponding flat name of
                  % this base.

DELAY   TheoryBaseName(x,y,z,u) UNTIL GROUND(x) &
                               ((GROUND(y) & GROUND(z)) \/ GROUND(u)).

PREDICATE   TheoryConstructorName :

  Theory   % Representation of a theory.
* String   % Name of this theory.
* String   % Name of a constructor.
* Integer   % Arity of this constructor.
* Name.   % Representation of the corresponding flat name of
                  % this constructor.

DELAY   TheoryConstructorName(x,y,z,u,v) UNTIL GROUND(x) &
              ((GROUND(y) & GROUND(z) & GROUND(u)) \/ GROUND(v)).

PREDICATE   TheoryConstantName :

  Theory   % Representation of a theory.
* String   % Name of this theory.
* String   % Name of a constant.
* Name.   % Representation of the corresponding flat name of
                  % this constant.

DELAY   TheoryConstantName(x,y,z,u) UNTIL GROUND(x) &
                               ((GROUND(y) & GROUND(z)) \/ GROUND(u)).

PREDICATE   TheoryFunctionName :

  Theory   % Representation of a theory.

```
* String            % Name of this theory.
* String            % Name of a function.
* Integer           % Arity of this function.
* Name.             % Representation of the corresponding flat name of
                    % this function.

DELAY       TheoryFunctionName(x,y,z,u,v) UNTIL GROUND(x) &
                    ((GROUND(y) & GROUND(z) & GROUND(u)) \/ GROUND(v)).

PREDICATE   TheoryPropositionName :

  Theory            % Representation of a theory.
* String            % Name of this theory.
* String            % Name of a proposition.
* Name.             % Representation of the corresponding flat name of
                    % this proposition.

DELAY       TheoryPropositionName(x,y,z,u) UNTIL GROUND(x) &
                    ((GROUND(y) & GROUND(z)) \/ GROUND(u)).

PREDICATE   TheoryPredicateName :

  Theory            % Representation of a theory.
* String            % Name of this theory.
* String            % Name of a predicate.
* Integer           % Arity of this predicate.
* Name.             % Representation of the corresponding flat name of
                    % this predicate.

DELAY       TheoryPredicateName(x,y,z,u,v) UNTIL GROUND(x) &
                    ((GROUND(y) & GROUND(z) & GROUND(u)) \/ GROUND(v)).

PREDICATE   AxiomInTheory :

  Theory            % Representation of a theory.
* Formula.          % Representation of an axiom in this theory.

DELAY       AxiomInTheory(x,_) UNTIL GROUND(x).
```

PREDICATE BaseInTheory :

  Theory   % Representation of a theory.
 * Name   % Representation of the flat name of a base accessible
               % to this theory.
 * String.   % Name of theory or system module in which this base
               % is declared.

DELAY   BaseInTheory(x,_,_) UNTIL GROUND(x).

PREDICATE ConstructorInTheory :

  Theory   % Representation of a theory.
 * Name   % Representation of the flat name of a constructor
               % accessible to this theory.
 * Integer   % Arity of this constructor.
 * String.   % Name of theory or system module in which this
               % constructor is declared.

DELAY   ConstructorInTheory(x,_,_,_) UNTIL GROUND(x).

PREDICATE ConstantInTheory :

  Theory   % Representation of a theory.
 * Name   % Representation of the flat name of a constant
               % accessible to this theory.
 * Type   % Representation of the type of this constant.
 * String.   % Name of theory or system module in which this
               % constant is declared.

DELAY   ConstantInTheory(x,_,_,_) UNTIL GROUND(x).

PREDICATE FunctionInTheory :

  Theory   % Representation of a theory.
 * Name   % Representation of the flat name of a function
               % accessible to this theory.

```
 * Integer            % Arity of this function.
 * FunctionInd        % Indicator for this function.
 * List(Type)         % List of the representations of the domain types of
                      % this function.
 * Type               % Representation of the range type of this function.
 * String.            % Name of theory or system module in which this
                      % function is declared.

DELAY       FunctionInTheory(x,_,_,_,_,_,_) UNTIL GROUND(x).


PREDICATE  PropositionInTheory :

   Theory              % Representation of a theory.
 * Name                % Representation of the flat name of a proposition
                       % accessible to this theory.
 * String.             % Name of theory or system module in which this
                       % proposition is declared.

DELAY       PropositionInTheory(x,_,_) UNTIL GROUND(x).


PREDICATE  PredicateInTheory :

   Theory              % Representation of a theory.
 * Name                % Representation of the flat name of a predicate
                       % accessible to this theory.
 * Integer             % Arity of this predicate.
 * PredicateInd        % Indicator for this predicate.
 * List(Type)          % List of the representations of the types for this
                       % predicate.
 * String.             % Name of theory or system module in which this
                       % predicate is declared.

DELAY       PredicateInTheory(x,_,_,_,_,_) UNTIL GROUND(x).


PREDICATE  ImportInTheory :

   Theory              % Representation of a theory.
```

```
  * String.          % Name of a module appearing in an IMPORT declaration
                     % in this theory.


  DELAY        ImportInTheory(x,_) UNTIL GROUND(x).


  PREDICATE  NewTheory :

    String           % A string.
  * Theory.          % Representation of an empty theory with this string
                     % as the name of the theory.


  DELAY        NewTheory(x,_) UNTIL GROUND(x).


  PREDICATE  InsertTheoryBase :

    Theory           % Representation of a theory.
  * Name             % Representation of the flat name of a base not
                     % declared in this theory.
  * Theory.          % Representation of a theory which differs from the
                     % theory in the first argument only in that it also
                     % contains the declaration of this base.


  DELAY        InsertTheoryBase(x,y,_) UNTIL GROUND(x) & GROUND(y).


  PREDICATE  DeleteTheoryBase :

    Theory           % Representation of a theory.
  * Name             % Representation of the flat name of a base declared
                     % in this theory.
  * Theory.          % Representation of a theory which differs from the
                     % theory in the first argument only in that it does
                     % not contain the declaration of this base.

  DELAY        DeleteTheoryBase(x,_,_) UNTIL GROUND(x).
```

```
PREDICATE   InsertTheoryConstructor :

  Theory            % Representation of a theory.
* Name              % Representation of the flat name of a constructor not
                    % declared in this theory.
* Integer           % Arity of this constructor.
* Theory.           % Representation of a theory which differs from the
                    % theory in the first argument only in that it also
                    % contains the declaration of this constructor.

DELAY       InsertTheoryConstructor(x,y,z,_) UNTIL GROUND(x) &
                                         GROUND(y) & GROUND(z).


PREDICATE   DeleteTheoryConstructor :

  Theory            % Representation of a theory.
* Name              % Representation of the flat name of a constructor
                    % declared in this theory.
* Integer           % Arity of this constructor.
* Theory.           % Representation of a theory which differs from the
                    % theory in the first argument only in that it does
                    % not contain the declaration of this constructor.

DELAY       DeleteTheoryConstructor(x,_,_,_) UNTIL GROUND(x).


PREDICATE   InsertTheoryConstant :

  Theory            % Representation of a theory.
* Name              % Representation of the flat name of a constant not
                    % declared in this theory.
* Type              % Representation of the type of this constant.
* Theory.           % Representation of a theory which differs from the
                    % theory in the first argument only in that it also
                    % contains the declaration of this constant.

DELAY       InsertTheoryConstant(x,y,z,_) UNTIL GROUND(x) & GROUND(y) &
                                         GROUND(z).
```

PREDICATE   DeleteTheoryConstant :

  Theory   % Representation of a theory.
* Name   % Representation of the flat name of a constant
                 % declared in this theory.
* Type   % Representation of the type of this constant.
* Theory.   % Representation of a theory which differs from the
                 % theory in the first argument only in that it does
                 % not contain the declaration of this constant.

DELAY   DeleteTheoryConstant(x,_,_,_) UNTIL GROUND(x).

PREDICATE   InsertTheoryFunction :

  Theory   % Representation of a theory.
* Name   % Representation of the flat name of a function not
                 % declared in this theory.
* FunctionInd   % Indicator for this function.
* List(Type)   % List of the representations of the domain types of
                 % this function.
* Type   % Representation of the range type of this function.
* Theory.   % Representation of a theory which differs from the
                 % theory in the first argument only in that it also
                 % contains the declaration of this function.

DELAY   InsertTheoryFunction(x,y,z,u,v,_) UNTIL GROUND(x) &
                     GROUND(y) & GROUND(z) & GROUND(u) & GROUND(v).

PREDICATE   DeleteTheoryFunction :

  Theory   % Representation of a theory.
* Name   % Representation of the flat name of a function
                 % declared in this theory.
* FunctionInd   % Indicator for this function.
* List(Type)   % List of the representations of the domain types of
                 % this function.
* Type   % Representation of the range type of this function.

```
  * Theory.          % Representation of a theory which differs from the
                     % theory in the first argument only in that it does
                     % not contain the declaration of this function.

  DELAY      DeleteTheoryFunction(x,_,_,_,_,_) UNTIL GROUND(x).


  PREDICATE  InsertTheoryProposition :

    Theory           % Representation of a theory.
  * Name             % Representation of the flat name of a proposition not
                     % declared in this theory.
  * Theory.          % Representation of a theory which differs from the
                     % theory in the first argument only in that it also
                     % contains the declaration of this proposition.

  DELAY      InsertTheoryProposition(x,y,_) UNTIL GROUND(x) & GROUND(y).


  PREDICATE  DeleteTheoryProposition :

    Theory           % Representation of a theory.
  * Name             % Representation of the flat name of a proposition
                     % declared in this theory.
  * Theory.          % Representation of a theory which differs from the
                     % theory in the first argument only in that it does
                     % not contain the declaration of this proposition.

  DELAY      DeleteTheoryProposition(x,_,_) UNTIL GROUND(x).


  PREDICATE  InsertTheoryPredicate :

    Theory           % Representation of a theory.
  * Name             % Representation of the flat name of a predicate not
                     % declared in this theory.
  * PredicateInd     % Indicator for this predicate.
  * List(Type)       % List of the representations of the types of this
                     % predicate.
  * Theory.          % Representation of a theory which differs from the
```

```
                        % theory in the first argument only in that it also
                        % contains the declaration of this predicate.

DELAY       InsertTheoryPredicate(x,y,z,u,_) UNTIL GROUND(x) &
                                    GROUND(y) & GROUND(z) & GROUND(u).


PREDICATE  DeleteTheoryPredicate :

  Theory             % Representation of a theory.
* Name               % Representation of the flat name of a predicate
                     % declared in this theory.
* PredicateInd       % Indicator for this predicate.
* List(Type)         % List of the representations of the types of this
                     % predicate.
* Theory.            % Representation of a theory which differs from the
                     % theory in the first argument only in that it does
                     % not contain the declaration of this predicate.

DELAY       DeleteTheoryPredicate(x,_,_,_,_) UNTIL GROUND(x).


PREDICATE  InsertTheoryImport :

  Theory             % Representation of a theory.
* String             % Name of a system module not imported into the
                     % theory.
* Theory.            % Representation of a theory which differs from the
                     % theory in the first argument only in that it also
                     % contains the IMPORT declaration importing the module
                     % in the second argument.

DELAY       InsertTheoryImport(x,y,_) UNTIL GROUND(x) & GROUND(y).


PREDICATE  DeleteTheoryImport :

  Theory             % Representation of a theory.
* String             % Name of a system module imported into the theory.
* Theory.            % Representation of a theory which differs from the
```

```
                    % theory in the first argument only in that it does
                    % not contain the IMPORT declaration importing the
                    % module in the second argument.

DELAY       DeleteTheoryImport(x,_,_) UNTIL GROUND(x).


PREDICATE   InsertAxiom :

   Theory           % Representation of a theory.
 * Formula          % Representation of a formula in the flat language of
                    % this theory.
 * Theory.          % Representation of a theory which differs from the
                    % theory in the first argument only in that it also
                    % contains this formula as an axiom.

DELAY       InsertAxiom(x,y,_) UNTIL GROUND(x) & GROUND(y).


PREDICATE   DeleteAxiom :

   Theory           % Representation of a theory.
 * Formula          % Representation of a formula in the flat language of
                    % this theory which is an axiom in this theory.
 * Theory.          % Representation of a theory which differs from the
                    % theory in the first argument only in that it does
                    % not contain this formula as an axiom.

DELAY       DeleteAxiom(x,_,_) UNTIL GROUND(x).


PREDICATE   Prove :

   Theory           % Representation of a theory.
 * Formula.         % Representation of a theorem of this theory.

DELAY       Prove(x,y) UNTIL GROUND(x) & GROUND(y).
```

13.15 IO

EXPORT   IO.

% Module providing basic input/output facilities.

IMPORT   Strings.

BASE   InputStream, OutputStream.
%
% Stream types.

BASE   ResultOfFind.
%
% Type of result indicating the success or failure of an attempt to open
% a stream.

CONSTANT   StdIn : InputStream.
%
% Built-in stream corresponding to standard input.

CONSTANT   StdOut, StdErr : OutputStream.
%
% Built-in streams corresponding to standard output and standard error,
% respectively.

CONSTANT   NotFound : ResultOfFind.
%
% Indicates stream could not be opened.

FUNCTION   In : InputStream -> ResultOfFind.
%
% Indicates input stream was opened successfully.

FUNCTION   Out : OutputStream -> ResultOfFind.
%

% Indicates output stream was opened successfully.

PREDICATE FindInput :

  String   % Name of file.
* ResultOfFind.   % In(stream), where stream is the new input stream
                 % pointing to the beginning of the file, if the attempt
                 % to open the file was successful;
                 % otherwise, NotFound, if file could not be opened.

DELAY   FindInput(x,_) UNTIL GROUND(x).

PREDICATE FindOutput :

  String   % Name of file.
* ResultOfFind.   % Out(stream), where stream is the new output stream
                 % pointing to the beginning of the file, if the attempt
                 % to open the file was successful;
                 % otherwise, NotFound, if file could not be opened.

% If the file already exists it is truncated, otherwise an empty file
% with the given name is created.

DELAY   FindOutput(x,_) UNTIL GROUND(x).

PREDICATE FindUpdate :

  String   % Name of file.
* ResultOfFind.   % Out(stream), where stream is the new output stream
                 % pointing to the end of the file, if the attempt
                 % to open the file was successful;
                 % otherwise, NotFound, if file could not be opened.

% The file pointer is set to the end of the file if it already exists.
% Otherwise, an empty file with the given name is created.

DELAY   FindUpdate(x,_) UNTIL GROUND(x).

% The previous three predicates are guaranteed to succeed if the file
% argument is instantiated and the result argument is uninstantiated. If
% the result argument is NotFound, subsequent read, write and close
% operations on the stream will fail.

PREDICATE EndInput :

  InputStream.   % An open input stream to be closed.

DELAY   EndInput(x) UNTIL GROUND(x).

PREDICATE EndOutput :

  OutputStream. % An open output stream to be closed.

DELAY   EndOutput(x) UNTIL GROUND(x).

% Closing one of the fixed streams StdIn, StdOut, or StdErr will succeed,
% but the stream is immediately reopened.

PREDICATE Get :

  InputStream   % An open input stream.
* Integer.   % The ASCII code of the next character read from the
                   % stream or -1 if the end of the file has been reached.

DELAY   Get(x,_) UNTIL GROUND(x).

PREDICATE ReadChar :

  InputStream   % An open input stream.
* String.   % A string of length 1 containing the next character
                   % read from the stream or the empty string if the end
                   % of the file has been reached.

DELAY   ReadChar(x,_) UNTIL GROUND(x).

PREDICATE Put :

  OutputStream   % An open output stream.
* Integer.   % An integer between 0 and 127. The character which
                    % has this ASCII code is written to the stream.

DELAY   Put(x,y) UNTIL GROUND(x) & GROUND(y).

PREDICATE WriteString :

  OutputStream   % An open output stream.
* String.   % A string of characters, which are written to the
                    % stream.

DELAY   WriteString(x,y) UNTIL GROUND(x) & GROUND(y).

PREDICATE NewLine :

  OutputStream.   % An open output stream, to which a newline character
                    % is written.

DELAY   NewLine(x) UNTIL GROUND(x).

PREDICATE Flush :

  OutputStream.   % An open output stream.

% Calling Flush forces any characters that have been written to the
% stream, but are buffered internally, to be physically written to the
% output device.

DELAY   Flush(x) UNTIL GROUND(x).

13.16   NumbersIO

EXPORT   NumbersIO.

% Module providing input/output for integers, rationals, and
% floating-point numbers.

IMPORT   IO, Numbers.

BASE   FileInfo.
%
% Type for constants indicating end of file.

CONSTANT   EOF, NotEOF : FileInfo.
%
% Constants indicating end of file and not end of file, respectively.

PREDICATE   ReadInteger :

  InputStream   % An open input stream.
* Integer   % An integer read from the stream unless the end of
                    % the file has already been reached.
* FileInfo.   % EOF if already end of file; otherwise, NotEOF.

DELAY   ReadInteger(x,_,_) UNTIL GROUND(x).

% ReadInteger skips over layout characters to find the next token
% (or pair of tokens) which should be an integer. If the next token
% (or pair of tokens) is not an integer, ReadInteger fails. If end of
% file has already been reached (or if there are only layout
% characters before the end of file), ReadInteger succeeds with 0 in
% the second argument and EOF in the third. If end of file has not
% been reached and ReadInteger succeeds, then NotEOF is returned in
% the third argument.

PREDICATE   ReadRational :

   InputStream   % An open input stream.
 * Rational   % A rational read from the stream unless the end of
                      % the file has already been reached.
 * FileInfo.   % EOF if already end of file; otherwise, NotEOF.

DELAY   ReadRational(x,_,_) UNTIL GROUND(x).

% ReadRational skips over layout characters to find the next sequence
% of tokens which should be a rational. If the next sequence of tokens
% is not a rational, ReadRational fails. If end of file has already
% been reached (or if there are only layout characters before the end
% of file), ReadRational succeeds with 0 in the second argument and
% EOF in the third. If end of file has not been reached and
% ReadRational succeeds, then NotEOF is returned in the third argument.

PREDICATE   ReadFloat :

   InputStream   % An open input stream.
 * Float   % A floating-point number read from the stream unless
                      % the end of the file has already been reached.
 * FileInfo.   % EOF if already end of file; otherwise, NotEOF.

DELAY   ReadFloat(x,_,_) UNTIL GROUND(x).

% ReadFloat skips over layout characters to find the next token (or
% pair of tokens) which should be a floating-point number. If the
% next token (or pair of tokens) is not a floating-point number,
% ReadFloat fails. If end of file has already been reached (or if
% there are only layout characters before the end of file),
% ReadFloat succeeds with 0 in the second argument and EOF in the
% third. If end of file has not been reached and ReadFloat succeeds,
% then NotEOF is returned in the third argument.

PREDICATE   WriteInteger :

```
  OutputStream    % An open output stream.
* Integer.        % An integer which is written to the stream.

DELAY       WriteInteger(x,y) UNTIL GROUND(x) & GROUND(y).


PREDICATE   WriteRational :

  OutputStream    % An open output stream.
* Rational.       % A rational which is written in its standard form
                  % a/b to the stream.

DELAY       WriteRational(x,y) UNTIL GROUND(x) & GROUND(y).


PREDICATE   WriteFloat :

  OutputStream    % An open output stream.
* Float.          % A floating-point number which is written in its
                  % standard form decimal representation to the stream.

DELAY       WriteFloat(x,y) UNTIL GROUND(x) & GROUND(y).
```

13.17 FlocksIO

EXPORT   FlocksIO.

% Module providing input/output for flocks.

IMPORT   IO, Flocks.

PREDICATE   GetFlock :

  InputStream   % An open input stream corresponding to a file with a
                  % .flk extension.
* Flock.   % The representation of the flock in the file
                  % corresponding to the input stream in the first
                  % argument is read into this argument.

DELAY   GetFlock(x,_) UNTIL GROUND(x).

PREDICATE   PutFlock :

  OutputStream   % An open output stream corresponding to a file with a
                  % .flk extension.
* Flock.   % The representation of the flock in this argument is
                  % written to the output stream in the first argument.

DELAY   PutFlock(x,y) UNTIL GROUND(x) & GROUND(y).

PREDICATE   FlockCompile :

  String   % The name of a file from which a flock is read.
* Flock.   % The representation of this flock.

DELAY   FlockCompile(x,_) UNTIL GROUND(x).

PREDICATE   FlockDecompile :

  Flock   % The representation of a flock.
* String.   % The name of a file to which this flock is written.

DELAY   FlockDecompile(x,y) UNTIL GROUND(x) & GROUND(y).

13.18 ProgramsIO

EXPORT   ProgramsIO.

% Module providing input/output for the ground representation of
% Goedel programs.

IMPORT   IO, Programs.

PREDICATE   GetProgram :

  InputStream   % An open input stream corresponding to a file with a
                     % .prm extension.
* Program.   % The ground representation of the program in the file
                     % corresponding to the input stream in the first
                     % argument is read into this argument.

DELAY   GetProgram(x,_) UNTIL GROUND(x).

PREDICATE   PutProgram :

  OutputStream   % An open output stream corresponding to a file with a
                     % .prm extension.
* Program.   % The ground representation of the program in this
                     % argument is written to the output stream in the first
                     % argument.

DELAY   PutProgram(x,y) UNTIL GROUND(x) & GROUND(y).

PREDICATE   ProgramCompile :

  String   % The name of the main module of a program.
* Program.   % The ground representation of this program.

DELAY   ProgramCompile(x,_) UNTIL GROUND(x).

PREDICATE   ProgramDecompile :

  Program.   % The ground representation of a program which is
               % written to files containing the modules of this
               % program.

DELAY   ProgramDecompile(x) UNTIL GROUND(x).

13.19   ScriptsIO

EXPORT   ScriptsIO.

% Module providing input/output for the ground representation of
% Goedel scripts.

IMPORT   IO, Scripts.

PREDICATE   GetScript :

  InputStream   % An open input stream corresponding to a file with a
                   % .scr extension.
* Script.   % The ground representation of the script in the file
                   % corresponding to the input stream in the first
                   % argument is read into this argument.

DELAY   GetScript(x,_) UNTIL GROUND(x).

PREDICATE   PutScript :

  OutputStream   % An open output stream corresponding to a file with a
                   % .scr extension.
* Script.   % The ground representation of the script in this
                   % argument is written to the output stream in the first
                   % argument.

DELAY   PutScript(x,y) UNTIL GROUND(x) & GROUND(y).

13.20   TheoriesIO

EXPORT   TheoriesIO.

% Module providing input/output for the ground representation of
% polymorphic many-sorted theories.

IMPORT   IO, Theories.

PREDICATE   GetTheory :

  InputStream   % An open input stream corresponding to a file with a
                 % .thy extension.
* Theory.   % The ground representation of the theory in the file
                 % corresponding to the input stream in the first
                 % argument is read into this argument.

DELAY   GetTheory(x,_) UNTIL GROUND(x).

PREDICATE   PutTheory :

  OutputStream   % An open output stream corresponding to a file with a
                 % .thy extension.
* Theory.   % The ground representation of the theory in this
                 % argument is written to the output stream in the first
                 % argument.

DELAY   PutTheory(x,y) UNTIL GROUND(x) & GROUND(y).

PREDICATE   TheoryCompile :

  String   % The name of a theory.
* Theory.   % The ground representation of this theory.

DELAY   TheoryCompile(x,_) UNTIL GROUND(x).

```
PREDICATE      TheoryDecompile :

   Theory.            % The ground representation of a theory which is
                      % written to a file containing this theory.

DELAY          TheoryDecompile(x) UNTIL GROUND(x).
```

13.21 System Utilities

First, some file naming conventions:

- The file containing the export part of the module *Name* is called *Name*.exp.
- The file containing the local part of the module *Name* is called *Name*.loc.
- The file containing the theory *Name* is called *Name*.axm.
- A file containing the representation of a program has extension .prm.
- A file containing the representation of a theory has extension .thy.
- A file containing the representation of a flock has extension .flk.
- A file containing the representation of a script has extension .scr.

Now here is a brief description of the system utilities provided by Gödel. For more information, consult the reference manual of an implementation.

- flock-compile "*File*" "*Flock*"
  This takes a file *File* containing a flock and produces a file *Flock*.flk containing the representation of this flock.
- flock-decompile "*Flock*" "*File*"
  This takes a file *Flock*.flk containing the representation of a flock and produces a file *File* containing this flock.
- program-compile *Name*
  This takes a program with main module *Name* and produces the ground representation of the program in a file *Name*.prm.
- program-decompile "*File*"
  This takes a file *File*.prm which contains the ground representation of a program and produces files containing the modules of this program.
- theory-compile *Name*
  This takes a file containing the theory *Name* and produces the ground representation of the theory in the file *Name*.thy.
- theory-decompile "*File*"
  This takes a file *File*.thy which contains the ground representation of a theory and produces a file containing this theory.
- script-view *Name*
  This allows viewing of the script whose ground representation is in the file *Name*.scr.

A Polymorphic Many-Sorted Logic

Many-sorted first order logic generalizes ordinary (unsorted) first order logic ([7], [16]) in that it has sort declarations for the variables, constants, functions, and predicates. We can regard (unsorted) logic as a special case in which there is only one sort. In the general case, there are a number of (possibly infinitely many) sorts. Each constant, for example, is then specified as having a particular sort. There is also a natural definition of what it means for an expression to be a formula in the many-sorted language. For the declarative semantics, we have to generalize the usual notions of interpretation, logical consequence, and so on. The key idea here is that a many-sorted interpretation has a domain for every sort (instead of just one domain for an unsorted logic). Then each constant, for example, is assigned by the interpretation an element of the domain corresponding to its sort. The remainder of the declarative concepts can be developed in a natural way. Polymorphism is introduced by adding parameters, which are sort variables, and constructors. Generally speaking, the development of the theory of (unsorted) logic can be carried through with only minor changes for the more general case of polymorphic many-sorted logic. For further discussion on many-sorted logic beyond that given in this appendix, see [7]. There is also some discussion of many-sorted logic with applications to deductive database systems in [15]. In the following, to conform to the terminology normally used in programming languages, we refer to a sort as a *type*. For clarity, we treat many-sorted logic in detail first, then consider polymorphic many-sorted logic. We also give definitions of the basic logic programming concepts of program, completion, and correct answer in the setting of polymorphic many-sorted logic.

A.1   Many-sortedness

The alphabet of a many-sorted language contains types, variables, constants, functions, propositions, predicates, connectives, and quantifiers. In general, there is at least one type. Also there are zero or more constants and functions, and at least one proposition or predicate. Types are denoted by Greek letters such as τ and σ. Variables and constants have types such as τ. For each type τ, there are denumerably many variables v_τ^1, v_τ^2, ... of type τ. Occasionally it will be convenient to omit the superscript on a variable. Functions of arity n have types of the form $\tau_1 \times \ldots \times \tau_n \to \tau$, and predicates of arity n have types of the form $\tau_1 \times \ldots \times \tau_n$. If f has type $\tau_1 \times \ldots \times \tau_n \to \tau$, we say f has *range type* τ. For each type τ, there is a universal quantifier $\forall_\tau$ and an existential quantifier $\exists_\tau$.

Definition A *term* is defined inductively as follows:

1. A variable of type τ is a term of type τ.

2. A constant of type τ is a term of type τ.

3. If f is an n-ary function of type $\tau_1 \times \ldots \times \tau_n \rightarrow \tau$ and t_i is a term of type τ_i $(i = 1, \ldots, n)$, then $f(t_1, \ldots, t_n)$ is a term of type τ.

Next we define many-sorted formulas. These formulas will be *rectified*, in the sense that no variable can be bound by more than one quantifier and no variable can be both bound and free.

Definition A *many-sorted formula* is defined inductively as follows:

1. If p is a proposition, then p is a many-sorted atomic formula.

2. If p is an n-ary predicate of type $\tau_1 \times \ldots \times \tau_n$ and t_i is a term of type τ_i $(i = 1, \ldots, n)$, then $p(t_1, \ldots, t_n)$ is a many-sorted atomic formula.

3. If F and G are many-sorted formulas (whose common variables are free in both formulas), then so are $\sim F$, $F \wedge G$, $F \vee G$, $F \rightarrow G$, $F \leftarrow G$, and $F \leftrightarrow G$.

4. If F is a many-sorted formula and v_τ is a variable (free in F) of type τ, then $\forall_\tau v_\tau \, F$ and $\exists_\tau v_\tau \, F$ are many-sorted formulas.

Definition The *many-sorted language* given by an alphabet consists of the set of all many-sorted formulas constructed from the symbols of the alphabet.

We let $\forall(F)$ denote the universal closure of the formula F and $\exists(F)$ denote the existential closure. The universal closure of F is the closed formula obtained by prefixing F with universal quantifiers, each one corresponding to a free variable in F. The existential closure is defined analogously.

Now we turn to the declarative semantics of many-sorted languages.

Definition A *pre-interpretation* of a many-sorted language consists of the following:

1. For each type τ, a non-empty set D_τ, called the *domain of type τ*.

2. For each constant of type τ, the assignment of an element in D_τ.

3. For each n-ary function of type $\tau_1 \times \ldots \times \tau_n \rightarrow \tau$, the assignment of a mapping from $D_{\tau_1} \times \ldots \times D_{\tau_n}$ to D_τ.

Definition An *interpretation* of a many-sorted language consists of a pre-interpretation with domains $\{D_\tau\}$ together with the following:

1. For each proposition, the assignment of a value, true or false.

2. For each n-ary predicate of type $\tau_1 \times \ldots \times \tau_n$, the assignment of a mapping from $D_{\tau_1} \times \ldots \times D_{\tau_n}$ to {true, false} (or, equivalently, a relation on $D_{\tau_1} \times \ldots \times D_{\tau_n}$).

Definition Let J be a pre-interpretation of a many-sorted language. A *variable assignment (with respect to J)* is an assignment to each variable of type τ of an element in the domain D_τ of J, for each type τ.

Definition Let J be a pre-interpretation with domains $\{D_\tau\}$ of a many-sorted language L and let V be a variable assignment. The *term assignment (with respect to J and V)* of the terms in L is defined as follows:

1. Each variable is given its assignment according to V.

2. Each constant is given its assignment according to J.

3. If $t'_1, \ldots, t'_n$ are the term assignments of $t_1, \ldots, t_n$ and f' is the assignment of the n-ary function f of range type τ, then $f'(t'_1, \ldots, t'_n) \in D_\tau$ is the term assignment of $f(t_1, \ldots, t_n)$.

Definition Let I be an interpretation with domains $\{D_\tau\}$ of a many-sorted language L and let V be a variable assignment. Then a formula in L can be given a *truth value*, true or false, (*with respect to I and V*) as follows:

1. If the formula is a proposition p, then the truth value of the formula is the same as the value assigned to p by I.

2. If the formula is an atom $p(t_1, \ldots, t_n)$, then the truth value is obtained by calculating the value of $p'(t'_1, \ldots, t'_n)$, where p' is the mapping assigned to p by I and $t'_1, \ldots, t'_n$ are the term assignments of $t_1, \ldots, t_n$ with respect to I and V.

3. If the formula has the form $\sim F$, $F \wedge G$, $F \vee G$, $F \rightarrow G$, $F \leftarrow G$, or $F \leftrightarrow G$, then the truth value of the formula is given by the following table:

F	G	$\sim F$	$F \wedge G$	$F \vee G$	$F \rightarrow G$	$F \leftarrow G$	$F \leftrightarrow G$
true	true	false	true	true	true	true	true
true	false	false	false	true	false	true	false
false	true	true	false	true	true	false	false
false	false	true	false	false	true	true	true

4. If the formula has the form $\exists_\tau v_\tau \, F$, then the truth value of the formula is true if there exists $d \in D_\tau$ such that F has truth value true with respect to I and $V(v_\tau/d)$, where $V(v_\tau/d)$ is V except that v_τ is assigned d; otherwise, its truth value is false.

5. If the formula has the form $\forall_\tau v_\tau\ F$, then the truth value of the formula is true if, for all $d \in D_\tau$, we have that F has truth value true with respect to I and $V(v_\tau/d)$; otherwise, its truth value is false.

The truth value of a closed formula does not depend on the variable assignment. Consequently, we can speak unambiguously of the truth value of a closed formula with respect to an interpretation. If the truth value of a closed formula with respect to an interpretation is true (resp., false), we say the formula is true (resp., false) with respect to the interpretation.

Definition Let I be an interpretation of a many-sorted language L and let F be a closed formula of L. Then I is a *model* for F if F is true with respect to I.

The concept of a model of a closed formula can easily be extended to a model of a set of closed formulas.

Definition Let S be a set of closed formulas of a many-sorted language L and let I be an interpretation of L. We say I is a *model* for S if I is a model for each formula of S.

Now we can give the definition of the important concept of logical consequence.

Definition Let S be a set of closed formulas and F be a closed formula of a many-sorted language L. We say F is a *logical consequence* of S if, for every interpretation I of L, I is a model for S implies that I is a model for F.

Definition A *many-sorted theory* consists of a many-sorted language and a set of axioms which is a designated subset of closed formulas in the language of the theory.

Definition Let T be a many-sorted theory and let L be the language of T. A *model* for T is an interpretation for L which is a model for the set of axioms of T.

If T has a model, we say T is *consistent*.

There is a transformation of many-sorted theories into (unsorted) theories, which shows that the apparent extra generality provided by many-sorted logics is illusory [7]. This transformation allows one to reduce the proof of a theorem in many-sorted logic to a corresponding theorem in (unsorted) logic. The existence of this transformation makes many-sorted logic a mathematically trivial extension of (unsorted) logic and explains why so few logic books even mention many-sorted logic. However, many-sorted logic is more expressive than (unsorted) logic and it avoids having to use the type predicates that are introduced in the mapping to (unsorted) logic.

A.2 Polymorphism

Next we introduce (parametric) polymorphism into the logic. For this, we extend the alphabet by adding parameters, bases, and constructors. Parameters are type variables, bases correspond to what were called types in the many-sorted case, and constructors have an arity and are used to construct new types. In contrast to the many-sorted case, there is now a single polymorphic universal quantifier $\forall$ and a single polymorphic existential quantifier $\exists$. Also variables do not have fixed types as in the many-sorted case, but have their types inferred from the context in which they occur. We assume that there are denumerably many variables v^1, v^2, ...

Definition A *type* is defined inductively as follows:

1. A parameter is a type.

2. A base is a type.

3. If c is a constructor of arity n and $\tau_1, \ldots, \tau_n$ are types, then $c(\tau_1, \ldots, \tau_n)$ is a type.

A *ground type* is a type not containing parameters.

In a polymorphic many-sorted language, constants have types such as τ, functions have types of the form $\tau_1 \times \ldots \times \tau_n \to \tau$, and predicates have types of the form $\tau_1 \times \ldots \times \tau_n$ (where $\tau, \tau_1, \ldots, \tau_n$ are types defined according to the preceding definition). A symbol is *polymorphic* if its type contains a parameter; otherwise, it is *monomorphic*. A polymorphic symbol can be intuitively understood as representing a collection of (monomorphic) symbols, one for each ground instance of its type. (This is explained later.)

We now define the concept of a term t of type τ so that each subterm of t has a type in t and multiple occurrences of a variable in t all have the same type in t.

Definition A *term* is defined inductively as follows:

1. A variable v is a term of type a, where a is a parameter, and the subterm v has the type a in v.

2. A constant c of type τ is a term of type τ and the subterm c has type τ in c.

3. Let f be a function of type $\tau_1 \times \ldots \times \tau_n \to \tau$ and let t_i be a term of type σ_i, for $i = 1, \ldots, n$. Suppose that the parameters in $\tau_1 \times \ldots \times \tau_n \to \tau$ and the parameters of each σ_i, taken together with the parameters in the types in t_i of each of the subterms of t_i, are standardized apart. Consider the set of equations
$$\sigma_1 = \tau_1, \ldots, \sigma_n = \tau_n$$
augmented with equations of the form
$$\rho_{i_1} = \rho_{i_2} = \ldots = \rho_{i_k}$$

for each variable having an occurrence in the terms $t_{i_1}, \ldots, t_{i_k}$ ($\{i_1, \ldots, i_k\} \subseteq \{1, \ldots, n\}$, $k > 1$), say, and where the variable is assigned the type ρ_{i_j} in t_{i_j} ($j = 1, \ldots, k$). Then we say that $f(t_1, \ldots, t_n)$ is a term if and only if this set of equations has a most general unifier θ, say. In this case, $f(t_1, \ldots, t_n)$ has type $\tau\theta$ and the subterm $f(t_1, \ldots, t_n)$ has type $\tau\theta$ in $f(t_1, \ldots, t_n)$. A strict subterm of $f(t_1, \ldots, t_n)$, which must be a subterm of some t_i and has type σ, say, in t_i, has type $\sigma\theta$ in $f(t_1, \ldots, t_n)$.

Note that multiple occurrences of a variable in $f(t_1, \ldots, t_n)$ all have the same type in $f(t_1, \ldots, t_n)$. Also the type of $f(t_1, \ldots, t_n)$ and the type in $f(t_1, \ldots, t_n)$ of each of its subterms is unique up to variants.

Next we define the concept of an atom A so that each subterm of A has a type in A and multiple occurrences of a variable in A all have the same type in A.

Definition An *atom* is defined as follows:

1. A proposition p is an atom.

2. Let p be a predicate with type $\tau_1 \times \ldots \times \tau_n$ and let t_i be a term of type σ_i, for $i = 1, \ldots, n$. Suppose that the parameters in $\tau_1 \times \ldots \times \tau_n$ and the parameters of each σ_i, taken together with the parameters in the types in t_i of each of the subterms of t_i, are standardized apart. Consider the set of equations
   $$\sigma_1 = \tau_1, \ldots, \sigma_n = \tau_n$$
   augmented with equations of the form
   $$\rho_{i_1} = \rho_{i_2} = \ldots = \rho_{i_k}$$
   for each variable having an occurrence in the terms $t_{i_1}, \ldots, t_{i_k}$ ($\{i_1, \ldots, i_k\} \subseteq \{1, \ldots, n\}$, $k > 1$), say, and where the variable has the type ρ_{i_j} in t_{i_j} ($j = 1, \ldots, k$). Then we say that $p(t_1, \ldots, t_n)$ is an atom if and only if this set of equations has a most general unifier θ, say. In this case, a subterm of $p(t_1, \ldots, t_n)$, which must be a subterm of some t_i and has type σ, say, in t_i, has the type $\sigma\theta$ in $p(t_1, \ldots, t_n)$.

Note that multiple occurrences of a variable in $p(t_1, \ldots, t_n)$ all have the same type in $p(t_1, \ldots, t_n)$. Also the type in $p(t_1, \ldots, t_n)$ of each of its subterms is unique up to variants.

Now we can give the definition of a polymorphic many-sorted formula F so that each subterm of F has a type in F and multiple occurrences of a variable in F all have the same type in F.

Definition A *polymorphic many-sorted formula* is defined inductively as follows:

1. An atom is a formula. Each subterm of the atom having type τ in the atom has the type τ in the formula.

2. If F is a formula, then so is $\sim F$. Each subterm of F having type τ in F has type τ in $\sim F$.

3. Let F and G be formulas, whose common variables are free in both formulas. Suppose that the parameters in types of subterms of F are standardized apart from the parameters in types of subterms of G. For each variable in common with F and G, form the equation

   $\rho = \sigma$

   where ρ is the type assigned to the variable in F and σ is the type assigned to the variable in G. Then $F \wedge G$ (resp., $F \vee G$, $F \rightarrow G$, $F \leftarrow G$, $F \leftrightarrow G$) is a formula if and only if the set of equations has a most general unifier θ, say. In this case, a subterm of $F \wedge G$ (resp., $F \vee G$, $F \rightarrow G$, $F \leftarrow G$, $F \leftrightarrow G$), which must be a subterm of either F or G and has type ρ in F or G, has type $\rho\theta$ in $F \wedge G$ (resp., $F \vee G$, $F \rightarrow G$, $F \leftarrow G$, $F \leftrightarrow G$).

4. Let F be a formula containing a free variable v. Then $\forall v\, F$ is a formula and every subterm of $\forall v\, F$ has the same type in this formula as it has in F.

5. Let F be a formula containing a free variable v. Then $\exists v\, F$ is a formula and every subterm of $\exists v\, F$ has the same type in this formula as it has in F.

Note that multiple occurrences of a variable in a formula have the same type in the formula. Also the types of subterms of a formula are unique up to variants.

The universal closure and existential closure of a polymorphic formula can be defined by obvious extensions of the many-sorted definitions.

Definition The *polymorphic many-sorted language* given by an alphabet consists of the set of all polymorphic many-sorted formulas constructed from the symbols of the alphabet.

Definition A *polymorphic many-sorted theory* consists of a polymorphic many-sorted language and a set of axioms which is a designated subset of closed formulas in the language of the theory.

A polymorphic formula can be intuitively understood as representing a collection of (monomorphic) formulas. We now make this idea more precise.

Definition Let L be a polymorphic many-sorted language. The *underlying many-sorted language* of L is the (monomorphic) many-sorted language L^* with the following alphabet:

1. The types of L^* are the ground types of L. (Any structure in a ground type is ignored.)

2. For each ground type δ in L, there are denumerably many variables v_δ^1, v_δ^2, ... in L^*.

3. For each constant c of type τ in L and ground instance δ of τ, there is a constant c_δ of type δ in L^*.

4. For each function f of type $\tau_1 \times \ldots \times \tau_n \to \tau$ in L and ground instance $\delta_1 \times \ldots \times \delta_n \to \delta$ of $\tau_1 \times \ldots \times \tau_n \to \tau$, there is a function $f_{\delta_1 \times \ldots \times \delta_n \to \delta}$ of type $\delta_1 \times \ldots \times \delta_n \to \delta$ in L^*.

5. The propositions of L^* are the propositions of L.

6. For each predicate p of type $\tau_1 \times \ldots \times \tau_n$ in L and ground instance $\delta_1 \times \ldots \times \delta_n$ of $\tau_1 \times \ldots \times \tau_n$, there is a predicate $p_{\delta_1 \times \ldots \times \delta_n}$ of type $\delta_1 \times \ldots \times \delta_n$ in L^*.

Definition Let F be a formula in a polymorphic many-sorted language. Each occurrence of a variable, constant, function, or predicate in F has a *relative type* in F defined as follows.

1. The relative type of an occurrence of a variable v in F is the type of v in F.

2. The relative type of an occurrence of a constant c in F is the type of the subterm c in F.

3. Consider an occurrence of the function f in the subterm $f(t_1, \ldots, t_n)$ of F. Suppose the subterm $f(t_1, \ldots, t_n)$ has type τ in F and the subterm t_i has type τ_i in F ($i = 1, \ldots, n$). Then the relative type of this occurrence of f in F is $\tau_1 \times \ldots \times \tau_n \to \tau$.

4. Consider an occurrence of the predicate p in the atom $p(t_1, \ldots, t_n)$ of F. Suppose the subterm t_i has type τ_i in F ($i = 1, \ldots, n$). Then the relative type of this occurrence of p in F is $\tau_1 \times \ldots \times \tau_n$.

Note that the relative type of a constant in a formula is an instance of its type in the language. A similar comment applies to functions and predicates.

Definition Let F be a formula in a polymorphic many-sorted language. A *grounding type substitution* is a type substitution which binds all the parameters appearing in relative types of symbols in F to ground types.

Definition Let F be a formula in a polymorphic many-sorted language L and Ψ be a grounding type substitution for F. The many-sorted formula F_Ψ in the language L^* is obtained by replacing all occurrences of symbols in F as follows:

1. For an occurrence of a variable v of relative type τ appearing in F, replace v by the variable $v_{\tau\Psi}$.

2. For an occurrence of a constant c of relative type τ appearing in F, replace c by the constant $c_{\tau\Psi}$.

3. For an occurrence of a function f of relative type $\tau_1 \times \ldots \times \tau_n \to \tau$ appearing in F, replace f by the function $f_{\tau_1 \Psi \times \ldots \times \tau_n \Psi \to \tau \Psi}$.

4. For an occurrence of a predicate p of relative type $\tau_1 \times \ldots \times \tau_n$ appearing in F, replace p by the predicate $p_{\tau_1 \Psi \times \ldots \times \tau_n \Psi}$.

5. For an occurrence of a quantifier $\forall$ for a variable of relative type τ appearing in F, replace $\forall$ by $\forall_{\tau \Psi}$.

6. For an occurrence of a quantifier $\exists$ for a variable of relative type τ appearing in F, replace $\exists$ by $\forall_{\tau \Psi}$.

Now we can give precise meaning to the intuitive concept of a polymorphic many-sorted formula representing a set of (monomorphic) many-sorted formulas.

Definition Let F be a formula in a polymorphic many-sorted language. The set

$$\{F_\Psi : \Psi \text{ is a grounding type substitution for } F\}$$

is called the *set of many-sorted formulas underlying F*.

Now we turn to the declarative semantics of polymorphic many-sorted languages.

Definition A *pre-interpretation* of a polymorphic many-sorted language consists of the following:

1. For each ground type δ, a non-empty set D_δ, called the *domain of type δ*.

2. For each constant of type τ and for each ground instance δ of τ, the assignment of an element in D_δ.

3. For each n-ary function of type $\tau_1 \times \ldots \times \tau_n \to \tau$ and for each ground instance $\delta_1 \times \ldots \times \delta_n \to \delta$ of $\tau_1 \times \ldots \times \tau_n \to \tau$, the assignment of a mapping from $D_{\delta_1} \times \ldots \times D_{\delta_n}$ to D_δ.

Definition An *interpretation* I of a polymorphic many-sorted language consists of a pre-interpretation J with domains $\{D_\delta\}$ together with the following:

1. For each proposition, the assignment of a value, true or false.

2. For each n-ary predicate of type $\tau_1 \times \ldots \times \tau_n$ and for each ground instance $\delta_1 \times \ldots \times \delta_n$ of $\tau_1 \times \ldots \times \tau_n$, the assignment of a mapping from $D_{\delta_1} \times \ldots \times D_{\delta_n}$ to $\{\text{true, false}\}$ (or, equivalently, a relation on $D_{\delta_1} \times \ldots \times D_{\delta_n}$).

An interpretation for a polymorphic many-sorted language L can also be regarded as an interpretation for the many-sorted language L^* underlying L in the obvious way.

Definition Let I be an interpretation of a polymorphic many-sorted language L and F be a closed formula of L. The truth value of F with respect to I is true if, for every grounding type substitution Ψ for F, the truth value of F_Ψ is true with respect to I. The truth value of F with respect to I is false if, for every grounding type substitution Ψ for F, the truth value of F_Ψ is false with respect to I.

If the truth value of a closed formula with respect to an interpretation is true (resp., false), we say the formula is true (resp,. false) with respect to the interpretation.

We now give the definitions of model, consistency, and logical consequence, which are analogous to the many-sorted case.

Definition Let I be an interpretation of a polymorphic many-sorted language L and F be a closed formula of L. Then I is a *model* for F if F is true with respect to I.

Definition Let S be a set of closed formulas of a polymorphic many-sorted language L and let I be an interpretation of L. We say I is a *model* for S if I is a model for each formula of S.

Definition Let S be a set of closed formulas and F be a closed formula of a polymorphic many-sorted language L. We say F is a *logical consequence* of S if, for every interpretation I of L, I is a model for S implies that I is a model for F.

Definition Let T be a polymorphic many-sorted theory and let L be the language of T. A *model* for T is an interpretation for L which is a model for the set of axioms of T. If T has a model, we say T is *consistent*.

We conclude this section with the definition of a variable typing and some related concepts. The definitions are given in the context of some alphabet and corresponding language.

Definition A *variable typing* is a finite set of the form $\{v_1/\tau_1, \ldots, v_n/\tau_n\}$, where each v_i is a variable, each τ_i is a type, and the variables are distinct. Each v_i/τ_i is called a *binding*.

Definition Let Θ and Φ be variable typings. The *combination* $\Theta\Phi$ of Θ and Φ is the variable typing defined as follows. For each variable v, say, which has a binding v/τ_1 in one variable typing and a binding v/τ_2 in the other variable typing, form the equation $\tau_1 = \tau_2$, and consider the set of all such equations. If this set of equations has an mgu α, then $\Theta\Phi$ consists of the set of all bindings of the form $u/\tau\alpha$, where u/τ occurs in Θ or Φ; otherwise, the combination of Θ and Φ is not defined.

Note that the combination of two variable typings is commutative. Finally, we give the definition of the type of a term with respect to a variable typing.

Definition Let t be a term and Θ a variable typing. The *type of t with respect to Θ* is defined as follows. Suppose t has type τ and Φ is the variable typing given by the types of the variables in t. If $\Theta\Phi$ is defined and α is the mgu associated with this combination given in the previous definition, then the type of t with respect to Θ is $\tau\alpha$. Otherwise, $\Theta\Phi$ is not defined and the type of t with respect to Θ is also not defined.

A.3 Logic Programming Concepts

In this section, we give the definitions of the basic declarative logic programming concepts of program, completion, and correct answer in the context of polymorphic many-sorted logic with equality. Throughout this section, we suppose the definitions are given in the context of some fixed, but arbitrary, polymorphic many-sorted language with equality. We also suppose that function declarations are transparent and that statements (defined below) satisfy the head condition. These assumptions are needed to ensure that the completion of a program is well-defined.

Definition A *statement* is a polymorphic many-sorted formula of the form

$$A \leftarrow W$$

where A is an atom and W is a polymorphic many-sorted formula. The formula W may be absent. Any variables in A and any free variables in W are assumed to be universally quantified at the front of the statement. A is called the *head* and W the *body* of the statement.

Definition A *program* is a finite set of statements.

Definition A *goal* is a polymorphic many-sorted formula of the form

$$\leftarrow W$$

where W is a polymorphic many-sorted formula and any free variables of W are assumed to be universally quantified at the front of the goal.

Note that equality can appear in the body of a statement or goal, but not in the head of a statement. Next we give the definition of the completion of a program.

Definition The *definition* of a proposition or predicate p appearing in a program P is the set of all statements in P which have p in their head.

Definition Suppose the definition of a proposition or predicate p of arity $n \geq 0$ in a program is

$$A_1 \leftarrow W_1$$
$$\cdots$$
$$A_k \leftarrow W_k$$

Then the *completed definition* of p is the formula

$$\forall x_1 \ldots \forall x_n (p(x_1, \ldots, x_n) \leftrightarrow E_1 \vee \ldots \vee E_k)$$

where E_i is $\exists y_1 \ldots \exists y_d ((x_1 = t_1) \wedge \ldots \wedge (x_n = t_n) \wedge W_i)$, A_i is $p(t_1, \ldots, t_n)$, $y_1, \ldots, y_d$ are the variables in A_i and the free variables in W_i, and $x_1, \ldots, x_n$ are variables not appearing anywhere in the definition of p.

Example Let the definition of p be
$p(x) \leftarrow q(x, y)$
$p(b) \leftarrow$
Then the completed definition for p is

$$\forall z (p(z) \leftrightarrow (\exists x \exists y ((z = x) \wedge q(x, y)) \vee (z = b))).$$

Definition Let P be a program and p a proposition or predicate occurring in P. Suppose there is no program statement in P with p in its head. Then the *completed definition* of p is the formula

$$\forall x_1 \ldots \forall x_n \sim p(x_1, \ldots, x_n).$$

The *equality theory* for a program consists of all axioms of the following form (where $s \neq t$ is an abbreviation for $\sim (s = t)$):

1. $c \neq d$, for all pairs c, d of distinct constants whose types have a common instance.

2. $\forall (f(x_1, \ldots, x_n) \neq g(y_1, \ldots, y_m))$, for all pairs f, g of distinct functions whose range types have a common instance.

3. $\forall (f(x_1, \ldots, x_n) \neq c)$, for each constant c and function f such that the type of c and the range type of f have a common instance.

4. $\forall (t[x] \neq x)$, for each term $t[x]$ containing x and different from x.

5. $\forall((x_1 \neq y_1) \vee \ldots \vee (x_n \neq y_n) \rightarrow f(x_1, \ldots, x_n) \neq f(y_1, \ldots, y_n))$, for each function f.

6. $\forall x(x = x)$.

7. $\forall((x_1 = y_1) \wedge \ldots \wedge (x_n = y_n) \rightarrow f(x_1, \ldots, x_n) = f(y_1, \ldots, y_n))$, for each function f.

8. $\forall((x_1 = y_1) \wedge \ldots \wedge (x_n = y_n) \rightarrow (p(x_1, \ldots, x_n) \rightarrow p(y_1, \ldots, y_n)))$, for each predicate p (including $=$).

In axiom 4, it is understood that only those expressions of the form $\forall(t[x] \neq x)$ which are actually formulas appear there.

Definition Let P be a program. The *completion* of P, denoted by $comp(P)$, is the collection of completed definitions of propositions and predicates in P together with the above equality theory.

Definition Let P be a program, G a goal $\leftarrow W$, and θ an answer for $P \cup \{G\}$. We say θ is a *correct answer* for $comp(P) \cup \{G\}$ if $\forall(W\theta)$ is a logical consequence of $comp(P)$.

The concept of a correct answer gives a declarative description of the desired output from a goal and program.

Bibliography

[1] *Language Independent Arithmetic, ISO/IEC CD 10967-1:1992.* August 1992. Second Committee Draft (Version 4.0); JTC1/SC22/WG11 N318, ANSI X3T2 92-064.

[2] *Standard for Binary Floating-Point Arithmetic.* 1985. ANSI/IEEE Std 754-1985.

[3] K.A. Bowen and R.A. Kowalski. Amalgamating language and metalanguage in logic programming. In K.L. Clark and S.-A. Tarnlund, editors, *Logic Programming*, pages 153–172, Academic Press, 1982.

[4] A.F. Bowers. *Representing Gödel Object Programs in Gödel.* Technical Report CSTR-92-31, Department of Computer Science, University of Bristol, 1992.

[5] K. L. Clark, F. G. McCabe, and S. Gregory. IC-Prolog language features. In K.L. Clark and S.-A. Tarnlund, editors, *Logic Programming*, pages 253–266, Academic Press, 1982.

[6] A. Dovier, E.G. Omodeo, E. Pontelli, and G. Rossi. {Log}: a logic programming language with finite sets. In K. Furukawa, editor, *Proceedings of the Eighth International Conference on Logic Programming*, pages 111–124, Paris, 1991.

[7] H. B. Enderton. *A Mathematical Introduction to Logic.* Academic Press, 1972.

[8] C.A. Gurr. *A Self-Applicable Partial Evaluator for the Logic Programming Language Gödel.* PhD thesis, Department of Computer Science, University of Bristol, 1993. Submitted August 1993.

[9] C.A. Gurr. Specialising the ground representation in the logic programming language Gödel. In K.K. Lau and T. Clement, editors, *Proceedings of the Third International Workshop on Logic Program Synthesis and Transformation (LOPSTR'93)*, 1993. To be published by Springer-Verlag in the "Workshops in Computing" series.

[10] P.M. Hill and J.W. Lloyd. Analysis of meta-programs. In H.D. Abramson and M.H. Rogers, editors, *Meta-Programming in Logic Programming*, pages 23–52, MIT Press, 1989. Proceedings of the Meta88 Workshop, June 1988.

[11] P.M. Hill and J.W. Lloyd. *Meta-Programming for Dynamic Knowledge Bases.* Technical Report CS-88-18, Department of Computer Science, University of Bristol, 1988.

[12] P.M. Hill, J.W. Lloyd, and J.C. Shepherdson. Properties of a pruning operator. *Journal of Logic and Computation*, 1(1):99–143, 1990.

[13] P.M. Hill and R.W. Topor. A semantics for typed logic programs. In F. Pfenning, editor, *Types in Logic Programming*, pages 1–62, MIT Press, 1992.

[14] J.-L. Lassez and K. McAloon. A canonical form for generalized linear constraints. *J. Symbolic Computation*, 13:1–24, 1992.

[15] J.W. Lloyd. *Foundations of Logic Programming.* Springer-Verlag, second edition, 1987.

[16] E. Mendelson. *Introduction to Mathematical Logic.* 3rd Edition, Van Nostrand, 1987.

[17] A. Mycroft and R. A. O'Keefe. A polymorphic type system for Prolog. *Artificial Intelligence*, 23:295–307, 1984.

[18] L. Naish. Negation and quantifiers in NU-Prolog. In E. Shapiro, editor, *Proceedings of the Third International Conference on Logic Programming*, London, pages 624–634, Lecture Notes in Computer Science 225, Springer-Verlag, 1986.

[19] E. Shapiro. The family of concurrent logic programming languages. *ACM Computing Surveys*, 21(3):412–510, 1989.

[20] L. Sterling and E. Shapiro. *The Art of Prolog.* MIT Press, 1986.

[21] J. A. Thom and J. Zobel. *NU-Prolog Reference Manual, Version 1.3.* Technical Report, Machine Intelligence Project, Department of Computer Science, University of Melbourne, 1988.

System Index

General Index

∃, 326, 331
∀, 189, 326, 331
:, 31
=, 39
&, 29
->, 29
<-, 29
<->, 29
\", 64
\, 64
\/, 29
\\, 64
\b, 64
\n, 64
\t, 64
{...}, 87, 89
{...}_n, 87, 89
|, 15, 87
~, 29
_, 30, 41
.axm, 323
.exp, 323
.flk, 323
.loc, 323
.prm, 323
.scr, 323
.thy, 323
~=, 39
1-import, 56, 176
1-redeclare, 56, 176

abstract data type, 6
accessible to, 51, 56, 176
ALL, 29
ambiguity, 58
assert, 12, 14
associated program, 122
associated script, 122
associativity, 35
atom, 330

bar commit, 7, 15, 87, 190
BASE, 19
base, 19, 329
binding in a variable typing, 334
body, 25, 60, 94, 335
built-in predicate, 39, 41
built-in proposition, 41

canonical form of a body, 187
canonical form of a definition, 189
canonical form of a statement, 188
category, 19
CLOSED, 51
closed module, 53, 178
closed part of a script, 122
colon, 31
combination of variable typings, 334
commit, 7, 87
commit label, 92
completed definition, 336
completion, 337
completion of a program, 189
computation rule, 7, 79, 190
conditional, 31, 32
consistent, 328, 334
CONSTANT, 19
constant, 19
constraint solving, 7, 44, 47
constraint-free atom, 83
CONSTRUCTOR, 19
constructor, 19, 21, 329
control, 7, 79
control component of a program, 4
control declaration, 7, 19, 80, 82, 177
correct answer, 187, 190, 337
current goal, 190
cut node, 97

declarative semantics, 187
declare a symbol, 19, 51, 56, 176
declared name, 111
definite body, 185
definite goal, 184
definite resultant, 184
definite statement, 184
definition, 335
DELAY declaration, 7, 79, 82, 177, 191
depends upon, 57, 174
disequality, 39
domain of a type, 326, 333

eager pruning, 98
elimination step, 191
equality, 39
equality theory, 336
equality theory for a program, 189
error message, 45

Logic Programming

Ehud Shapiro, editor
Koichi Furukawa, Jean-Louis Lassez, Fernando Pereira, and David H. D. Warren, associate editors

The Art of Prolog: Advanced Programming Techniques, Leon Sterling and Ehud Shapiro, 1986

Logic Programming: Proceedings of the Fourth International Conference (volumes 1 and 2), edited by Jean-Louis Lassez, 1987

Concurrent Prolog: Collected Papers (volumes 1 and 2), edited by Ehud Shapiro, 1987

Logic Programming: Proceedings of the Fifth International Conference and Symposium (volumes 1 and 2), edited by Robert A. Kowalski and Kenneth A. Bowen, 1988

Constraint Satisfaction in Logic Programming, Pascal Van Hentenryck, 1989

Logic-Based Knowledge Representation, edited by Peter Jackson, Han Reichgelt, and Frank van Harmelen, 1989

Logic Programming: Proceedings of the Sixth International Conference, edited by Giorgio Levi and Maurizio Martelli, 1989

Meta-Programming in Logic Programming, edited by Harvey Abramson and M. H. Rogers, 1989

Logic Programming: Proceedings of the North American Conference 1989 (volumes 1 and 2), edited by Ewing L. Lusk and Ross A. Overbeek, 1989

Logic Programming: Proceedings of the 1990 North American Conference, edited by Saumya Debray and Manuel Hermenegildo, 1990

Logic Programming: Proceedings of the Seventh International Conference, edited by David H. D. Warren and Peter Szeredi, 1990

The Craft of Prolog, Richard A. O'Keefe, 1990

The Practice of Prolog, edited by Leon S. Sterling, 1990

Eco-Logic: Logic-Based Approaches to Ecological Modelling, David Robertson, Alan Bundy, Robert Muetzelfeldt, Mandy Haggith, and Michael Uschold, 1991

Warren's Abstract Machine: A Tutorial Reconstruction, Hassan Aït-Kaci, 1991

Parallel Logic Programming, Evan Tick, 1991

Logic Programming: Proceedings of the Eighth International Conference, edited by Koichi Furukawa, 1991

Logic Programming: Proceedings of the 1991 International Symposium, edited by Vijay Saraswat and Kazunori Ueda, 1991

Foundations of Disjunctive Logic Programming, Jorge Lobo, Jack Minker, and Arcot Rajasekar, 1992

Types in Logic Programming, edited by Frank Pfenning, 1992

Logic Programming: Proceedings of the Joint International Conference and Symposium on Logic Programming, edited by Krzysztof Apt, 1992

Concurrent Constraint Programming, Vijay A. Saraswat, 1993

Logic Programming Languages: Constraints, Functions, and Objects, edited by K. R. Apt, J. W. de Bakker, and J. J. M. M. Rutten, 1993

Logic Programming: Proceedings of the Tenth International Conference on Logic Programming, edited by David S. Warren, 1993

Constraint Logic Programming: Selected Research, edited by Frédéric Benhamou and Alain Colmerauer, 1993

A Grammatical View of Logic Programming, Pierre Deransart and Jan Małuszyński, 1993

Logic Programming: Proceedings of the 1993 International Symposium, edited by Dale Miller, 1993

The Gödel Programming Language, Patricia Hill and John Lloyd, 1994